Maharaja Ranjit Singh (1780–1839). Sikh, Punjab Plains, *c.* 1835–1840
(Pages 117–123)

VICTORIA AND ALBERT MUSEUM

Paintings of the Sikhs

W. G. ARCHER

LONDON

HER MAJESTY'S STATIONERY OFFICE

1966

Printed in England for Her Majesty's Stationery Office
by The Curwen Press, London, E.13

I do not know whether it is an optical illusion but I am greatly pleased with the Punjab and all its inhabitants. Perhaps you will say it is because I see them through a rain of gold; but the unsophisticated Sikhs of these parts have a simplicity and frank courtesy of manner which a European appreciates all the more after staying or travelling about in India for two years.

JACQUEMONT, *Letters from India, 1829–1832*

ACKNOWLEDGMENTS

For support and encouragement in preparing this book, I am greatly indebted to Sardar Pratap Singh Kairon, former Chief Minister, Punjab Government and to Sri Amar Nath Vidyalankar, Minister for Education.

I must also express my deep gratitude to Mildred Archer for constant help and advice, to Mr S. C. Sutton, c.b.e., Librarian, India Office Library, for limitless facilities, to Lady Edith C. Broun Lindsay, Mr and Mrs T. W. F. Scott, Mr Robert Skelton and Mrs Hilda Moorhouse for generous grants of information, to Mr Charles Gibbs-Smith for valued co-operation and to Mr John Wiltshire and Miss Ann Opie of the Indian Section, Victoria and Albert Museum for devoted help in assembling the text and illustrations.

Above all, I must thank Dr M. S. Randhawa at whose instance I was first led to undertake this research and whose unflagging friendship, stimulus and support have been more precious than any 'rain of gold'.

For courtesy in permitting the reproduction of certain pictures, grateful acknowledgments are made to the following owners, institutions and authorities: Sardar Mohan Singh (Figs. 1–6), Maharaja Manvindra Shah of Tehri Garhwal (Fig. 7), Punjab Museum, Chandigarh (Figs. 8, 11, 38), Sri Kasturbhai Lalbhai (Fig. 12), British Museum, London (Figs. 13, 16, 41, 55, 58, 59, 60), Sir A. Chester Beatty and the Librarian, Chester Beatty Library, Dublin (Fig. 15), Archaeological Museum, Bikaner (Fig. 25), Mr and Mrs T. W. F. Scott (Figs. 28, 35, 40), Secretary of State for Commonwealth Relations and Librarian, India Office Library, London (Figs. 34, 56, 61, 64, 68, 92–95), Sikh Museum, Lahore, Pakistan, and Dr F. A. Khan, Director of Archaeology, Pakistan (Figs. 43–45) and Mrs A. E. Anson (Fig. 62).

September 1964   W. G. ARCHER

CONTENTS

ILLUSTRATIONS

12. Maharaja Ranjit Singh (1780–1839) carousing with a Kangra lady. Gouache. Kangra, *c.* 1830–1835. Kasturbhai Lalbhai collection, Ahmedabad, Gujerat. *See p. 27.*

13. Youth in Sikh costume and turban, perhaps Hira Singh, dallying with a Kangra lady on a bed beneath a canopy, a maid-servant in attendance; in the bottom right-hand corner a chair in Sikh style, on it a sword and shield. The lady's anklets are on the bed. In the background, a gathering storm. Gouache. Kangra, *c.* 1835. British Museum, 1925-4-6-03. *See p. 27.*

14. Maharaja Ranjit Singh (1780–1839) on horseback. Gouache. Sikh, Punjab Plains, *c.* 1835–1840. Victoria and Albert Museum, I.S. 480–1950. Cat. no. 4. *See pp. 126–127.*

15. Maharaja Ranjit Singh (1780–1839) in darbar with his head astrologer, pandits and Rajput courtiers. Gouache. Sikh, Punjab Plains, *c.* 1830–1835. Chester Beatty Library, Dublin, 195. *See pp. 33, 34, 36.*

16. The funeral of Ranjit Singh. Gouache. Kangra, *c.* 1840. British Museum, 1925-4-6-03. *See pp. 27–30.*

17. Maharaja Ranjit Singh (1780–1839) on horseback. Gouache. Sikh, Punjab Plains, *c.* 1838–1840. Victoria and Albert Museum, I.S. 111–1953. Cat. no. 5. *See pp. 127–128.*

18. Maharaja Ranjit Singh (1780–1839) on horseback. Gouache. Sikh, Punjab Plains, *c.* 1838–1840. Victoria and Albert Museum, I.S. 112–1953. Cat. no. 6. *See pp. 128–129.*

19. Maharaja Ranjit Singh (1780–1839) and Hira Singh (*c.* 1816–1844). Gouache. Sikh, Punjab Plains, *c.* 1838–1840. Victoria and Albert Museum, I.S. 114–1953. Cat. no. 7. *See p. 129.*

20. Hira Singh (*c.* 1816–1844) with attendant. Gouache. Sikh, Punjab Plains, *c.* 1838–1840. Victoria and Albert Museum, I.S. 115–1953. Cat. no. 8. *See p. 132.*

21. Maharaja Kharak Singh (1802–1840) on horseback. Gouache. Sikh, Punjab Plains, *c.* 1838–1840. Victoria and Albert Museum, I.S. 113–1953. Cat. no. 9. *See p. 133.*

22. Maharaja Kharak Singh (1802–1840) seated. Gouache. Sikh, Punjab Plains, *c.* 1835–1840. Victoria and Albert Museum, I.S. 338–1951. Cat. no. 12. *See p. 138.*

23. Raja Suchet Singh (1801–1844) and Raja Dhian Singh (1796–1843) seated. Gouache. Sikh, Punjab Plains, *c.* 1840. Victoria and Albert Museum, I.S. 264–1953. Cat. no. 13. *See p. 139.*

24. Raja Dhian Singh (1796–1843) seated on ground with Raja Nau Nihal Singh (1821–1840) in chair. Gouache. Sikh, Punjab Plains, *c.* 1840. Victoria and Albert Museum, I.S. 116–1953. Cat. no. 10. *See pp. 136–137.*

25. Maharaja Ranjit Singh (1780–1839) seated in a chair, Raja Dhian Singh (1796–1843) standing before him. Gouache. Sikh, Punjab Plains, *c.* 1845. Archaeological Museum, Bikaner, Rajasthan, 738–56. *See pp. 51, 131.*

26. Maharaja Ranjit Singh (1780–1839) seated. Lithograph after an original drawing by Emily Eden, Lahore, December 1838. Published: Emily Eden, *Portraits of the Princes and People of India* (London, 1844), pl. 13. *See pp. 51, 130, 131.*

27. Maharaja Ranjit Singh (1780–1839) on horseback. Gouache. Sikh, Punjab Plains, *c.* 1840. Victoria and Albert Museum, I.M. 56–1936. Cat. no. 14. *See p. 139.*

28. Maharaja Ranjit Singh (1780–1839) seated. Gouache. Sikh, Punjab Plains, *c.* 1840. Mr and Mrs T. W. F. Scott collection, London. *See pp. 37, 129, 130.*

29. Hira Singh (*c.* 1816–1844) seated. Gouache. Sikh, Punjab Plains, *c.* 1840. Victoria and Albert Museum, I.M. 60–1936. Cat. no. 18. *See pp. 141–142.*

30. Raja Dhian Singh (1796–1843) seated on a chair. Gouache. Sikh, Punjab Plains, *c.* 1838–1840. Victoria and Albert Museum, I.S. 117–1953. Cat. no. 11. *See pp. 137–138.*

31. Maharaja Kharak Singh (1802–1840) seated. Gouache. Sikh, Punjab Plains, *c.* 1840. Victoria and Albert Museum, I.M. 57–1936. Cat. no. 15. *See p. 140.*

32. Raja Nau Nihal Singh (1821–1840) seated. Gouache. Sikh, Punjab Plains, *c.* 1840. Victoria and Albert Museum, I.M. 58–1936. Cat. no. 16. *See pp. 140–141.*

33. Raja Dhian Singh (1796–1843) on horseback. Gouache. Sikh, Punjab Plains, *c.* 1840. Victoria and Albert Museum, I.M. 59–1936. Cat. no. 17. *See p. 141.*

34. Raja Gulab Singh (1792–1857) of Jammu on horseback. Gouache. Sikh, Punjab Plains, *c.* 1840–1845. India Office Library, London. Add. Or. 707. *See p. 143.*

35. Raja Dhian Singh (1796–1843) seated on a terrace to the right, facing right to left, Maharaja Kharak Singh (1802–1840), Nau Nihal Singh (1821–1840) and Hira Singh (*c.* 1816–1844). Gouache. Sikh, Punjab Plains, *c.* 1840. Mr and Mrs T. W. F. Scott collection, London. *See pp. 37, 132, 133.*

36. Sikh sardar, perhaps Lehna Singh Majithia, receiving petitions. Gouache. Sikh, Punjab Plains, *c.* 1840. Victoria and Albert Museum, I.S. 43–1960. Cat. no. 19. *See pp. 20, 21, 142.*

37. Maharaja Gulab Singh (1792–1857) taking his bath prior to worship. Gouache. Sikh, Punjab Plains, *c.* 1835–1840. Victoria and Albert Museum, I.S. 37–1949. Cat. no. 20. *See pp. 53, 54, 143.*

38. Maharaja Sher Singh (1807–1843) seated on a bed after bathing. Gouache. Kangra, *c.* 1830. Punjab Museum, Chandigarh. *See pp. 25, 26, 167.*

39. Maharaja Sher Singh (1807–1843). Lithograph (London, 1842) after an original drawing by G. T. Vigne, Punjab, 1838. Published: G. T. Vigne, *Travels in Kashmir, Ladak, Iskardo* (London, 1842), I, frontispiece. *See p. 167.*

40. Maharaja Sher Singh (1807–1843) seated. Gouache. Sikh, Punjab Plains, *c.* 1840. Mr and Mrs T. W. F. Scott collection, London. *See pp. 37, 167, 168.*

41. Maharaja Sher Singh (1807–1843) seated. Gouache. Sikh, Punjab Plains, *c.* 1840–1845. British Museum, 1956–10–13–03. *See p. 168.*

42. Maharaja Sher Singh (1807–1843). Lithograph after an original drawing by Emily Eden, Lahore, December 1838. Published: Emily Eden, *Portraits of the Princes and People of India* (London, 1844), pl. 2. *See pp. 42, 168.*

56. The first and second sons of Maharaja Gulab Singh (1792–1857) of Jammu and Kashmir; left, Udham Singh (?–1840); right, Sohan (Randhir) Singh (?–1844). Gouache. Sikh, Lahore, c. 1840–1846. India Office Library, London. Add. Or. 708. *See pp. 55, 149.*

57. Maharaja Gulab Singh (1792–1857) of Jammu and Kashmir, left; his third son, Ranbir Singh (?–1885), right. Gouache. Sikh, Lahore, c. 1846. Victoria and Albert Museum, I.S. 13–1956. Cat. no. 26. *See pp. 55, 148.*

58. Raja Ranbir Singh (?–1885) of Jammu left, seated on a terrace conversing with a secretary. Gouache. Sikh, Lahore, c. 1846. British Museum, 1915–9–15–02. *See pp. 55, 150.*

59. The second Lahore Darbar of 26 December 1846 (detail). Gouache. Sikh, Lahore, c. 1846–1847. British Museum, P. C. Manuk and Miss G. M. Coles collection, 1948–10–9–0109. *See pp. 55, 150, 151.*

60. The second Lahore Durbar of 26 December 1846, showing from left to right, front row, Henry Lawrence, Lord Gough (Commander-in-Chief), Lord Hardinge (Governor-General), Sheikh Imam-ud-din, Raja Ranbir Singh (proxy for Gulab Singh), one person unidentified, the child Maharaja Dalip Singh, Frederick Currie (Foreign Secretary). Gouache. Sikh, Lahore, c. 1846–1847. British Museum, P. C. Manuk and Miss G. M. Coles collection, 1948–10–9–0109. *See pp. 55, 150, 151.*

61. Maharaja Dalip Singh (1837–1893) in darbar, December 1845. Seated from left to right: (1) Labh Singh (2) standing attendant with cloth and yak's tail fly-whisk (3) Tej Singh (4) Maharaja Dalip Singh, a shot-gun in the left hand, his pet lap-dog at his feet (5) Dina Nath (6) Nur-ud-din. Gouache. By Hasan-al-din, Sikh, Lahore, 1845–1846. India Office Library, London, Add. Or. 710. *See pp. 66, 173.*

62. Maharaja Dalip Singh (1837–1893) in darbar, November 1843. Seated clockwise from left to right: (1) ? (2) Labh Singh (3) ? (4) ? (5) Pandit Jalla (6) Hira Singh (7) standing attendant (8) Maharaja Dalip Singh, petting a lap-dog (9) Dina Nath (10) Jawahir Singh (11) Lal Singh (12) Tej Singh (13) Gulab Singh (14) Suchet Singh (15) Chattar Singh Atariwala (16) Sher Singh Atariwala. Gouache. Style of Hasan-al-din, Sikh, Lahore, c. 1843. Mrs A. E. Anson collection, Chiswick, London. *See pp. 65–66, 172–173.*

63. Jawahir Singh (?–1845), brother of Rani Jindan in darbar. Seated from left to right: (1) Labh Singh (2) Lal Singh. Lithograph after a Sikh painting in style of Hasan-al-din (figs. 61, 62), c. 1845. Published: W. L. McGregor, *The History of the Sikhs* (London, 1846), II, frontispiece. *See pp. 66, 182.*

64. Henry Lawrence, British Resident at Lahore, 1846–1848, dictating instructions to Dina Nath, ex-Finance Minister. Gouache. Style of Hasan-al-din, Sikh, Lahore, c. 1847. India Office Library, London (photo). *See pp. 66, 161.*

65. Youth with attendant. Gouache. Sikh, Punjab Plains, c. 1832–1835. Victoria and Albert Museum, J. C. French collection, I.S. 193–1955. Cat. no. 3. *See p. 125.*

82. Sikh sardar. Sketch. Sikh, Punjab Plains, *c.* 1835–1845. Victoria and Albert Museum, I.S. 10–1957. Cat. no. 35. *See pp. 34, 161.*

83. Ajit Singh Sandhawalia (?–1843) with attendant. Sketch. Sikh, Punjab Plains, *c.* 1835–1840. Victoria and Albert Museum, I.S. 171–1953. Cat. no. 33. *See p. 159.*

84. Brahmin (?). Sketch. Sikh, Punjab Plains, *c.* 1835–1845. Victoria and Albert Museum, I.S. 14–1957. Cat. no. 37. *See p. 162.*

85. Sikh sardar. Sketch. Sikh, Punjab Plains, *c.* 1835–1845. Victoria and Albert Museum, I.S. 16–1957. Cat. no. 40. *See pp. 34, 163.*

86. Sikh sardar. Sketch. Sikh, Punjab Plains, *c.* 1835–1845. Victoria and Albert Museum, I.S. 15–1957. Cat. no. 39. *See pp. 34, 162.*

87. Sikh sardar. Sketch. Sikh, Punjab Plains, *c.* 1835–1845. Victoria and Albert Museum, I.S. 12–1957. Cat. no. 36. *See pp. 34, 162.*

88. Sikh sardar. Sketch. Sikh, Punjab Plains, *c.* 1835–1845. Victoria and Albert Museum, I.S. 13–1957. Cat. no. 38. *See pp. 34, 162.*

89. Sikh sardar. Sketch. Sikh, Punjab Plains, *c.* 1835–1845. Victoria and Albert Museum, I.S. 17–1957. Cat. no. 42. *See pp. 34, 163.*

90. Raja Dhian Singh (1796–1843). Sketch. Sikh, Punjab Plains, *c.* 1835–1840. Victoria and Albert Museum, I.S. 92–1960. Cat. no. 43. *See p. 163.*

91. Sikh sardar. Sketch. Sikh, Punjab Plains, *c.* 1835–1845. Victoria and Albert Museum, I.S. 172–1953. Cat. no. 41. *See pp. 34, 163.*

92. Maharaja Sher Singh (1807–1843) seated on an oval rug. Water-colour. Sikh, Lahore, *c.* 1860. India Office Library, London, Add. Or. 1454. *See pp. 51, 59, 169.*

93. Sher Singh Atariwala seated on a chair. Water-colour. Sikh, Lahore, *c.* 1860. India Office Library, London, Add. Or. 1404a. *See pp. 59, 178.*

94. Sham Singh Atariwala seated on a chair. Water-colour. Sikh, Lahore, *c.* 1860. India Office Library, London, Add. Or. 1403a. *See pp. 59, 179.*

95. Maharaja Ranbir Singh (?–1885) of Jammu and Kashmir, seated on a chair. Water-colour. Sikh, Lahore, *c.* 1860. India Office Library, London, Add. Or. 1402b. *See pp. 59, 151.*

96. Maharaja Dalip Singh (1837–1893) Ivory. Sikh, Lahore, *c.* 1850–1870. Victoria and Albert Museum, I.S. 143–1954. Cat. no. 49. *See p. 172.*

97. Rani Jindan (?–1861). Ivory. Sikh, Lahore, *c.* 1850–1870. Victoria and Albert Museum, 03597 I.S. Cat. no. 51. *See pp. 175–176.*

98. Tej Singh. Ivory. Sikh, Lahore, *c.* 1850–1870. Victoria and Albert Museum, 03595 I.S. Cat. no. 64. *See pp. 67, 180.*

99. Chattar Singh Atariwala. Ivory. Sikh, Lahore, *c.* 1850–1870. Victoria and Albert Museum, 03592 I.S. Cat. no. 62. *See pp. 66, 180.*

PREFACE

Until quite recently, historians of Indian art have tended to adopt a cautious, even at times, a caustic attitude to paintings of the Sikhs. The Sikhs, they imply, are humble products of the Punjab Plains, newcomers to Indian culture and, in origin, rough and simple peasants. They are a non-artistic race—as non-artistic, it is urged, as that other 'barbarous' people, the Scots. Like Scotsmen, Sikhs have many good qualities—industry, courage, intelligence and tenacity. They indulge at times in outbreaks of berserk frenzy. But they are great fighters and soldiers; they are hard workers and, like the Scots, they have spread all over the globe. Go anywhere and you will find two persons—a Scotsman and a Sikh. Scottish qualities are also reflected in Sikh religion. Its founder, Guru Nanak, is the exact counterpart of John Knox and Sikh worship has a plain simplicity, a quiet suspicion of aesthetic graces that reminds one of Presbyterianism itself. We can take the analogy still further for, in politics, both peoples are devoted to their homelands and each has a similar ideal—a Punjab for the Sikhs, a Scotland for the Scots. Even in dress, they have the same obsessive need to assert their own identities. The hardened Scot despises coat and trousers and flaunts a kilt, sporan and tam-o'-shanter. A true Sikh wears coat and trousers but faithfully parades a beard and turban. These traits of character have given both peoples a marked individuality. But, as to painting, critics have asked, where is it? In 1858, Ruskin said of the Scots: '(Here) you have a people careless of art, and apparently incapable of it, their utmost efforts hitherto reaching no farther than to the variations of the bars of colour in square chequers.' His remarks are quite unjust for they totally ignore —to cite only a few examples—the portrait painting of Allan, Willison, Ramsay, Wilkie, Runciman and Raeburn. But what Ruskin said about the Scots, other writers have hinted about the Sikhs.

The purpose of the present book is to correct this false impression. I have had two aims: to catalogue Sikh pictures in the Victoria and Albert Museum—a collection unrivalled in scope and quality—and, at the same time, to provide the basic materials necessary for its study. Like painting of the Scots, Sikh painting is chiefly an art of portraiture. It is concerned with historic characters and we can only grasp its significance by knowing who these were. Not only must we get their names right but we must have some idea of the part they played in events, what they were like as people and how they were regarded by their own and later times. We must understand why particular persons were chosen for portrayal, what Sikh needs were satisfied by portraiture and why Sikh painting focused on this type of art. Since the Sikh religion frowned on art, we must explain how Sikh painting began, where painters of the Sikhs came from, what styles they employed and how they were influenced by the Sikh environment. Finally—since Sikh painting is a product of the nineteenth century—we must consider the influence of European artists and the role of the British in Sikh affairs.

The problem of deciding who is who admits, at first sight, of easy solution. Sikh portraiture abounds in inscriptions and one would think that, granted care, identification would be simple. Yet it is surprising what mistakes have hitherto been made. The astute and massive Gulab Singh has been confused with the frail half-wit Kharak, later with his brother, Dhian and even with his son, Ranbir. The child maharaja, Dalip, has been taken for his mother, Rani Jindan, and certain characters, such as Ranbir Singh and his brothers Udham and Sohan have gone unrecognised. These mistakes have been due to one simple cause: the want of adequate collation. The evidence exists but it has never been presented. It is to remedy this omission that I have supplied biographical notes and included in them as full a list as possible of inscribed portraits.

Inscriptions alone, however, are not, in every case, sufficient and to identify a sitter correctly we may also need to know his character. If this precaution had been taken, Kharak could never have been confused with Gulab. In certain cases, inscribed portraits do not exist and personality then becomes the only clue to identity. There is no doubt, therefore, that we must have studies of character. The problem is where to find them and which to use.

Unlike the Mughal emperor Jahangir, whose memoirs give us a vivid self-portrait, no Sikh wrote or dictated an autobiography. Contemporary impressions by Indian observers are few and those that exist have one great weakness: they are so tactful that they tell us nothing. Aziz-ud-din, Foreign Minister to Maharaja Ranjit Singh, is a case in point. Asked by an English officer in 1831 in which eye Ranjit Singh was blind, he said: 'The splendour of the Maharaja's face is such that I have never been able to look close enough to discover.' We are compelled, therefore, to use accounts by Europeans. Yet here a different problem confronts us: if Indian accounts are too tactful, these, it might be said, are too outspoken.

No one can assess the Sikh attitude to painting without appreciating the character of Ranjit Singh. One of the greatest figures in Indian history, he had certain controversial traits and to understand him we must flinch from nothing. There are groups in modern India who would pull down the medieval temple of Konarak in Orissa—the 'black pagoda' of early voyagers, famous for its erotic sculptures. They would ban the *Kama Sutra* and *Koka Shastra*, India's contribution to the science and art of love. They would insist that Radha—Krishna's principal love, a married milkmaid with a cowherd husband—was, in fact, Krishna's lawfully wedded spouse. Over everything they would draw a grey veil of wan respectability. Historical characters would cease to exist: they would become, instead, mere projections of puritanical ideals.

Khushwant Singh, the latest and best biographer of Ranjit Singh, is only too well aware of this problem. Defending his own interpretation, he writes:

'Ranjit Singh has been poorly served by his biographers. Hindu and Sikh admirers deified him as a virtuous man and a selfless patriot. This academic apo-theosis reduced a full-blooded man and an astute politician to an anaemic saint and a simple-minded nationalist. Muslim historians were unduly harsh in describing him as an avaricious free-booter. English writers, who took their material largely from Muslim sources, portrayed him as a cunning man, devoid of moral considera-tions, whose only redeeming feature was his friendship with the English. They were not only not averse to picking up any gossip they could (every oriental court has always been a whispering gallery of rumours) but also gave them currency by incorporating them in works of history. . . . Ranjit Singh was neither a selfless patriot nor an avaricious free-booter. He was neither a model of virtue nor a lascivious sensualist. He was too warm and lively a character to have his life-story told in a lifeless catalogue of facts, figures and footnotes.'[1]

This passage sensibly expresses a modern outlook. Yet the writer surely goes a little too far; and to certain of the British he is less than just. The first historians— Cunningham and Prinsep—may well have relied too much on Muslim sources. Early British and European visitors to the Punjab did not. Jacquemont, Masson, Vigne, Hugel, Osborne, Emily Eden and Honigberger tell us how Ranjit Singh struck them. They saw him in camp and at headquarters; they met his courtiers and ministers; some of them personally drew and sketched Sikh characters. Much of what they saw was distinctly 'un-British'; indeed it was only too obvious that Ranjit Singh was no Queen Victoria or Prince Consort. But all were agreed on two things: his very evident greatness and his personal charm. Jacquemont described him as 'an imaginary invalid', dilated on other weaknesses but ended a letter with the words: 'Do love him a little for my sake.' Emily Eden, a tart and shrewish

[1] Khushwant Singh, *Ranjit Singh*, 7–8.

spinster, was aghast at his hard drinking but marvelled at his gentle manners and perfect courtesy. Her nephew, Osborne, was in a similar dilemma. He was baffled by what appeared to be contradictions in Ranjit's character but he was forced to admit that in spite of everything, he was a truly great person. Such genuine admiration ill accords with wilful fabrication of slanderous lies. None of these travellers had any motive for inventing stories. They were fascinated by the Sikh leader and merely sought to describe him as he was.

The correct attitude is perhaps suggested by a Victorian biographer, Sir Lepel Griffin. Griffin knew and loved the Punjab and wrote with keen appreciation of Ranjit the man:

'Ranjit Singh, although short of stature and disfigured, was the *beau idéal* of a soldier, strong, spare, active, courageous, and enduring. An excellent horseman, he would remain the whole day in the saddle without showing any sign of fatigue. His love for horses amounted to a passion and he maintained an enormous stud. He was also a keen sportsman and an accomplished swordsman. His dress was scrupulously simple. In winter and spring he wore generally a warm dress of saffron-coloured Kashmir cloth; in hot weather white muslin without jewel or ornament, except on occasions of special display or state.

The Maharaja was endowed with some of the most conspicuous signs of greatness. Judged from a commonplace ethical standpoint, he had no moral character at all. His moral being seemed, at a superficial glance, as dwarfed and distorted as its physical envelope. He was selfish, false and avaricious; grossly superstitious, shamelessly and openly drunken and debauched. In the respectable virtues he had no part; but in their default he was still great. With him, as with the most illustrious leaders of men, from Caesar and Alexander to Napoleon, intellectual strength was not allied to moral rectitude. He was great because he possessed the qualities without which the highest success cannot be attained. He was a born ruler with the natural genius of command. Men obeyed him by instinct and because they had no power to disobey. The control which he exercised over the whole Sikh people, nobles, priests and people, was the measure of his greatness.

'Although it would be to violate the truth of history to conceal or disguise the many faults and vices of Ranjit Singh, yet it would be trivial to judge him or them without full consideration of the society in which he lived. . . . In the days of the Georges, our ancestors drank as heavily and ostentatiously as any of the sirdars of the Lahore Court. "Drunk as a lord" was a popular saying which very fairly expressed the habits of the aristocracy in England in the eighteenth century. Today the fashion has changed and men drink more or less secretly. In the matter of relations between the sexes the morality of the Punjab was low. . . . But if we accept contemporary literature as sufficient evidence, the society of Paris today is fully as corrupt as that of the Punjab in 1830; and the bazaars of Lahore, while Ranjit Singh was celebrating the festival of the Holi, were not so shameless as Piccadilly at night in 1892.'[1]

It is Griffin's attitude that I have tried to emulate in the present catalogue. Believing that some impression of character is necessary, I have included comments from British sources—the name of the traveller appearing first, the comment later. Such comments are often as revealing of the writer as of the subject but provided we allow for this basic limitation, they can help to bring a character to life. On one major point, I have shrunk from commitment. Almost all British travellers and historians in the nineteenth century were convinced that Ranjit Singh had only one true son, Kharak and that the others—Sher, Tara, Multana, Kashmira, Peshaura, and Dalip—were 'fictitious' offspring, wished on him by various of his ranis but accepted and recognised by Ranjit for political or diplomatic reasons. This view is naturally unpalatable to present-day Sikhs and it has been hotly contested by the modern Sikh historian, Khushwant Singh. I have no wish to enter this thorny field. For Sikh painting, only two sons—Sher and Dalip —are relevant since only these succeeded to the Sikh throne. Modern Sikhs would certainly regard both as truly legitimate and since they were accepted by Ranjit as true sons, that is how they were treated in their life-times. In referring to them, therefore, I have sometimes used the word 'accepted' to distinguish them from Ranjit's first-born, Kharak but I have otherwise conformed to modern Sikh usage.

Two final questions must be briefly discussed: why were certain Sikhs painted and why has portraiture been the main Sikh contribution to Indian art? The answers to both questions will, I hope, become clear as the book proceeds. They can, in fact, be given in only one way—by recourse to Sikh history. Like another Indian sect, the Jains, the Sikhs began as a separate religious community and dispensed with the Hindu scriptures which underlie so much of Hindu painting. The Sikhs had no traditional mythology or imagery and, as their history shows, they also had no feudal system. Their history is, in essence, a struggle for two kinds of freedom—spiritual and political. The first was achieved through the teaching of their ten leaders or Gurus. The second was won by Maharaja Ranjit Singh. Sikh portraiture developed from this struggle and it is only by realising the roles which certain individuals played that we can understand their place in painting. For this reason, therefore, I have prefaced my account with a brief historical survey, for only by relating them to history do paintings of the Sikhs become intelligible.

[1] Griffin, *Ranjit Singh*, 89–94.

xxi

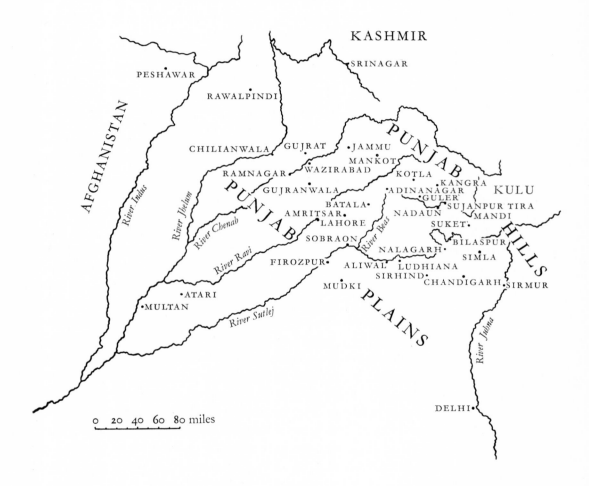

KASHMIR

SRINAGAR

PESHAWAR

RAWALPINDI

AFGHANISTAN

PUNJAB

CHILIANWALA   GUJRAT   • JAMMU

MANKOT

RAMNAGAR   WAZIRABAD   KOTLA

KANGRA   KULU

GUJRANWALA   ADINANAGAR

GULER

BATALA   SUJANPUR TIRA

AMRITSAR   NADAUN   MANDI

LAHORE   SUKET

SOBRAON   BILASPUR

HILLS

NALAGARH

SIMLA

FIROZPUR   ALIWAL   LUDHIANA

SIRHIND

MUDKI   CHANDIGARH   SIRMUR

PLAINS

ATARI

MULTAN

River Indus

River Jhelum

River Chenab

River Ravi

River Beas

River Sutlej

River Jumna

DELHI •

0   20 40 60 80 miles

xxii

Introduction

I THE SIKHS

(i) TEN GURUS

Among the peoples of India, the Sikhs are marked by a distinctive religion and by intense devotion to their homeland, the Punjab. Their brotherhood was founded in northern India at the end of the fifteenth century by a wandering teacher, Guru Nanak, whose message was first transmitted through three successors, Angad, Amar Das and Ram Das.[1] Teaching the worship of God as Truth and repudiating mosques and Hindu temples, these Gurus appealed especially to the Jats, the sturdy but unlettered peasants of the Punjab and soon a new community was formed, whose members used separate meeting-houses for prayer and hymn-singing. They were called Sikh from *sikh*, the Punjabi term for 'disciple' or 'learner'.

Under a fifth Guru, Arjun, the town of Amritsar was proclaimed the centre of Sikhism and a place of pilgrimage. A holy book, the *Adi Granth*, was compiled from the writings of Guru Nanak, his successors and certain Hindu and Muslim thinkers. Fixed rules for religious and social conduct were framed and with a view to husbanding resources, special contributions were levied.

These steps gave the Sikhs a firm organisation; but, just as the medieval Christian church in Europe came into conflict with secular power once it began to own property, Guru Arjun's dabblings in politics brought disaster. He rebelled against the Mughal emperor, Jahangir, the ruler of the Punjab and was executed in 1606. His death is a turning-point in Sikh history for it changed a gentle sect into a ruthless soldiery.

Until this time, however tough and sturdy their character, the Sikhs were, by inclination, quiet mystics. But they were never tame or servile. The death of Guru Arjun warned and provoked them. His son, Har Govind, the sixth Guru, armed his followers and formed a personal bodyguard; and from this action there dates a cult of the sword which has ever since been part of Sikh discipline. To Guru Har Govind, the sword symbolised both spiritual and secular authority and in personally

[1]Note I, p. 71.

I

wearing two swords, he expressed his resolve as Guru to maintain Sikhism as a faith and protect its adherents from oppression. The result was a gradual emergence of two kinds of Sikh. Many continued as able, steady cultivators, anxious to avoid conflict. Others made fighting a life-long profession. Between these two types there was no rigid division. Cultivators became fighters when occasion demanded it and fighters blended with villagers when events forced them 'underground'. The connecting link was faith in the Guru as head of the community, devotion to the *Granth* or Holy Bible and the resolve to fight rather than to be oppressed. Both kinds are equally typical but it was the Sikhs as fighters who were now to influence events.

During the thirty years, 1645 to 1675, quarrels between families led to the nebulous position of the seventh Guru, Har Rai, the choice of an infant, Har Kishan, as eighth Guru, and finally the uncertain status of the ninth Guru, Tegh Bahadur. None of these leaders had fixed headquarters and although they were regarded as continuations of the founder, Guru Nanak, their personal influence was no longer vital. Sikh beliefs had become clarified through the spread of copies of the *Granth*; religion was a morning and evening exercise practised either in public under the direction of a prominent disciple, or privately in the house. The community, in fact, could be compared to a network of cells spread across the Punjab. For part of this period, there was a lull in persecution by the Mughals. But in 1658 the bigoted Aurangzeb became emperor and began to harass all non-Muslims, including the Sikhs. On his return to the Punjab from Assam and Bihar, where he had gone to spread Sikhism, Tegh Bahadur gathered leading Sikhs about him and advocated passive resistance. So effective was his quiet teaching that he was arraigned before the Emperor, taken to Delhi in 1675, tortured and beheaded.

His son, Govind Singh, was fifteen years old when his father was executed. He was viewed with suspicion by the Emperor and, due to Sikh dissensions was not, at first, unanimously accepted as tenth Guru. He therefore lived in retirement for twenty years and it was not until 1695 that he emerged and applied himself to two projects. The first was political—the liberation of Sikhs from Mughal rule and the achievement of a daring new ideal, an independent Sikh state. The second was spiritual—the reanimation of Sikhism itself and the expression of Guru Nanak's ideas in new forms. Both projects were revolutionary and from their launching dates the gradual rise to power of the Sikh people.

Govind Singh's first aim was to rid the Punjab of the Mughals. At the end of the seventeenth century, the region fell into three rough divisions—the Punjab Plains, the Punjab Hills and a tract of broken country between them. It was part of the Mughal empire and was administered by Mughal governors. Two of these were based on Sirhind and Lahore, while a third occupied the great fort of Kangra and supervised the Kangra Hills. The governors' chief functions in the Plains were to collect imperial revenues and maintain Mughal authority, while the governor at Kangra received annual tribute from the Hill rajas but, for the rest, left them to their own concerns. Provided, in fact, annual tribute was paid, the Hill rulers were free to fight each other, annex each other's territories and live as they pleased. The three areas were part of the same Punjabi region but differed greatly in communications and accessibility. It was easy to move in the Plains, difficult in the Hills, while the belt of country in-between, with its low hills and jungle, gave excellent shelter to bands of marauders. Here they could avoid capture and organise brigandage and revolt. Mughal control was strongest at each governor's headquarters but order was never wholly preserved. Handicapped by weak or absentee emperors, Mughal governors were often forced to rely on their own armies.

Under these conditions the Sikhs grew in strength. They could often visit Amritsar and keep in contact with their Gurus. They could suddenly erupt as mobile squads of fighters, rally round a leader and become an army. The middle belt of country provided them with gathering points for aggression. It was also a retreat to which they could withdraw. A Sikh state might not be practicable at once, but it was far from impossible. And Guru Govind Singh, inspired by his father, began to plan accordingly.

Basing himself on the lower hills, he quietly assembled a band of fighters. He built five forts to serve as strongholds and defeated the Hill rajas of Sirmur and Nalagarh, two minor states between the Hills and the Plains. Then, in alliance with the Raja of Bilaspur, he beat off attacks by the Mughal governor of Kangra and other Hill rulers. By 1699 he was well established as a small but independent power and at this point he began to revise the whole Sikh structure.

So far as doctrine was concerned, he directed his followers to worship the One Invisible God, revere the memory of Nanak and other Gurus, employ the watchword 'Hail Guru', concentrate on the *Granth*, and, above all, honour steel. He saw Sikhism, in fact, as a warring creed. He himself was in no sense holy or divine and indeed he ordered that all individual gurus must be deemed to end with him. It was the *Granth* that should be worshipped and through it the ten Gurus would receive symbolic representation.

To create this idea of militant brotherhood, Guru Govind Singh devised two sacraments: the first, a form of baptism with consecrated water stirred by a sword or dagger; the second, the joint partaking of a mixture of flour, sugar and butter, which broke caste. The brotherhood, created by these rites, was called the *Khālsā* or 'the Pure'. They abstained from smoking; they had no intercourse with Muslim women; they avoided meat killed by Muslims. At the same time, a member of the

3

Khālsā observed 'the five K's': his hair (*kesh*) was unshaven, he wore a wooden comb (*kanghā*) in his hair, he had an iron bracelet (*karā*) on his wrist, he wore shorts (*kach*) and he carried a sword or *kirpān*. In addition, the members of the brotherhood adopted the name of Singh or lion. With these observances, the Sikhs took on the appearance by which they are known today.[1]

These reforms completed, Guru Govind Singh turned to arms but here his enemies were successful. He sought refuge in two of his forts and though he escaped after five years, he was hotly pursued and four of his sons were slain. At Dam Dama, 'the breathing place', he paused and for a year compiled further scriptures—the *Dasam Granth* or Tenth Book. But the soldier in him was not to be suppressed. In 1707, the death of Aurangzeb brought a change in Mughal policy. Guru Govind Singh supported his successor, Bahadur Shah, and perhaps in the hope of obtaining a *quid pro quo* in the Punjab, he took his horsemen to the Deccan to confront the emperor's rival. A year later he was dead, murdered by Muslim assassins.

So hapless a *débâcle* might well have ended Sikh aspirations. But the Sikhs were now a militant body. Guru Govind Singh had been not only a guru but a warrior; and despite its seeming failure, there remained the ideal of Sikh independence. Within a century, this was suddenly to be achieved.

(ii) TWELVE MISLS

The death of Guru Govind Singh did not depress the Sikhs; it rather stung them to action. Banda, a convert from Hinduism, called them to arms, and for a brief eight years, a savage rebellion raged. In 1716, Banda was captured and executed and just as failure had dogged Guru Govind Singh, defeat drove the Sikhs once more into 'underground' resistance. With neither leader nor state, they were none the less united by religious ideals. As roving bands of warriors they kept together, and despite twenty years of Mughal oppression they maintained their identity. Gradually Mughal rule at Delhi weakened and, with its collapse, the Sikhs rose again.

By 1750, sixty-five bands were raiding the Punjab. They functioned under locally chosen leaders and it was this acceptance of local spheres of influence which gave them their vitality. Gradually, however, larger units were formed—several bands uniting to form a *misl* or confederacy. As the century advanced, twelve *misls* were recognised, some named after their leaders, some from the areas where they operated. Each was independent of the others, yet each believed itself part of the

[1]Note II, p. 71.

4

Sikh community. Each *misl* had its own tract of country where it levied protection money, constructed forts and exercised its rule. Whenever possible the *misls* met twice a year at Amritsar to formulate a policy and discuss Sikh affairs, and at these meetings, leaders of certain *misls* impressed themselves on others by sheer force of character and personality.

This organisation was encouraged by the waning of Mughal authority. In 1738 and 1739, the Persian Nadir Shah invaded India, marched across the Punjab, captured and looted Delhi and withdrew carrying much booty. His invasion was followed by incursions of the Afghans. Indeed between 1748 and 1767 the Afghan, Ahmad Shah Durani, passed through the Punjab on nine occasions. At the same time, Maratha forces were threatening Mughal rule from the southwest, while the British were slowly coming up from the south and east. Taking advantage of this chaos, the Sikh bands plundered Persian and Afghan invaders as well as Muslim towns and villages in the Punjab. In the course of these struggles, battles on a large scale took place and key towns and cities changed hands. In 1757, 1759 and 1761 the Sikhs occupied Lahore for short periods and Amritsar was several times seized. Afghan armies were heavily engaged. In 1762, Afghan forces severely defeated the Sikhs, killing, it is said, twenty to thirty thousand men. Yet so numerous were the Sikhs that only a few months later they defeated Afghan forces at Amritsar and recaptured most of the southern Punjab. During this time, Mughal rule finally collapsed. In 1761 the Afghans routed the Marathas at Panipat but, failing to establish a permanent rule of their own, abandoned the Punjab to its factions. In 1767 Lahore fell to the Sikhs. Afghan kings still claimed sovereignty but, for practical purposes, the unforeseen had happened—the Punjab was under Sikh control.

To overrun the Punjab, however, was not to unite it and almost immediately the limits of Sikh power became apparent. Success in arms had had its dangers; it had led to the ownership of lands and property which resulted in family rivalries and jealousy. Each *misl* was racked by intrigues; leadership tended to stay in one family but no one knew when a rival family might suddenly seize it. *Misls* quarrelled amongst themselves and even *misl* territories were never stable. From being a loose confederation of local commands, staunchly attached to one ideal, Sikh *misls* came to resemble a 'devouring pack' each obstinately independent, each voraciously preying on the others.

At the end of the eighteenth century, the largest and most powerful *misls* were known as the Bhangis, the Kanheyas, the Ramgharias and the Sukerchakias. These *misls* lay north of the Sutlej river and were strung out across the Punjab. They were not, however, confined to the Plains. From the middle of the century they had interfered in Hill affairs, aiding one Rajput ruler against another, plundering towns and exacting tribute. In these ventures, Sikh frequently fought Sikh and inter-*misl* rivalries were as virulent and as strong as in the Plains. It was on to this violent, anarchic scene that the greatest political leader the Sikhs had ever had, Maharaja Ranjit Singh, was now to come.

(iii) MAHARAJA RANJIT SINGH

Ranjit Singh was twelve years old when in 1792 he succeeded his father as chief of the Sukerchakia *misl*. This *misl* already dominated the Punjab and the father, Maha Singh, had strengthened it by linking it with the Kanheyas. Ranjit was married as a child to Jai Singh Kanheya's grand-daughter and the union provided him with armed support. His mother-in-law, Sada Kaur, was able and astute, and in the crucial years following his succession, her guidance helped to consolidate his position.

Like the young Akbar who became third Mughal emperor at the age of thirteen and Raja Sansar Chand who succeeded to Kangra at ten, Ranjit Singh at twelve was already fit to rule. His aim was to unify the Sikhs and found a Sikh state. The Sukerchakia troops backed him; in 1796 he mauled the Ramgharias; he then attacked other *misls*. Finally, in 1798, he obtained from the Afghan ruler, Shah Zaman, the title of Maharaja and the right to take and hold the city of Lahore. A year later, it became his capital.

From this strong position, Ranjit Singh gradually expanded his power and influence. The Sikhs were fighters who were best controlled when actively engaged. He therefore planned to establish a Sikh 'empire'—adding first one piece of territory and then another and employing the Sikhs to gain new glory.

The Punjab Hills were an obvious target. Jammu had already been overrun by Sikh bands. The lower part of the Kangra valley and Guler were disturbed. Sansar Chand of Kangra was becoming too prominent a figure and when in 1809 he was still besieged by the Gurkhas, Ranjit Singh seized his chance. He ousted the invaders but in the process subdued the Kangra ruler and compelled him to give tribute. He appointed a Sikh sardar, Desa Singh Majithia, as Governor of the Kangra Hills and in 1811 and 1813 he annexed first Kotla and then Guler. Further west he made similar encroachments. He took the small state of Jasrota and overawed the Raja of Jammu, replacing him in 1820 with a Raja of his own making. In 1828 he annexed Kangra itself. Certain Hill states kept a precarious independence but not a state dared to thwart or defy him. Similar expansion took place in other directions: in 1819 he moved west and took Multan; in 1820 he annexed

Rawalpindi and invaded Kashmir; in 1833 he absorbed Ladakh and in 1834 Peshawar.

Such expansion built up Ranjit Singh's personal prestige. The more battles he won, and the more territory he acquired, the greater became his name. Yet alongside ruthless daring went cunning prudence and perhaps his greatest success was the containment of the British. While the Sikh *misls* had been battling in the eighteenth century, the British had been steadily moving north. In 1803 they took Delhi and in 1805 routed the Marathas. Since Mughal rule was over, no other power rivalled them. But to the north lay Afghanistan, Persia and Russia with the Punjab in-between. It was vital to their safety to secure northern India; but the means of doing so was far from clear. Should they fight the Sikhs, annex the Punjab, invade Afghanistan? Or should they pause and negotiate? Ranjit Singh's skill and brilliance made them choose peace. In 1809 he sought to subdue the six Sikh *misls* south of the river Sutlej. The British objected and occupied Patiala. Then, instead of declaring war, they signed a treaty. By this agreement, both Ranjit and the British accepted the Sutlej as a permanent boundary between them. They promised 'perpetual friendship' and although neither side entirely trusted the other, necessity kept them at peace. In 1838, the year before Ranjit died, Vigne, the British traveller, noted: 'He was jealous of every European, and particularly of Englishmen, and could he have done so, would not easily have been persuaded to allow any English traveller to cross his frontier. But courtesy and hospitality, which he has so frequently displayed, were cheap and unavoidable returns for the perpetual friendship that existed between him and the East India Company.'[1] It is not too much to claim that by this subtle exercise of patience Ranjit Singh ensured his rule for thirty years.

In forming a Sikh state, Ranjit Singh was helped over the years by a number of able assistants. These engineers of his success can be divided into four groups. In his early years he owed much to Sada Kaur, his firm mother-in-law. He also acted, at this time, through and with his fellow Sikhs. Yet soon he sensed that in a world of vehement rivalries and inter-*misl* conflicts, his best counsellors were non-Sikhs. Only men with no exterior allegiances, whose entire position, status and career depended on himself, could be fully trusted. He therefore discarded Sikh confidants and recruited instead an inner council of outsiders. The Brahmin Dina Nath, an expert in taxation, organised his finances. Aziz-ud-din, a young Muslim physician whose intelligence and sympathy had won his confidence, became Foreign Minister. Khushala, a Brahmin from Meerut, who had joined Ranjit's bodyguard and fired him with his personal attractions, became his intimate favourite, adopted Sikhism and was known as Jamadar Khushal Singh. From 1811 until 1818 he

[1] Vigne, *Travels in Kashmir*, II, 425.

7

swayed the household as Lord Chamberlain, determining who should have access to Ranjit and on what terms. Although he was later seconded to the army, he was never wholly superceded.

But it was rather a third group, three Dogra brothers, who attracted public attention and gave panache to Ranjit's court. In 1810, a young member of the Jammu junior line, a Dogra Rajput named Gulab Singh, had entered Ranjit's army. A little later he was joined by two handsome brothers, Dhian Singh and Suchet Singh. Fascinated above all by the polished Dhian, Ranjit made him first a porter in the palace, then, in 1818, chamberlain or lord of the privy chamber and finally in 1828 Chief Minister. In this capacity Dhian Singh amassed wealth, became master of a great tract on the borders of Kashmir and maintained an army of 25,000 men. His young son, Hira, became Ranjit's inseparable companion, even sitting in a chair beside him, while his own father deferentially stood. Dhian's appointment led to the promotion of his two brothers—Suchet, who hovered round the court as a 'gay courtier and gallant soldier', and Gulab Singh, the most enterprising of the three. He usually remained in the Hills, but from time to time visited the court. In 1820 he was made Raja of Jammu, replacing the senior line and holding the state in semi-independent charge. Eventually he was to become the most powerful of all Ranjit Singh's associates.

There remains a fourth group to whom he owed some of his success. These were various European adventurers who were employed as officers after 1822 to organise his army. Two Italians, Ventura and Avitabile, trained his infantry and also held civil charges. A Frenchman, Allard, commanded cavalry, while the most efficient of his troops, the artillery, were trained by a series of Europeans including the Frenchman, General Court, and the Irish-American Colonel Gardner. Others, such as Van Cortlandt, were also given commands. Under the leadership of these Europeans, Ranjit Singh's army became perhaps the most effective force in the whole of India, the only one to rival the Company's army.

It was ultimately, however, from Ranjit's own personality that his power sprang. Though small and ugly, his charm was irresistible. William Osborne, A.D.C. to the Governor-General, Lord Auckland, met him in 1838, a year before he died, and his journal, *The Court and Camp of Runjeet Sing*, describes how the Maharaja impressed him: 'The more I see of Runjeet Sing, the more he strikes me as an extraordinary man. Cunning and distrustful himself, he has succeeded in inspiring his followers with a strong and devoted attachment to his person; with a quick talent at reading men's minds, he is an equal adept at concealing his own; and it is curious to see the sort of quiet indifference with which he listens to the absurd reports of his own motives and actions which are daily poured into his ears at the Durbar, without giving any opinion of his own, and without rendering it possible to guess what his final decision on any subject will be, till the moment for action has arrived.

Though he is by profession a Sikh, in religion he is in reality a sceptic, and it is difficult to say whether his superstition is real, or only a mask assumed to gratify and conciliate his people.

He is mild and merciful as a ruler, but faithless and deceitful; perfectly uneducated, unable even to read or write, he has by his own natural and unassisted intellect raised himself from the situation of a private individual to that of a despotic monarch over a turbulent and powerful nation. By sheer force of mind, personal energy and courage (though at the commencement of his career he was feared and detested rather than loved), he has established his throne on a firmer foundation than that of any other eastern sovereign, and but for the watchful jealousy of the British government, would long ere this have added Scinde, if not Afghanistan, to his present kingdom.'[1]

Another traveller, Baron Hugel, had formed the same impression:

'When he seats himself in a common English armchair, with his feet drawn under him, the position is one particularly unfavourable to him; but as soon as he mounts his horse, and with his black shield at his back, puts him on his mettle, his whole form seems animated by the spirit within, and assumes a certain grace, of which nobody could believe it susceptible. In spite of the paralysis affecting one side, he manages his horse with the greatest ease.

If nature has been niggardly to him in respect of personal appearance, she has recompensed him very richly by the power which he exercises over everyone who approaches him. He can in a moment take up a subject of conversation, follow it up closely by questions and answers, which convey other questions in themselves, and these are always so exactly to the purpose, that they put the understanding of his respondent to the test.

With a voice naturally rough and unpleasant, he can assume a tone of much fascination whenever he wishes to flatter; and his influence over the people of northern India amounts to something like enchantment.'[2]

Aided by his courtiers and advisers but above all, through sheer force of character, Ranjit Singh had united the Punjab, created a separate Sikh state and realised the seemingly impossible.

[1] Osborne, *Court and Camp*, 92–94.
[2] Hugel, *Travels*, 380–381.

Ranjit Singh died in June 1839 and almost immediately the cherished ideal of a strong Sikh state began to dissolve. His son, the half-witted Kharak Singh, succeeded but within two months was set aside by his own son, Nau Nihal. Ranjit's peaceful tactics lapsed and almost at once the Sikhs resorted to political killings. Chet Singh, favourite and Chief Minister of Kharak, was promptly murdered. Kharak Singh himself died in November 1840 and by coincidence or design Nau Nihal Singh was killed a day later by a fall of masonry while returning from his father's funeral. Dhian Singh, the former Chief Minister, had assisted Nau Nihal in his coup and for a time had kept the Sikh army steady. He now sided with Sher Singh, another son of Ranjit, in a strenuous battle for the succession. Sher and Dhian Singh succeeded but a rival clique led by prominent members of the Sandhawalia *misl* bided its time. Three years later, in September 1843, they struck, and, in the manner of Elizabethan melodrama, violent deaths followed in grim succession. Sher Singh, his son the young Pratap and the veteran minister Dhian were all killed by Lehna and Ajit Singh Sandhawalia. Dhian Singh's son—the Hira Singh of Ranjit Singh's doting fancies—struck back. He killed both Sandhawalias and then installed as Maharaja his own nominee, the boy Dalip Singh, the youngest of Ranjit's accepted offspring.

Hira was opposed by another Sandhawalia leader, Attar Singh, by Dalip's own mother, Rani Jindan, and by her brother, Jawahir Singh. He withstood them for a time, executing, in the process, Attar Singh. Then their manœuvres succeeded and in December 1844 Hira Singh too was murdered. Jawahir Singh and his sister, Rani Jindan, seized power; the Rani was made Regent for the young Dalip and Jawahir became Chief Minister. His rule, however, lasted for only a few months for in September 1845 the Sikh army intervened and he was summarily executed. Rani Jindan and the child Maharaja were then left, but, with the army getting more and more truculent, the Sikh government faced an ever-worsening crisis.

While the Sandhawalias, Dhian Singh, Hira Singh and Ranjit's heirs manœuvred for position, the army had gone its own way. Discipline had lapsed and the highly organised body which Ranjit Singh had trained through his foreign military advisers reverted to the roving bands which had preceded the *misls*. The Sikh instinct for democracy again asserted itself, but this time with disastrous consequences. Committees of the troops, not their officers, commanded; there was much agitation for pay; there was no respect for orders. In desperation, Nau Nihal Singh had sent a part of the army under General Ventura to attack Mandi and Suket—not because these harmless Hill states threatened Sikh power, but because any diversion was better than no employment. And, in a similar way, other contingents had been sent to assist Gulab Singh in a campaign that brought in Ladakh and parts of Baltistan. But these campaigns were long since over; and now, it seemed, only a major war could unite the army and make it once again a strong organ of Sikh rule.

Similar ideas had been occurring to the British. South of the Sutlej river, they had been growing impatient. So long as Ranjit lived, 'perpetual friendship' between Sikhs and British had been joint policy. Both parties had needed to be powerful: the British had respected Ranjit because he was strong; they had also valued his position as a buffer between themselves and the Afghans. As they watched anarchy increasing, they felt their own security threatened. Reverses on the Afghan front had shaken their morale; they were beginning to think that soon they must intervene in Sikh affairs. In such circumstances, Rani Jindan appointed Sardar Tej Singh as Commander-in-Chief; and believing as her husband, Ranjit Singh, had done before her, that private intimacy was a good qualification for high office, she made her lover, Lal Singh, Chief Minister. It was now November 1845. In two months' time, the Sikhs would be at war.

(V) THE UNSEEN RIVAL

During the years following Ranjit Singh's death, Raja Gulab Singh of Jammu, brother of Ranjit's Chief Minister, Dhian, had maintained the Rajput 'Dogra brothers'' interests and had created a powerful military state of his own. Nominally subservient to Ranjit and the Sikh court, he had proved, in practice, toughly independent. Gulab's own appearances before Ranjit had been few and after his death he preferred to watch events from his fortress town in Jammu rather than become involved in the dangerous intrigues of Lahore. He had normally, though not always, supported his brother, Dhian, and after the latter's murder in October 1843, he had opposed Hira Singh, his own nephew and Dhian's son. From October 1843 until his own murder in December 1844, Hira Singh was Chief Minister. He had been defied, however, by his uncle, the third 'Dogra brother', Raja Suchet Singh. Suchet rebelled in March 1844 but was killed while fighting. His estates in Jammu were claimed by Gulab for his son, Ranbir Singh, whom the childless Suchet had earlier adopted. As Chief Minister, Hira declared these estates forfeited to the Sikh government and although a compromise was effected, his death in December 1844 induced Rani Jindan and the new Chief Minister, her lover, Lal Singh, to intervene. They fined Gulab Singh three crores of rupees for insubordination and demanded the return of all of Hira Singh's estates in Jammu. Gulab Singh resisted; Sikh armies were sent against him and a confused period ensued in which much of Gulab Singh's Jammu 'empire' was overrun. Gulab was able, however, to suborn some of the Sikh regiments and, his safety guaranteed, went to Lahore to settle matters personally with Rani Jindan. He arrived, in Latif's words, 'half in triumph and half in bondage'. He remained in Lahore until August 1845 during which time he was first imprisoned by Rani Jindan, and then released as a result of clamour by the Sikh army. He was then severely fined, but was allowed to return to Jammu. When he left, he was even more popular with the Sikh soldiers than when he came.

It is against this background that we must set the first Anglo-Sikh War. In December 1845 Sikh forces crossed the Sutlej river. Their first battle at Mudki was inconclusive; but the British suffered heavy casualties and the Sikhs were encouraged. They pressed on but first at Ferozshah and then at Aliwal their advance was halted. So far, they had not been crushingly defeated but it was plain that the British were stronger than they had imagined. Doubts began to assail them; Lal Singh and Tej Singh lost their nerve, and in the moment of crisis, Gulab Singh intervened.

When war was imminent in December 1845, he was away in Jammu, but had at once protested to Rani Jindan: 'The British authorities have not acted contrary to the agreement. Neither have they broken their word. So to fight them without any reason is wrong. Though you killed my brothers and their sons without reason, who had been loyal subjects and faithful servants of the departed Majesty, I have the same feeling of loyalty to his present Majesty. I cannot question your right to do whatever you please within your territories in his name. But do not interfere in the affairs of the British.'[1] His advice had not been taken but as the Sikhs suffered reverses, the demand for Gulab Singh reached vast dimensions. He was believed to be the man of the hour—the only person who could save the Punjab and retrieve the situation. Rani Jindan accepted the position but when she sent for him Gulab Singh at first declined to come. Then, late in January 1846, he yielded to popular pressure, went to Lahore and was installed as Chief Minister. Opposed to the war from the start, he at once reproached the Sikhs for rashly attacking so colossal a neighbour. But it was too late to affect the outcome. In February 1846, the Sikhs were routed at the battle of Sobraon and it devolved on Gulab Singh to make peace.

In the negotiations that followed, two facts stand out. The first is Gulab Singh's loyalty to the young Maharaja, Dalip, and his determination to rescue the Sikh state. The second is his resolve to achieve the final independence of his own kingdom, Jammu. He would salvage the Punjab but he would sever it from Jammu. These two objects were achieved by separate treaties—the first Treaty of Lahore (8th March 1846) and the Treaty of Amritsar (16th March 1846).

[1]Panikkar, *Founding of the Kashmir State*, 91.

By the first treaty of Lahore, the Sikh empire was curtailed, a crore of rupees was levied as indemnity and Kashmir, taken by Ranjit in 1819, was annexed by the British. Sikh independence, however, was preserved. Dalip Singh was maintained as Maharaja, but as an insurance against anarchy, Henry Lawrence was made resident at Lahore and British garrisons were posted to the Punjab. Early in March these articles were agreed and the British celebrated their success:

'On the 5th of March, the Governor-General (Lord Hardinge) gave a grand dinner at Lahore at which all the officers of the army, including the Commander-in-Chief (Sir Hugh Gough) and Sir Charles Napier, were present. Toasts and speeches followed, in which the officers bestowed warm eulogies on one another and on the army at large, for the bravery displayed in the field. Every face flushed with joy, and at the conclusion of the entertainment the outburst of "hip, hip, hip hurrah" was deafening.'[1]

On 8th March 1846, the treaty itself was signed, Lawrence and the Foreign Secretary, Currie, representing Hardinge, the Governor-General; and there then followed a great darbar:

'On the afternoon of the following day (9th March), the treaty of peace was ratified by the Governor-General in his State tent, in the presence of the young Maharaja, who was attended by Raja Lal Singh, Raja Gulab Singh, Sardar Tej Singh and about thirty other sardars and civil officers, the Commander-in-Chief (Gough) and staff, the Governor of Sindh (Sir Charles Napier) and staff, the generals of divisions, the brigadiers, the heads of each department and all officers commanding corps, with one native officer from every British regiment being also present. The Governor-General was, on this occasion, seated on the throne, with the Maharaja on another throne on his right, and Prince Waldemar, a distinguished guest, on his left. The British officers were ranged on one side of the tent, and the Sikh chiefs on the other. On the treaty being duly ratified and duplicates executed and exchanged the Governor-General addressed the chiefs, his speech being translated, sentence by sentence, by the Chief Secretary, Mr Currie . . . At the close of this speech, the chiefs present expressed their deep gratitude to His Excellency for all the kindness he had shown to the young Maharaja and the valuable advice he had given.'[2]

This expression of gratitude should not be taken too literally for already undercurrents of intrigue and enmity were at work. Hardly had peace been declared than Rani Jindan repudiated Gulab Singh, and replaced him as Chief Minister by her

[1] Latif, *History*, 552.
[2] *Ibid.*, 552–553.

13

lover, Lal. The change did not perturb Gulab Singh; for his Jammu army was still intact; it had not been used in the war, and his shrewd policy of seeking terms had been amply vindicated. Lawrence, the Resident, knew and admired him. Gulab himself valued Jammu rather than the Punjab, and by the Treaty of Amritsar, concluded only eight days after the Treaty of Lahore he obtained all he desired. He was recognised by the British as independent Maharaja of Jammu and then, by a sudden stroke of brilliant diplomacy, he was allowed to take Kashmir in exchange for paying most of the war indemnity levied from the Sikhs. By this treaty, therefore, the British rid themselves of Kashmir—an area which they did not greatly want—and in return received almost a crore of rupees—a sum of money which they greatly needed. Gulab Singh, for his part, more than doubled his territories, and became Maharaja not merely of Jammu but of Jammu and Kashmir.

Such a bargain satisfied all parties; but trouble was not entirely over. Rani Jindan's lover and Chief Minister, Lal Singh, secretly instigated the Governor of Kashmir, Sheikh Imam-ud-din, to oppose the treaty. Three armies—a British force under Lawrence, a Jammu force under Gulab's son, Ranbir, and a Sikh army from Lahore had therefore to invade Kashmir and only when resistance appeared useless did he accept the decision. On 7th November 1846 he left for Lahore and on 9th November Gulab Singh entered Srinagar, the Kashmir capital.

On Lawrence's return to Lahore, the problem of how to restore Sikh government was re-examined. Lal Singh was removed and after a trial early in December, he was exiled to Banaras. Dalip's mother, Rani Jindan, was held to be a dangerous intriguer and on 16th December 1846 a second Treaty of Lahore deprived her of all power and set up a Regency Council of eight ministers and chiefs. They included the old Finance Minister, Dina Nath, the former Commander-in-Chief, Tej Singh, Sardar Sher Singh of Atari and Fakir Nur-ud-din, brother of Ranjit's Foreign Minister, Aziz-ud-din. The Regency Council was to be directed by Lawrence who in turn became permanent Resident at Lahore.

This treaty was ratified by a darbar on 26th December 1846. Lord Hardinge, Governor-General, Gough, Commander-in-Chief, and Henry Lawrence, were arrayed on one side, and amongst others present was Lawrence's assistant, Henry Vansittart. His wife, Mary Amelia, was also in the party and the following is her graphic account of the ceremony:

'The morning of the 26th December 1846 dawned cold and frosty. The Governor General's camp was pitched on the Beas (river) opposite to Byrowal Ghat where shone the red and yellow silk tents of the boy King Dhulip Singh. In the north rose the snow-capped hills of the Himalayas and to the east the dismantled towers of Kapurtallah, the residence of the once powerful Aloowala Chief.

Lord Hardinge had determined to reenact the scene performed at Ferozepoor in 1841, to have a personal interview with the Maharajah of the Punjab. The scene is the same, divested of its pomp and circumstance.

The Heroes of Jullalabad and Candahar are removed far above the pomps and vanities of this world, the frank hearted Shere Singh and his gallant boy Purtaub Singh, and Arch-enemy Dyan Singh, and the restless Atar Singh—the murdered and murderers have passed away to that "bourne from whence no traveller returns".

The nasty and corrupt accountant Deena Nath, the plodding and untalented Sirdar Tej Singh, the boy Dhulip Singh, the son of a profligate mother, by a disputed father; Lord Hardinge the fortunate, and Lord Gough the brave, are actors now.

The troops have formed down the long line of white canvas tents when a royal salute of twenty-nine guns announces the auspicious moment of the departure of the Maharajah Dhulip Singh. He had crossed the bridge of boats, throwing a largesse of 150 rupees among the boatmen, the scramble for the money is over, the now treasonable cry of "May the Raj of the Khalsah far be extended" has died away, and an A.D.C. on his flea-bitten arab has galloped down the line announcing the approach of the cavalcade.

A train of elephants trapped in red cloth and glittering with gold are looming in the distance, the bands have struck up "God Save the Queen", the elephant of the Lord Sahib is kneeling. Mr. Currie is asking "Where is His Lordship? He ought to have met them at the other end of the street." Then he adds "Why, it is only the Commander-in-Chief!" And Lord Gough, venerable with age but firm in tread and carriage, dismounts.

But another A.D.C. gallops down the line. Lord Hardinge and his staff have clambered up the elephants, again the bands play, and as the first gun of the salute is fired, the boy Dhulip Singh is lifted into the Howdah of the Governor General. A frightened child of eight years dressed in yellow silk with a falcon's feather, a clasp of jewels in his turban, is seated by the side of the old soldier and successful statesman.

The press at the door of the Durbar is over. European officers have filed off to the left, and the Sikh Sirdars are seated on the right.

At the head of the tent is Lord Hardinge, to his right sits the boy Dhulip Singh, and on the back of his chair Lady Gough is leaning. To the left is Lord Gough, his foot resting on a bag of gold Mohurs, his hand on the hilt of his sword, and his face shaded with white locks, is turned towards the Governor General.

The Sirdars, shabbily dressed in Afghan chogars (loose coats) have been presented and their nuzzurs accepted. A tray of shawls and kincob have been given to each, the contents have been rolled together by practised hands, and the value of

15

the stuffs been estimated, as a clothesman would estimate old clothes. A small table is pushed forwards, Dhulip Singh signs the draft of the new treaty, the band plays "Rule Britannia" and a royal salute announces to the world that the evil day of annexation is postponed, that Colonel Lawrence is Regent, and that the sun of the independence of the Punjab has set, never to rise again. The Governor General makes a short and pertinent speech, the Secretary translates it into a long and flowery Persian oration, and the Durbar is over.'[1]

At this darbar, two other significant figures were also included. 'Among the chiefs present', Latif records, 'was the famous Sheikh Imam-ud-din'—a passive witness, we must assume, to the transfer of Kashmir.[2] The other figure was Ranbir, son of Gulab Singh himself. Following the capture of Srinagar, Ranbir had hurried back to Lahore with Lawrence to attend the enquiry into Lal Singh. His father was too preoccupied to come in person and Ranbir had therefore attended as his proxy. The result was a darbar which ratified not merely one but two agreements. The first was the second Treaty of Lahore (16th December 1846), which replaced Rani Jindan and established the Regency Council. The second was the earlier Treaty of Amritsar (16th March 1846) which had granted Gulab Singh Kashmir, but which Imam-ud-din had contested. Which of the two treaties was to prove more important will soon become apparent.

(vi) THE END OF A PHASE

December 1846 was a triumph for Henry Lawrence. He admired and respected the Sikhs; he did not want a British Punjab; he desired rather a new and independent Sikh state—aided by the British but not controlled by them. What he did not want was annexation. Yet events and personalities were to prove too much for him. Sikh restlessness was ever present; Lawrence himself was more arrogant than certain Sikhs could tolerate; the replacement of Rani Jindan by the Regency Council appeared a calculated insult to the Sikh monarchy. It was rumoured that further attacks on the Sikh way of life were on the way. In 1847, Lawrence was out of the Punjab and on leave; but even if he had been present, the Sikhs might still have risen. In April 1848 an incident at Multan led its governor, Mul Raj, to attack the British. British forces retaliated; more Sikh contingents revolted and the

---

[1] MSS. account, in the possession of Mrs Hilda Moorhouse, a descendant of Mrs Mary Amelia Vansittart.

[2] 'The treaty was ratified in a public Durbar held at Lahore on the 26th December, the Commander-in-Chief being present. Lord Hardinge, seated on a throne, delivered an address explaining the object of the British Government to be the welfare of that of Lahore. Among the chiefs who were present was the famous Sheikh Imam-ud-din. The speech was interpreted to the chiefs by Mr Currie and the Darbar closed with a profusion of nazars consisting of jewels, shawls, guns etc.'
(Latif, *History*, 556).

second Anglo-Sikh war had started. Battles followed at Ramnagar, Chilianwala and Gujarat but by March 1849 the British had once again won.

This time Lawrence was overruled. To the tidy British, annexation seemed now the only solution. Dalhousie, the Governor-General, strongly favoured it: the British dared not risk a further Sikh uprising; they needed a strong frontier to march with Afghanistan; they were tired of muddle, anarchy and intrigue; the child Dalip was no substitute for his great father, the astute and powerful Ranjit. Tidiness prevailed. On 21st March 1849, the Punjab was formally annexed to British India; the Regency Council was disbanded and Dalip was put in charge of a tutor guardian, Dr John Login. He remained in Lahore until 1850 and was then removed to Allahabad. There he grew up as a young British gentleman and in 1854 was taken to England where he bought a country estate and visited Queen Victoria. In the Punjab, British officers took charge of districts; Sikhs were absorbed into the British army; order was imposed, and for almost a century Sikhs and British lived side by side.

It is in the light of these developments that we must now consider the painting of the Sikhs.

II THE PUNJAB HILLS

(i) GULER

Until the second quarter of the nineteenth century, no painting that is truly Sikh can be said to exist. In the eighteenth century in the Punjab Plains, murals in a somewhat rough style had for long been common.[1] Miniature painting, as practised for the Mughals, however, had virtually lapsed and it was only in the Punjab Hills that artists painted for local princes and their courts. Their pictures fulfilled Rajput needs and while portraiture accounted for some of their activities, the chief subjects were taken from Hindi and Sanskrit poetry and Hindu religious texts. In 1800, Kangra was the chief centre of painting but Guler, where vital experiments had been made between 1740 and 1770, had also a nucleus of artists.

During the eighteenth century, the Sikhs had often interfered in Hill affairs, siding now with one state, now with another. Their interventions had been largely opportunist. States were looted rather than occupied and no attempt was made to bring them under permanent Sikh control. In 1809, however, this policy had been abruptly abandoned. Sansar Chand of Kangra had been replaced as suzerain by Ranjit Singh himself. The Kangra raja had been allowed to keep his state but a Sikh governor, Desa Singh Majithia, had been installed in the vast Kangra fort. All tribute previously paid to Sansar Chand was now taken by the Sikhs but difficulties in payment finally led to a revised policy of annexation. In 1811, Kotla, an offshoot of Guler and Nurpur, became a Sikh enclave and two years later, Guler itself was taken over.

'The plan,' writes Barnes, 'was skilfully and deliberately laid. The Raja was directed to raise a large force to assist some operations on the Indus and when the military strength of the population was drained off and the country lay defenceless, the Raja was summoned to Lahore. On the day that he expected leave to return, he was shamelessly arrested and told that he would not be allowed to go till he

[1] Note III, p. 71.

18

surrendered his kingdom and accepted a *jāgīr*. Without waiting for a reply, Desa Singh (Majithia) was sent off with an army of ten thousand Sikhs and the territory was quietly annexed to the growing rule of the Khalsa. The Raja was restored to liberty but spurned the offer of a *jāgīr*. He had, however, assigned 20,000 rupees during his own incumbency for the support of his female household; and Ranjit Singh left that maintenance untouched.'[1] The allowance in question was derived from twenty villages and three gardens in Nandpur and Haripur (the State capital) and in one or other of these places, the raja, Bhup Singh, maintained a dwindled establishment until his death in 1826.

This sudden replacement of Rajput rule by the Sikhs imposed on Guler a new pattern. Desa Singh Majithia superseded Bhup Singh as local head of state. Government was now by Sikh officers; Sikh landlords were inducted on Guler estates. The Guler royal family continued a parallel, if tenuous existence but along with other Rajput families, it was now subordinated to the Sikhs. Such a situation involved adjustments in both attitudes and manners and for the smoothness with which the new régime worked credit must go to Desa Singh, the Sikh Governor.

Tactful, affable and generous by nature, he had become warmly attached to the Kangra Hills. When not residing at the Kangra Fort or visiting other states, he lived in Guler and mingled with the local people. He also expressed his love for the area by marrying a hill woman who bore him a son, Ranjodh Singh. His gentle courtesy may well have mollified the embittered Bhup Singh and perhaps as a result, Guler artists began to shed their reliance on Rajput subjects and experiment with paintings for the Sikhs.

One such example is a series of pictures portraying the ten Sikh Gurus.[2] The pictures are in Guler style of about the years 1815 to 1820 and invest each Guru with calm, serene grace. The features are based on traditional accounts and it is significant that Guru Nanak is portrayed along with Guru Govind Singh—the last guru confronting the first. Although the subjects are Sikh, the treatment employs Guler settings such as terraces and landscapes as well as standard Guler idioms for all attendants and accessories.

Besides the Gurus, other Sikh characters were portrayed, and among them, a local person famous for his Sikh affiliations.[3] Amar Singh 'Darhiwala', a connection of the Kotla family, had so impressed Ranjit Singh with his stupendously long beard, that he was given a monthly stipend with which to cultivate it. Yet of all local figures, it was Desa Singh Majithia himself who may well have attracted most attention; and although no securely identified portraits of him have so far come to

[1] Barnes, *Settlement Report*, 11.
[2] Figs. 1–6, Notes I and IV, pp. 71, 72.
[3] Fig. 8.

light, there are two pictures in which we can confidently connect him with the presiding figure. In one of these[1] a Sikh officer is shown seated in a chair in a court-yard, while a group of gentry, part Sikh, part Hindu, sit ranged about him on the floor. To the left musicians are escorting a party bearing a spinning wheel, stool and baskets. These are conventional equipment for a bride and indeed the whole atmosphere strongly suggests a wedding. The central Sikh figure, however, has an air of command—he is the sole person to occupy a chair—and the only character likely to receive such magisterial homage is Desa Singh Majithia himself. The suspicion arises, then, that this is no ordinary ceremony but may well be the Governor's own wedding.

This interpretation is re-inforced by a second picture.[2] Here the same Sikh officer appears, once again seated on a chair but this time with a Hill lady opposite him. The two sit closely together drinking liquor from wine-cups.[3] The lady her-self and her maid have Guler-type features and the picture with its red screen is in Guler style of about the years 1815 to 1820. If the first picture records Desa Singh Majithia's wedding, this second picture may illustrate his domestic life.

Such a suggestion is supported by further evidence. In a much later picture[4] of about the year 1840, a bearded Sikh figure appears once again. He is clearly not the same as the person in our last two pictures yet he bears a close, even a family resemblance to him. He is shown sitting on a terrace floor, dictating notes to a secretary whose pen-case lies beside him. Low down in the left-hand corner is a crowd of clamouring soldiers, each grasping a petition and pestering him for notice. The situation is highly unusual and indeed we know of no other pictures in which a leading Sikh notable is portrayed in quite these circumstances—calmly conducting official business but at the same time remaining so accessible to petitioners. Yet it was this very quality—patient forbearance—which characterised Desa Singh Majithia's own son, Lehna Singh Majithia. When Desa Singh died in 1832, his son succeeded him as Nazim or Governor of the Kangra Hills. 'The Nazim', Barnes states, 'was not only entrusted with the entire receipts from this territory, but he was likewise responsible for all disbursements; the fiscal, military and miscellaneous charges were all paid by his authority out of the gross income. There was no stated time for rendering these accounts to the State—sometimes two or three years would be allowed to elapse before he was called upon to give an explanation of his stewardship. But he was obliged to be always prepared to give up his papers and to pay the balance whenever the Government might demand an adjustment.'[5] Lehna Singh Majithia, Barnes adds, 'did not reside permanently within the limits of his jurisdiction. He appointed his own agents to every principal town or seat of a parganah, and left the details of management in

[1]Fig. 10.   [2]Fig. 11.   [3]Note V, p. 72–73.   [4]Fig. 36.   [5]Barnes, *Settlement Report*, 50.

their hands. Once a year he made a periodical tour, took his accounts, heard and redressed complaints, and then returned to his native residence at Majithia, near Amritsar.'[1]

In three respects then—the payment of military charges, the taking of accounts and the hearing of complaints—the picture exactly tallies with Barnes's descriptions. Such duties had been carried out by other Sikhs. It was rather the kindly spirit in which he executed them which seems to have made Lehna Singh Majithia remarkable. 'Sirdar Lehna Singh', Barnes further writes, 'enjoys a good reputation in the hills; he was a mild and lenient Governor, his periodical visits were not made the pretence for oppressing and plundering the people; he maintained a friendly and generous intercourse with the deposed Hill Chiefs and contributed, by his conciliatory manners, to alleviate their fallen position. At the same time, he is held in favourable recollection by the peasantry. His assessments were moderate for a native system and, although he did not possess that force of character to keep his agents under proper control, yet he never oppressed himself, nor willingly countenanced oppression in others.'[2]

Lepel Griffin gives an equally warm impression: 'Lehna Singh was known as *Hasmuddaula*, the Sword of the State and was a man of considerable ability. He was a skilful mechanist and an original inventor. He much improved the Sikh ordnance. Among other things, he invented a clock which showed the hour, the day of the month and the changes of the moon. He was fond of astronomy and mathematics, and was master of several languages. As an administrator, he was very popular. The poor were never oppressed by him, his assessments were moderate and his decisions essentially just. As a statesman, he may be said to have been almost the only honest man in Lahore.'[3]

It is this character—the honest and popular administrator—which is so vividly presented in our picture. Is it not probable, then, that its subject is Lehna Singh Majithia and him alone? We have seen, however, that while not being the same person as in the previous two pictures, he markedly resembles him. Such an identification therefore would strongly reinforce our earlier suggestion that the figure presiding at the wedding and later carousing with the Guler lady is his father, Desa Singh Majithia.

These pictures are more than local studies of a Sikh outsider. At one level, they testify to the Governor's kindly nature; they prove his desire to fraternise with local people; they show that Rajput aloofness had already yielded to Sikh warmth and affability. But in some respects they go much further. Before Sikh rule in Guler, artists in the Punjab Hills were geared only to the Rajput order. It was Rajput, not Punjabi culture, that they interpreted. In these studies, their function

[1] *Ibid.*, 49.　　[2] *Ibid.*, 50.　　[3] Griffin, *Ranjit Singh*, 131.

sharply alters. A Sikh soldier-administrator has replaced a Rajput prince as subject and Sikh power in the Punjab has received its first artistic recognition. This step was only possible because Guler artists no longer felt estranged. They could approach their Sikh masters with confidence. They could feel at ease in their company. And it was this willing suspension of mistrust that was shortly to bring Guler artists to the Punjab plains.

(ii) KANGRA

Such a development will be discussed in the next chapter, but in Kangra also events were giving painting a Sikh colouring. So long as the Kangra ruler, Sansar Chand, lived, Rajput disdain for the Sikhs had remained. The Raja had paid his tribute but had kept aloof. With his death in December 1823, the results of Sikh sovereignty became clear. When Anirudh Chand—his son by 'Rani Suketan'—succeeded him, he waited on Ranjit Singh at his summer capital of Adinanagar, some thirty miles from Kangra. He paid a handsome succession fee and was duly recognised as Raja. In 1827, however, there occurred a fateful sequel. The son of Fateh Singh Ahluwalia, a leading Sikh general, was married in Lahore; and Anirudh, accompanied by his two sisters, was summoned to the wedding. While there, the party attracted the notice of Dhian Singh, Ranjit Singh's Chief Minister and father of the boy-favourite, Hira Singh. Hira was now eleven years old and the question of his own marriage was being actively discussed. Dhian Singh proposed one of Anirudh's sisters.

This proposal brought to a sudden head the whole problem of Rajput-Sikh relations. For sixty years—from 1760 onwards—Sikhs and Rajputs had had more and more to do with each other. The early savage hostility, mutual mistrust and active dislike had slowly weakened and again and again Rajput princes had gladly made Sikh political alliances. Rajputs had used Sikhs and Sikhs Rajputs. Yet despite occasional gestures of friendship, each had remained at heart separate and distinct. Rajputs still adhered with firm tenacity to their aristocratic customs and the most basic of these were the rules that governed marriage. A Rajput princess, the daughter of a ruling prince, could only marry the son of a ruling prince. His nephew was beneath her. The prince himself, on the other hand, could marry anywhere. Members of junior branches of a royal house—the ruling prince's brothers, uncles and nephews—were technically known as 'Mian'. By Rajput custom they could marry in 'Mian' families, but not in reigning ones and it was precisely this issue that the Sikh proposal now raised.

Hira Singh was son of Dhian Singh, who in turn was brother of Gulab Singh

22

and Suchet Singh. Although a boy, he had been made a 'Raja' by Ranjit Singh. His father and uncles were also 'Rajas'. His uncle, Gulab Singh was 'Raja' of Jammu. None, however, were 'reigning Rajas' (in the strict sense of the term) and although members of the Jammu royal house, all were descended from a junior branch. Their father was Kishor Singh, son of Zorawar Singh, who, in turn, was son of Surat Singh. Surat Singh had been third brother of Raja Ranjit Dev, a reigning Raja of Jammu. By Rajput standards they were inescapably 'Mian'. Ranjit Singh had ennobled them by making them 'Rajas', but in Rajput eyes, the Sikh title was no title. In asking for one of Anirudh's sisters, therefore, Dhian Singh and, through him, Ranjit Singh himself, were putting to the test the whole problem of Sikh 'nobility' or status. Had success in war given the Sikhs the same status as Rajputs? Were they now socially equal? Was Ranjit Singh himself a 'noble'? Had service for Ranjit Singh 'ennobled' the three Dogra brothers and the boy Hira Singh?

To Anirudh Chand the question permitted only one answer: 'No.' The marriage proposal, if acceded to, would mean the end of his self-respect as a reigning prince. He was unprepared to abase himself so grossly. Yet he dared not reject the demand out of hand. He appeared to acquiesce and for the moment did nothing. 'Time passed,' Hutchison and Vogel relate, 'and Dhian Singh, through the Maharaja, sent messages to hasten the marriage alliance. Anirudh used the pretext that his mother had recently died and he would give his sister a year later but he secretly sent away his property across the Sutlej river preparatory to flight. When the year was past, the Maharaja, at the instigation of his Minister, started for Nadaun to hasten on the marriage, if necessary by force.'[1] And it is this descent on Kangra by Ranjit Singh in 1828 which set in train a series of events and eventually gave to Kangra painting a new character.

Faced with Ranjit Singh's imminent arrival, Anirudh chose to abdicate rather than to lose his honour. He took his two sisters with him and escaped to distant Hardwar. So grave a slight to Ranjit could have only one consequence—the annexation of Kangra by the Sikhs. Until 1828 Sikh occupation had been confined to the Kangra fort and to the sixty-six villages whose revenues supplied the garrison. The rest had remained with its ruler. Now the entire state was occupied and a Sikh governor for Kangra, as distinct from a Governor-General for all the Kangra Hills, was appointed. In 1830 and 1831, he was Raja Sher Singh, accepted son and later a successor of Ranjit Singh himself. In 1832 he was Lehna Singh Majithia, the kindly administrator, whom we have just discussed. In place of the great castle at Kangra, Sujanpur became the centre of Sikh authority and thus, in almost every sense, Kangra was now Sikh.

[1] Hutchison and Vogel, *History*, I, 194.

Yet this was not the only result. When Anirudh and his sisters fled, their uncle Fateh Chand remained. So also did Nokhu, one of Sansar Chand's ranis—the Gaddan girl with whom he had had his famous romance.[1] With her stayed her two daughters, Mehtab Devi and Rajbanso and her son, Jodhbir Chand. These were admittedly offspring of a reigning prince, but they were half-Gaddi (the shepherd caste) and half-Rajput. They did not count as pure Rajputs and the son's status was at most a 'Mian'. Fateh Chand, as uncle of a reigning prince, was 'Mian' also. None of them, however, shared Anirudh's hostility to Hira Singh. Fateh Chand, for his part, had cultivated friendly relations with the Sikhs. He had served as his brother Sansar Chand's envoy when negotiating with Ranjit Singh for the relief of Kangra in 1809. More than any other member of the Kangra house, he was *persona grata* to the Sikhs. And it is this circumstance which explains what followed.

Fateh Chand was keenly alive to his own interests. Nothing, he felt, could be gained by obstinate boycott. Accordingly when Ranjit Singh reached Nadaun, the country residence of the Kangra court, Fateh Chand was present to receive him. He did not try to condone Anirudh's insulting behaviour. He rather mollified Ranjit Singh by suggesting that Hira Singh should be married to his own (Fateh Chand's) grand-daughter, the daughter of his son, Mian Ludar Chand. Since Fateh Chand had not himself been a ruler, this alliance was obviously not nearly so grand as the one which had been first proposed. Fateh Chand, however, was Sansar Chand's second brother and Hira Singh was descended from a mere third brother of the Jammu raja. By Rajput standards, it involved at least some loss of face to Fateh Chand and some gain to the Sikhs. If Ranjit Singh and his minister, Dhian Singh, had not got all they wanted, they had at least done much better than they could rightfully have expected. Fateh Chand's mediation was therefore accepted and later in 1829 his grand-daughter was married to Hira Singh.[2]

But besides placating Dhian Singh, Fateh Chand soothed the Maharaja's own vanity. He proposed that Sansar Chand's two daughters by Nokhu, the Gaddan rani, should marry Ranjit Singh himself. Since Ranjit Singh already had several ranis and a large female establishment, they could hardly expect the highest honours. Moreover, they were half-Gaddi and only half-Rajput. But they were, none the less, true offspring of Sansar Chand and in becoming Ranjit Singh's wives, they showed Rajput respect for Ranjit Singh's status. Subject to their being married in proper form, their mother, Nokhu, agreed. Ranjit Singh accordingly observed the customary rites. 'Their mother,' states Latif, 'insisted on the Maharaja's going through all the nuptial ceremonies, such as the wearing of garlands on the head, the putting on of the bridal chaplet, etc. The gay Mahajara went through these formalities with much pleasure.'[3]

[1] Note VI, p. 73.   [2] Barnes, *Settlement Report*, 33.   [3] Latif, *History*, 441.

24

The upshot, then, was that Kangra was no longer ruled by its Rajput prince. The Rajput royal house was finished. The Sikhs were everywhere supreme. Not only was there a Sikh governor but Sikh notables held estates and were scattered through the valley. At the same time, the aloofness that had marked Sansar Chand's dealings with Ranjit Singh had at last vanished. The marriage of Fateh Chand's grand-daughter to Hira Singh linked Kangra to Lahore and Ranjit Singh's own marriages to the Gaddan rani's two daughters strengthened the link still further. Kangra was now doubly Sikh and it is this new situation which is reflected in painting.

When Anirudh fled to Hardwar, he took a small portion of his father's pictures with him. They were those most relevant to his sisters' weddings, later negotiated with the Raja of Tehri in Garhwal. They comprised a great series illustrating the *Gita Govinda*[1] which had probably been painted by Manaku, a Kangra master-artist from Guler, in about 1780; and, secondly a series illustrating Bihari's poem, the *Sat Sai*, perhaps painted by Manaku's son, Khushala. Both sets celebrated the loves of Radha and Krishna and both were intimately linked to weddings. Bride and bridegroom were urged to 'love like Radha and Krishna' and the possession of such lavishly illustrated copies of the poems was thought to bring good luck; they were auguries of successful union. Yet if two great sets were brought to Tehri, almost all of Sansar Chand's collection remained in Kangra and with it most of his painters. The collection was split up and Kangra painters had now to face a new situation. There is no evidence that Anirudh had shared his father's enthusiasm for painting. From 1824 onwards, therefore, artists may well have been re-grouped, some remaining at Kangra itself, some at Sujanpur and Nadaun, the country residences of the Kangra court, others even migrating. One fact stood out. There was no longer a single great patron. They would need to find work as and where they could. Above all, they must come to terms with the new authority.

The first Sikh with whom Kangra painters made contact appears to have been Raja Sher Singh. A son of Ranjit Singh, he was twenty-three years old when in 1830 he was made Sikh governor of Kangra state. His great pastimes were hunting and dalliance and although in later portraits he was invariably shown brandishing a huge sword, he was, in fact, sensitive, amiable and gentle. He at once took a great liking to the Kangra Valley and delighted not only in its women but in its tranquil slopes. He was also sensitive to painting and while there are no great records of his day-to-day activities or portraits of his flashing physical presence, a patron in embryo is suggested by a Kangra sketch.[2] He is there shown seated on a

[1]M. S. Randhawa, *Kangra Paintings of the Gita Govinda* (New Delhi, 1963).
[2]Fig. 38.

25

stool, half-clad after taking his bath, and waited on by a Kangra maid-servant. In later life, Sher Singh was to show unusual interest in painting and also in the Kangra Valley and in this small drawing we obtain proof of that genial fraternisation which was to mould his future life and influence Sikh relations with the Hills.

A second public for art comprised the Sikh sardars inducted by Ranjit Singh on to Kangra estates. Their first duty was to collect revenue and to pay it to the Sikh administration. For the great part, however, they were no mere absentee landlords. They lived on their estates and perhaps guided by the example of the tactful and forbearing Majithias—the father Desa Singh Majithia, his son Lehna Singh Majithia—they broke down local suspicion and even evoked kindly regard. For Sikhs of this type, Kangra painters devised a new kind of picture. Under Sansar Chand, the leading Kangra style had been passionate and poetic, interpreting the moods of ideal lovers, the romance of Radha and Krishna and the courtly conventions of Rajput feudal life. So long as these subjects were Rajput, their pictures had little appeal to Sikhs. Yet their basic themes—the charms of courtly love, the need of graceful women for handsome lovers—touched the Sikh imagination. The upshot then was a type of picture[1] in which roles were subtly altered. The *nāyikā* or girl in love remained a Kangra lady; the *nāyaka* or lover became a Sikh. Pictures of this kind had no great vogue yet to certain Sikhs of Kangra, living in the valley in the turbulent years from 1829 to 1846, they may well have given a subtle satisfaction. Like self-made business-men in England, longing to be socially accepted, they may have secretly envied the Rajput lover and gone out of their way to demonstrate their new-found status. Kangra pictures flattered their pride and by portraying Sikhs as aristocrats and lovers testified to their success.

If Sikhs themselves provided Kangra painters with new opportunities, there remained a third class of patron—members of the Kangra royal house itself. Rajput families maintained their Rajput culture and despite Sikh supremacy demanded Rajput pictures. Indeed throughout the nineteenth century, Kangra pictures—Kangra in subject and in style—continued to be painted. But in one respect adjustments took place. Under Sansar Chand, boycott of Sikh subjects had been complete. Despite his long association first with Jai Singh Kanheya[2] and later with Ranjit Singh, no Sikh portraits appear to have entered his collection. After 1828 all was changed. Fateh Chand himself had died while returning to Nadaun after negotiating his grand-daughter's marriage to Hira Singh and after giving the Gaddan rani's daughters to the Maharaja. His son, Ludar Chand, however, had succeeded to the estate which Ranjit Singh had granted him. He became a great

[1] Fig. 76.   [2] Hutchison and Vogel, *History*, I, 177-180.

favourite and although this friendship later cooled, it was a determining factor in the years immediately succeeding.[1]

Following the three weddings, Kangra interest in Sikh affairs quickened. The fortunes of the two Gaddan ranis and of Fateh Chand's grand-daughter were closely followed. News from Lahore was eagerly awaited and both Maharaja Ranjit Singh and Raja Hira Singh were viewed in novel Kangra guises. Sikh topics which had formerly been unknown in Kangra painting now made unobtrusive entries and a first picture to reflect the changed attitude poeticises the marriage of Fateh Chand's grand-daughter.[2] A youth in Sikh trousers and turban, his features closely resembling Hira Singh's, is shown relaxing on a bed beneath a canopy, as black storm-clouds, lit with white cranes, loom in the sky. A Kangra lady sits on the bed, caressing his right foot, while the lover's hand tugs at her skirt. Behind him a maid servant, also with Kangra features, holds a box and peacock fan, and in the foreground, a chair in Sikh style supports a sword and shield. Painted in the Hills, the picture can scarcely be a true portrait of Hira Singh dallying with the Kangra lady who became his wife. It is rather a poetic reconstruction, a wishful interpretation of the role which Hira Singh as husband of a Kangra bride might be expected to sustain.

A similar interpretation may be placed on a second picture in which Ranjit Singh himself is shown drinking with a Kangra lady.[3] The Maharaja is seated on a Sikh chair while the lady sits opposite on a stool. Like other women in Kangra pictures, she could well be any Kangra beauty for her features correspond, not to those of any individual, but rather to an ideal type. Indeed her face is scarcely different from that of the girl who sits caressing Hira Singh's foot. Yet, despite her seeming anonymity, she is almost certainly intended as a real person. Such a lady would be one of Sansar Chand's Gaddan daughters whom Ranjit Singh espoused and the picture might well have been painted at Nadaun in Kangra state where her brother Jodhbir Chand resided. Like the picture of Hira Singh, it reflects a basic change in Kangra sentiment. It celebrates from afar the queenly role which family sentiment would fondly expect her to fulfil. Above all else, it reveals the Sikh Maharaja in a new light.

One last picture[4] shows how vivid an impress had been made by Ranjit Singh on the Kangra royal house through his marriage with the Gaddan ranis. When he died in 1839, his ranis were of two minds. *Sāti*, or the custom of a widow burning herself on her husband's funeral pyre, was a Rajput, not a Sikh, practice. There was no question, therefore, that his Sikh or non-Hindu wives should accompany

---

[1] For possible portraits of Ludar Chand see figs. 46 and 47.
[2] Fig. 13.   [3] Fig. 12. See Note V, pp. 72–73.
[4] Fig. 16. Note VII, p. 73.

the body to the flames. To the Gaddan rani who had survived, on the other hand, Rajput pride and breeding required this supreme act and as the obsequies proceeded, there followed a grim scene of awful grandeur.

'The Maharaja's body, having been bathed with fragrant waters and embalmed was dressed in rich clothes and decorated with ornaments, as in life. Four of the Maharaja's Ranis and seven of his slave-girls, of their own free will and accord, prepared to burn themselves along with the body of their lord and husband, animated with the hope, given them by their religion, of entering paradise with their earthly master. One of the Ranis who burnt themselves alive on the Maharaja's funeral pile, was Raj Devi daughter of the celebrated Sansar Chand, Raja of Kangra, whom the Maharaja had reduced to subjection.

All the Ranis who had prepared themselves for the horrible sacrifice, standing at the head of the Maharaja's body, called the Minister, Raja Dhian Singh, into their presence. The sacred book, *Siri Gitaji*, was placed on the Maharaja's chest, and Dhian Singh, having touched the body of his royal master and the sacred book, swore fealty to the new Maharaja, Kharak Singh, and solemnly promised to use his best endeavours to keep both Kharak Singh and Nau Nehal Singh on friendly terms.

The Maharaja's body was placed on a decorated bier in shape like a ship. It was wrought with gold, and the sails and flags were made of the richest silk, embroidered with gold. The vessel was placed on a board on which the body of the Maharaja lay, and was carried by a number of men. Thousands of people accompanied the funeral, and the procession moved slowly from the interior of the fortress towards the funeral pile, where originally existed a small, but beautiful garden.

As the funeral procession advanced, thousands of rupees were thrown among the crowd as alms, and scrambled for by the needy and poor. For the first time during their lives, the Ranis of the great Maharaja came out unveiled from the harem and meekly followed the corpse barefooted. They were dressed in pure white silk and wore no ornaments. They had distributed all their jewels and valuables among the poor before leaving the *zenana*. One of the Ranis who could not distribute all she had with her, had the remainder of her valuables carried by a man who walked by her side, and she gave them away to the poor with both hands, as she went to the horrible altar. In front of each Rani, at a distance of two or three paces, walked a man with his face turned towards her and moving backwards. He held a looking-glass before the Rani, in front of whom he walked, that she might see that her features were unaltered, and that her resolution to sacrifice her life had no effect on her appearance.

After the Ranis followed the seven slave-girls, also barefooted. Some of these appeared to be only fourteen or fifteen years of age. All seemed quite indifferent to the awful fate which awaited them, and which, indeed, they themselves sought. Dr Honigsberger, who was a personal witness of this melancholy scene, observes, 'Perhaps our hearts throbbed more at the view of the dismal train, than those of the poor victims themselves'.

The drums beat mournfully, the musicians sang melancholy dirges, and the sound of their instruments spread gloom and sorrow throughout the whole assembly. This, combined with the murmuring of a vast mourning crowd, whose anxious faces bore testimony to the grief and affliction inwardly felt by them, and to their love for the departed master, whom they adored, and who loved them, gave the whole scene a most melancholy aspect. The funeral pile was constructed of sandal wood and aloe, in the form of a square six feet high. Upon it were strewed inflammable substances, such as cotton seeds. The bier having been brought close to it, its valuable ornaments and costly covering were given away to the mob. The Brahmins and the Gurus then recited passages from their holy books and offered prayers for the benefit of the departed soul of the Maharaja. This occupied half an hour. The ascent to the funeral pile was by ladder. The ministers and the sardars first ascended and helped in gently removing the royal body from the bier and respectfully placing it in the middle of the pile, together with the board on which it lay. The four Ranis, with death-despising intrepidity, then ascended the fatal ladder, one by one, according to their rank, and occupied a place at the head of their royal husband, holding the head with their hands. The slave-girls, with equal courage and contempt for death, then ascended the ladder and placed themselves at the foot of their lord. The *sattis*, having thus seated themselves round the royal corpse, were covered with reed mats, on which oil had been profusely poured. Raja Dhian Singh, at this moment, approached the Ranis and begged them to offer prayers for the prosperity of the new Maharaja; but not a word was uttered by the Ranis, who, with eyes closed and hands stretched towards the head of the Maharaja, which they were holding, maintained a solemn silence in expectation of the fatal moment which was now near at hand. A strong thick mat of reeds was then brought and saturated with oil, with which all were covered. The Minister, Raja Dhian Singh, and the sardars then came down. The Raja seemed the most affected, and grief had so much overpowered him that he felt his own life a burden, and insisted on being burnt with the Ranis. Twice or thrice he even attempted to force his way forward; and it was with some difficulty that he was persuaded to refrain from sharing the fate of the *sattis*. Oil, otto and ghee were then profusely thrown on the pile. This being done, Prince Kharak Singh lighted the pile at each corner, and in a moment the whole was ablaze, the flames of which ascended to a prodigious height. In almost the twinkling of an eye the unfortunate creatures who had been covered with the mats, had ceased to exist, and in a short time, the whole mass was reduced to ashes.'[1]

When news of the Gaddan Rani's sacrifice reached Kangra, her Rajput heroism thrilled her family in Nadaun and in due course the scene was commemorated in a painting.[2] The picture was obviously painted by a local artist from hearsay for while certain details are correct, others do not tally. In the left hand corner is a bier 'shaped like a ship' but with flags and no sails. The corpse is laid on a long cot surmounted by a structure like a white pavilion. Four ranis and seven slave girls are grouped about it but of these only two are clearly ranis. There is no sign of 'sandal wood and aloe six feet high'. In place of a single roaring flame, three small fires are slowly rising. The picture lacks the majesty of great painting—there is no aura of tragic exaltation—yet its very existence shows the intense interest with which members of the Kangra house regarded developments at the Sikh court.

[1] Latif, *History*, 493–495.   [2] Fig. 16.

III THE PUNJAB PLAINS

(i) THE COURT OF RANJIT SINGH

The years 1810 to 1830 saw the first approach by Hill artists to Sikh patrons and the first expression of interest in painting by Sikhs themselves. The next decade was to advance this process much further and to see the development of painting in the Punjab Plains.

In 1830, Maharaja Ranjit Singh was fifty years old. He had succeeded more than any other Sikh; he had united the Punjab and created a strong Sikh state; he controlled an army which made a brave display and was a powerful fighting force. His keen sense of mercy, humour, love of riding and disregard for convention had made him the most popular sovereign of northern India.

It is no surprise that Guler painters began to look southwards to the Punjab Plains. Guler state adjoined Adinanagar, the little town which for a few hot months each year became Ranjit's summer capital. Their experience of Desa Singh Majithia's benign rule had drawn them to the Sikhs. In 1826, Raja Bhup Singh of Guler had died and local patronage may have dwindled. There was much to be said for prudent enterprise and in the early eighteen-thirties, we may assume that some of them abandoned the Hills and settled at Lahore and Amritsar.

Yet the situation confronting them there may well have daunted all but the most resolute. Although the most obvious subject for portraiture, Ranjit Singh was strongly averse to being painted. In 1832 when Bentinck, the Governor-General visited him, he sat to a Delhi artist, Jivan Ram. This circumstance was exceptional. The painter was attached to Bentinck's suite and it was only at Bentinck's express request that Ranjit agreed to be portrayed.[1] Normally he was reluctant to allow even Western painters to sketch him; and that Europeans should attach importance to drawing filled him with amazement. An anecdote related by an Austrian visitor, Baron Hugel, illustrates this trait. When Ranjit met the British geographer, Vigne, in January 1836, he turned to him and asked: 'And what can

[1] Archer, *Indian Painting for the British*, 67–68.

31

you do?' To which Vigne replied, 'I can draw'. 'The Maharaja', Hugel adds, 'did not seem to comprehend how an art so little esteemed by himself could possibly occupy the time of a great white man.'[1] His attitude, in fact, was one of amused tolerance and while he indulged Vigne so long as it did not inconvenience him—he arranged, for example, for a Bactrian camel and a white dromedary belonging to Hira Singh to be sent to Ventura's house so that Vigne might draw them—he teased and made fun of him when he requested a sitting.

This joking indifference to portraiture was, almost certainly, due in part to Ranjit's own appearance. As a child he had been ravaged by small-pox—the illness leaving his face pitted with pock-marks and, what was more important, blind in the left eye. It was a one-eyed person, therefore, who confronted visitors. To some, such as the French botanist, Jacquemont, a traveller in the Punjab from 1829 to 1832, this ugliness was of small account:

'He is a thin little man with an attractive face, though he has lost an eye from small-pox which has otherwise disfigured him little. His right eye, which remains, is very large, his nose is fine and slightly turned up, his mouth firm, his teeth excellent. He wears slight moustaches which he twists incessantly with his finger and a long thin white beard which falls to his chest. His expression shows nobility of thought, shrewdness and penetration.'[2]

Osborne, the nephew of Lord Auckland, felt much the same:

'Ill-looking as he undoubtedly is, the countenance of Runjeet Sing cannot fail to strike everyone as that of a very extraordinary man; and though at first his appearance gives rise to a disagreeable feeling almost amounting to disgust, a second look shows so much intelligence, and the restless wandering of his single fiery eye excites so much interest, that you get accustomed to his plainness, and are forced to confess that there is no common degree of intellect and acuteness developed in his countenance.'[3]

Baron Hugel, the Austrian traveller, on the other hand, was viciously repelled:

'I must call him the most ugly and unprepossessing man I saw throughout the Punjab. His left eye, which is quite closed, disfigures him less than the other, which is always rolling about, wide open, and is much distorted by disease. The scars of the small-pox on his face do not run into one another, but form so many dark pits in his greyish-brown skin, his short straight nose is swollen at the tip . . . and his head, which is sunk very much on his broad shoulders, is too large for his height and does not seem to move easily. He has a thick muscular neck, thin arms and legs, the left foot and the left arm dropping, and small well-formed hands. He will some-

[1] Hugel, *Travels*, 289.   [2] Garrett, *The Punjab*, 36.   [3] Osborne, *Court and Camp*, 81–82.

times hold a stranger's hand fast within his own for half an hour, and the nervous irritation of his mind is shown by the continued pressure on one's fingers. His costume always contributes to increase his ugliness being in winter the colour of gamboge.'[1]

To such ugliness, Ranjit himself was obviously very sensitive and while we know that by the end of his reign he was sometimes employing painters and even tolerating them in darbars, there is no evidence that he liked, or encouraged their activities.

So strong an allergy to portraiture was a serious obstacle to artists but a second circumstance may have handicapped them still further. Painting of the kind practised at Guler and Kangra had been part of the Rajput order. Sikhism had not availed of it and although portraits of the Sikh gurus had been produced in Guler, this was a new development in the Hills. During his rise to power, Ranjit Singh had been incensed by the behaviour of the Hill aristocracy. They had tended to regard him as a social inferior and to treat him with contempt. As a result, he was determined to assert Sikh identity, to humble his opponents and to supersede their culture by Sikh practises. Smoking the hookah—for Rajput princes a constant habit—had been forbidden to Sikhs by their Gurus and was therefore banned at court. Sikh dress, especially certain styles of turban and tightly fitting trousers, proclaimed essential differences. Sikh chairs, based on early nineteenth-century English examples but with a new kind of looped arm, replaced the broad, low seats on which Rajput rulers had been wont to relax; and the custom of wearing a great shield, strapped to the back, was also introduced. All these practices were, in varying degrees, un-Rajput and in the face of so general a boycott of Hill culture, it would be unrealistic to suppose that painting would be an exception. It was rather in the face of courtly prejudice that Guler artists established their position.

A first type of patronage to be achieved is suggested by a darbar picture[2] in the Chester Beatty Library, Dublin. Ranjit Singh with flowing white beard is seated in a chair holding as emblems of state a bow and arrow. The Rajput Minister Dhian Singh with customary deference stands obsequiously behind him, while Kharak Singh, his son, sits on a basket stool to the right. The boy favourite, Hira Singh, sits opposite his royal protector, commanding with his midget form the centre of the picture. Behind him to the right sitting on the floor are his two Rajput uncles, Gulab Singh and Suchet Singh. But it is three other figures, aligned before the Maharaja on the right, which tell us for whom the picture was painted. Each is identified by a Persian inscription and we learn that the one nearest Ranjit Singh is Joshi Kalan Shankar Nath, head astrologer; the next is Maksudan, the head pandit;

[1] Hugel, *Travel*, 380.
[2] Fig. 15. Note VIII, p. 73.

the third is the head pandit's son, Radha Krishna. In size each is on a slightly larger scale than any of the others. We know that Ranjit Singh never embarked on a project without taking omens and it is no surprise, therefore, that both astrologer and pandits should seemingly be members of his household and be treated with deference. Yet their size in the picture is unusual and we can only explain it on the assumption that either Joshi Shankar Nath or the pandit Maksudan desired a record of their close association with Ranjit Singh and themselves commissioned this painting.

Such a picture invites us to draw several conclusions. Of the persons included in the scene, it is the astrologer and the two pandits who are much the most carefully observed. On the artists' arrival in the Plains, in fact, it may have been minor persons such as these who were easiest of approach. If the Maharaja and his close associates appeared to be aloof, lesser figures could well be drawn from life. And it is significant that the Victoria and Albert Museum, the Museum of Fine Arts, Boston, and the Punjab Museum, Chandigarh all possess a number of portrait sketches, depicting not the most famous characters at court but humbler employees, army commanders or visiting sardars. Such portrait sketches appear to be from life and though, in certain cases, more finished pictures may possibly have been made later, they could well be trial ventures, increasing the artists' knowledge of Sikh character but perhaps going no further.

A second conclusion concerns the treatment of Ranjit Singh and his principal companions. If access to the court was difficult, artists must none the less have viewed the Maharaja from time to time and thus a standard impression of him had become their common property. There is nothing in the picture to suggest that a special darbar is in session and all the portraits, other than those of the astrologer and the two pandits, appear to be rough approximations to likenesses rather than telling life studies. If—as seems possible from the tiny figure of Hira Singh and the youngish appearances of the three Dogra brothers—the picture is a little after 1830 in date, it would support the view that, at any rate in the early eighteen-thirties, portraiture of major characters was rudimentary.

But it is the exact choice of courtiers which is perhaps of greatest significance. Part of Ranjit Singh's enigma was his attachment to the Dogra brothers. We have already seen that all were Rajput nobles, scions of the Jammu house. Only one, Dhian Singh, was Ranjit Singh's close intimate. The others, Gulab and Suchet, were normally far away, the former lording it in Jammu, the latter commanding an army. Yet to the public at large, all three were seemingly his indispensable associates. They far out-shone the clever accountant Dina Nath or the polished diplomat Aziz-ud-din. Indeed, in some mysterious way, they were vital parts of Ranjit Singh's own 'public image'.

Their personal characters partly explain this role. Of Dhian Singh, Osborne wrote in 1838:

'Rajah Dheean Sing is a noble specimen of the human race; rather above the usual height of natives, with a quick and intelligent eye, high handsome forehead, and aquiline features, he looked a model of manly beauty and intelligence. He is about thirty years of age and is very high, and by all accounts, justly so in his master's confidence. He is active, clever and intelligent, possessed of great influence over the Sikh people and in all probability will be one and not the least powerful or deserving candidate for the throne of the Punjab on Runjeet's decease. With enormous wealth and property and a large tract of country which he rules with mildness and justice, he presents a singular instance of a favourite and a man in power, whose talents and virtues are more appreciated than his power and influence are envied. Gentlemanlike, manly and unassuming in his manners, he is still cold and repulsive to Europeans whom he both fears and hates with more than common rancour and against whom he loses no opportunity of exerting influence with the Maharajah.'[1]

Suchet Singh was also unusually handsome while Gulab Singh was respected for his bluff bravery and astute intelligence.

Personality alone, however, can hardly explain their special positions and to understand why Ranjit Singh was so attached to them we must once again recall their Rajput status. Jealous and critical of Rajputs in general, he was perhaps for that very reason all the more moved by the loyal subservience of the three brothers; and by exalting their close association with him, he gave his court a more than Sikh aura.

The same trait may account for the prominence given in the picture to the boy, Hira Singh. Osborne was astounded in 1838 at the liberties he took with Ranjit:

'Rajah Heera Sing, the son of the minister, a boy of eighteen years of age, is a greater favourite with Runjeet Sing than any of his chiefs, not even excepting his father. His influence over Runjeet is extraordinary; and though acquired in a manner which in any other country would render him infamous for ever, here he is universally looked up to and respected.

He is the only individual who ever ventures to address Runjeet Sing without being spoken to, and whilst his father stands behind his master's chair, and never presumes to answer him with unclasped hands, this boy does not hesitate to interrupt and contradict him in the rudest manner. One instance of the way in which he presumes upon the kindness of Runjeet Sing was the subject of public conversation at Adeenanuggur upon our arrival. The yearly tribute from Cachemire had

[1] Osborne, *Court and Camp*, 74–75.

35

arrived, and was, as usual, opened and spread upon the floor in the Durbar for the inspection of the Maharajah. It consisted of shawls, arms, jewels, &c., to the amount of upwards of thirty thousand pounds. Young Heera Sing, without the slightest hesitation, addressed Runjeet and said, "Your Highness cannot require all these things; let me have them." The answer was, "You may take them."

Heera Singh is strikingly handsome, though rather effeminate in appearance. He was magnificently dressed, and almost entirely covered from the waist upwards with strings of pearls, diamonds, emeralds, and rubies; he is intelligent and clever, and has taken a fancy to learn English, which he studies for some hours every day, and in which he has already made considerable progress, being perhaps the only individual who would venture to do such a thing openly. Good-tempered, gentle-manlike, and amusing he is certainly one of the most amiable and popular persons at the court of Lahore.'[1]

Unlike his father who always stood before Ranjit, Hira Singh was habitually accommodated in a chair at his side—the only member of his court other than Kharak and Sher Singh to be granted this privilege. He also travelled in Ranjit Singh's own palanquin. Here too we must perhaps look beyond the special relationship. Like his father, Hira Singh was Rajput and in publicising the association, Ranjit Singh may once again have been investing it with Rajput glamour.

It is this strangely Rajput aura which may have fascinated and intrigued the Sikh public, contributing in no small part to Ranjit Singh's mystique. His own person with its odd blending of puny body and bright intelligence focused attention. So too did his son and grandson, Kharak and Nau Nihal—members of his family and participants in his greatness. For the rest it was his Rajput associates who seemed to proclaim his regal status, stress his unique splendour and enhance his prestige. From this point of view, the 'Chester Beatty' darbar scene is hardly an actual darbar at all. It is rather a symbolic rendering, a projection of Ranjit's 'public image', as it had grown up over the years. It was this image of Sikh royalty which in the years 1835 to 1841 was to be conveyed through standard portrait sets and to provide artists with a new patron—the public at large.

At Jodhpur in Rajasthan, in the early nineteenth century, pride in the feudal past as well as lively interest in baronial character had led painters to produce portrait sets of this kind[2]—picture after picture displaying local personages, past and present, in standardised postures. Each picture showed the same great horse, quietly walking or violently rearing, the same posse of small retainers, the same proud type of rider, sometimes smoking a hookah. Each employed similar devices—a plain background, often green or grey, serving as a foil to project the subject; a great stallion, coloured

---

[1] *Ibid.*, 76–78.   [2] Note IX, p. 74.

36

a rich brown, communicating a sense of martial vigour; above all, suavely simple forms stressing by their very rhythm the insolent dignity of the subject. Yet apart from the faces, almost every picture was the same. Projected through a standard type of composition, it was the feudal system rather than the individual that triumphed.

A similar phenomenon had occurred in the Punjab Hills. During the eighteenth century, at Basohli, Mankot, Mandi and Bilaspur, portrait sets of local princes and their nobles had also been produced.[1] Here too standard designs had been customary. Carpets, terraces, attendants, hookahs, swords and costumes varied little and it was rather the face that changed from portrait to portrait. Once again, it was the courtly order, its members reduced to units in a series, that dominated the painting. Faces were useful as sources of information but as studies of individual character, each portrait was neutral, as dimly objective as an entry in *Who's Who*.

Such portrait sets may well have given Guler painters in the Punjab Plains the stimulus and precedent they required. In a set of five pictures,[2] acquired by the astrologer Joshi Shankar Nath himself, one new figure, absent from the darbar, is included. He is Sher Singh, accepted son of Ranjit Singh and destined to succeed him in 1841. Nau Nihal, Ranjit's grandson, is also included but, otherwise, it is the darbar figures (barring only the astrologer and the pandits) who are present. Ranjit Singh is shown, nimbate, cross-legged in a massive, tub-shaped throne, an attendant fanning him with a white cloth. Gulab Singh bestrides a rearing charger, a state umbrella held above his head. Suchet Singh sits on a terrace floor fanned, like Ranjit, with a white cloth and gripping a falcon, the symbol of his might. Finally, in a more elaborate setting, the remaining four key figures are assembled. On the right is Dhian Singh and ranged in a row before him are Kharak Singh, Nau Nihal and the youth Hira. This last picture can hardly have been painted in the lifetime of Ranjit for it envisages the situation which arose immediately after his death. The picture of Sher Singh may also have been added when events were thrusting him to the fore. Joshi Shankar Nath had remained in court service until the murder of Sher Singh in 1843 but after that he had returned to his home in South India. All five pictures, then, must precede this date and perhaps their most likely time of execution was the second half of 1839 or the beginning of 1840—the time when Ranjit had only just died and public impressions of his greatness were overwhelmingly strong.

The same lure of courtly glamour explains two further sets, both in the Victoria and Albert Museum and both in similar style. Ranjit Singh is once again the cynosure, the true object of adoring regard but with him in each series are the same darbar figures and these alone.[3]

[1] Note IX, p. 74.   [2] Note X, p. 74. Figs. 28, 35, 40.   [3] Cat. nos. 5–11, 14–18.

Such sets can be matched in other collections and indeed we must assume that in the last two years of Ranjit's life, enthusiasm for the ageing monarch gave Guler artists in the Punjab Plains a novel kind of patronage. Popular, not courtly in character, it encouraged them to adjust their styles to Sikh taste, to incorporate new devices, and thus create an art that was vividly Sikh.

Their first innovation concerned Ranjit Singh himself. In one or two pictures, he is shown facing right, his good eye alone visible, his features gentle, tender and benign. In others—and these are far more numerous—the idealised rendering of the face is kept but his greatness is emphasised by means of a halo.[1] In Mughal and Rajasthani painting, emperors such as Jahangir, Shah Jahan and Aurangzeb and Rajput rulers such as Ram Singh of Jodhpur or Umed Singh of Kotah had all been granted this honouring convention. In the Punjab Hills, on the other hand, the fashion was virtually unknown. Raja Balvant Singh of Jammu, the great Sansar Chand of Kangra and even Raja Govardhan Chand of Guler were constantly portrayed yet in only one case was any of them provided with this flashing adjunct. By showing Ranjit, nimbate, the artists were therefore breaking with Hill conventions and adopting a foreign device. Exalting Ranjit above the Rajput aristocracy of the Hills, they connected him, by implication, with the older houses of Rajasthan, invested him with Mughal-like authority and thus endowed him with imperial majesty.

The state umbrella was a second novelty. In early India, umbrellas had been used to shade the royal head and had therefore been recognised as vivid symbols of royalty. The practice had been rarely adopted by the Mughals but in the Punjab Hills and Rajasthan, a small royal umbrella with bent handle was sometimes fixed in position behind a prince as he sat on an elephant or a throne. It was also, at times, held above him by an attendant or maid servant.[2] In the Punjab Plains, the artists not only changed its shape but enlarged and magnified it as a symbol of grandeur. In place of a bent handle, it was shown held aloft on a long straight stick while its great brims were widened to assure the recipient ample shade. Discarded when indoors, it was taken out when Ranjit or a member of his court went riding—the great umbrella rising above their heads as a badge of rank and being borne along by a footman who raced beside them. So large an emblem of royalty was new to Indian painting and in adopting it for Sikh portraiture, Guler artists not only gave their painting a Sikh flavour but invented new types of composition. In Hill portraits, rajas had often been shown smoking the hookah—the pipe with its bowl and straggling stem emphasising their status but also imbuing the picture with languid curling rhythm. In Sikh portraits, the umbrella honoured the rider but also gave the picture a sturdy flamboyance. What, in fact, the hookah had been to Hill painting, the state umbrella was to painting of the Sikhs.

[1]Note XI, p. 75.   [2]Note XII, p. 75.

Yet a third element made these pictures strongly Sikh. In contrast to Hill habits as they knew them, the painters included Sikh chairs, Sikh shields and Sikh turbans as integral parts of their compositions. In style, their painting might still recall Guler traditions. Barring a tendency to simplification, a harder firmness, an almost total boycott of the feminine, it was Guler-like in its fine and sensitive lines, its use of pink borders and blue margins—the latter decked with 'Kangra Valley' scrolls—its flat structures and sinuous rhythm. It was rather the total impact of its content and idioms and the incorporation of Sikh ingredients that made it un-Rajput and thus produced a novel Sikh effect.

One last feature must be mentioned. As Western missions, travellers and explorers traversed the Punjab, visited the Sikh court or watched the Sikh cavalry riding and drilling, all succumbed to the glittering dazzle of their dress, their handsome appearances, their great beards and turbans, above all, to the sheer sensuousness of Sikh colour. In May 1838 Osborne noted of Ranjit's bodyguard:

'Dismounting from our elephants at the gateway, we were conducted by two Sikh chiefs up a broad gravel walk about three hundred yards in length, lined by Runjeet's Goorcherras,[1] handsomely dressed in chain armour and quilted jackets, made of rich silk of either a bright yellow, green or scarlet colour, giving the walk, from the gateway to the palace, the appearance of a border of gaudy and gigantic tulips.'[2]

At a parade of troops in December 1838, Emily Eden commented:

'Behind us there was a large amphitheatre of elephants, belonging to our own camp or to the Sikhs and thousands of Runjeet's followers, all dressed in yellow or red satin, with quantities of their led horses, trapped in gold and silver tissues and all of them sparkling with jewels. I really never saw so dazzling a sight.'[3]

And of another review, she wrote:

'We drove for two miles and a half through a lane of Runjeet's "goocherras" or body-guard. The sun was up and shining on them, and I suppose there was not one who would not have made the fortune of a painter. One troop was dressed entirely in yellow satin, with gold scarfs and shawls; but the other half were in that cloth of gold which is called kincob—the *fond* being gold and the pattern scarlet or purple or yellow; their arms were all gold—many of them had collars of precious stones; their shields and lances were all studded with gold. They have long beards down to their waists, and most of them had a silver or gold tissue drapery which

---

[1]Body guards.   [2]Osborne, *Court and Camp*, 71.   [3]Eden, *Up the Country*, 205.

they bring over their heads and pass round their beards to keep them from the dust. In the distance there was a long line of troops extending four miles and a half, and which after much deliberation, I settled was a white wall with a red coping; I thought it could not possibly be alive; but it was—with 30,000 men.'[1]

Ranjit Singh himself might consciously affect a wilfully drab attire but his troops and courtiers exuded feverish brilliance. So strong a love for flashing, almost gaudy hues inevitably influenced the artists and it is hardly surprising that in evoking the splendours of Ranjit's 'public image' they adopted a gay and dazzling palette. Confining pallid greens and misty blues to backgrounds, they employed colours as bold and loud as the great scarlet areas so common in certain types of Guler painting. Rich blues and deep greens, blazing orange-reds and piercing yellows imbued their portraits with clamant gusto and by a strident heightening of tones, gave the Sikh community a vivid impression of Sikh majesty.

(ii) SHER SINGH: AESTHETE AND ANGLOPHIL

Such portrait sets were a tribute to Ranjit Singh. Produced despite his tepid opposition, they met a strong popular demand and in the upshot gratified Sikh pride. The death of Ranjit in no way lessened their appeal. Indeed as late as 1846, Herbert Edwardes could still obtain in Lahore portraits of Dhian and Gulab Singh executed in the same bright style.[2] Such painting was to last for a further ten years, and to include portrait studies of other Sikh characters as well as standard sets of Sikh horsemen.[3] Indeed, only with the foundering of the Sikh state in 1849 was this first type of Sikh painting to lose favour.

The painting we must now consider is of a different kind. Following Ranjit's death, the court had focused first on Kharak Singh and his minister, Chet Singh and then, from October the same year on Kharak's son, Nau Nihal and the former chief minister, Dhian. In September 1840, both Kharak and Nau Nihal had died and for a time it seemed that Kharak's widow, Chand Kaur, might seize power. This threat, however, was averted and in January 1841, Sher Singh became Maharaja. His accession provided the Sikh state with what appeared to be a stable emblem but, what is important for our purpose, it gave a different type of painting a sudden new prestige.

When Lord Auckland's nephew and A.D.C., Osborne, visited the Punjab, in May 1838, he had been struck by a strange happening. As his party neared Ranjit's camp at Adinanagar on 26 May, they were met not by one of Ranjit's sons but by

---

[1] *Ibid.*, 213–214. [2] India Office Library, Add. Or. 709 and 707 (present fig. 34). [3] Figs. 72–75.

a boy of seven, Pratap Singh. He was son of Sher Singh and had been sent to escort the party through the district. Osborne commented:

'Pertaub Sing was handsomely dressed, armed with a small ornamented shield, sword, and matchlock, all in miniature, covered with jewels, and escorted by a small party of Sikh cavalry and some guns. His horse was naturally of a white colour, but dyed with henna to a deep scarlet. He is one of the most intelligent boys I ever met with, very good looking, with singularly large and expressive eyes. His manners are in the highest degree attractive, polished, and gentleman-like, and totally free from all the *mauvaise honte* and awkwardness so generally found in European children of that age.

In the course of conversation I asked him if his matchlock was a real one, and if he ever shot with it. He jumped off his chair, highly indignant at the question, and after rapidly loading his musket, exclaimed "Now what shall I shoot?" I replied that I saw nothing in the camp at present it would be safe to shoot at, and asked him if he thought he could hit a man at a hundred yards' distance; to which he replied, without a moment's hesitation, pointing to the crowd of Sikh chiefs and soldiers that surrounded the tent, "These are all your friends; but shew me an enemy to the British government and you shall soon see what I can do".'[1]

When bidding farewell to Pertaub Singh, the mission presented him with a gold watch and chain 'as a token of remembrance on the part of the Governor-General. He expressed his thanks in graceful terms, and concluded by saying, "You may tell Lord Auckland that the British government will always find a friend in the son of Sher Sing". Then he gracefully raised his hand to his forehead and galloped off with his escort, curvetting and caracoling round him in circles till he was out of sight.'[2]

These strongly British sentiments struck Osborne as very odd and he was also puzzled by the absence of the father, Sher Singh. It appeared a strange breach of etiquette but he concluded that there must be some obvious explanation. He was not long in finding out. Sher Singh, it proved, was as much an anglophil as the child and it was suspicion on the part of Ranjit that had led to this diplomatic slight. Osborne noted:

'Sher Singh is dotingly fond of the boy; and when he was deputed last year by the Maharajah to escort Sir Henry Fane to the frontiers of the Punjab, took him with him; but such is Runjeet's jealousy of Europeans, that before they had got three marches, a regiment of cavalry was sent after them, with orders from the Maharajah to bring Pertaub Sing back with them, in order that he might remain a hostage until his father's return to the court.'[3]

[1] Osborne, *Court and Camp*, 57–60.　　[2] *Ibid.*, 59–60.　　[3] *Ibid.*, 58–59.

During Osborne's visit, Sher Singh assisted him with daily supplies but had, none the less, to be discreet. 'I have before adverted to Runjeet's jealousy of Europeans', wrote Osborne, 'and Sher Sing has unfortunately for himself shown so much attention to them and such attachment to their manners and customs, as effectually to rouse his master's vigilance; and whilst in his presence he hardly dared openly to accost us, when removed from observation, he, of all Sikh chiefs, appeared most inclined to be on friendly terms with us.'[1] And it was this strong desire to mix with British people which was shortly to affect Sikh painting.

Like other British men and women in India, Osborne had been trained to draw and as he travelled through the Punjab, he busied himself with pencil and sketch-book. Of no great natural skill, he viewed drawing as an amiable hobby—a means of whiling away his leisure hours and perhaps of imparting information on his return. He also kept a diary, hoping that it might amuse those 'who, blessed in the enjoyment of their native land, can little guess the shifts to which their less fortunate and exiled countrymen are reduced, to pass the tedious hours of a hot and sultry day, on the burning plains of the East'.[2] His diary and sketches, published as *The Court and Camp of Runjeet Sing* disclose how much he admired Sher Singh and it is no surprise that amongst the personages whom he sketched the future Mahajara was pre-eminent.

Osborne's drawing flattered Sher Singh's susceptibilities but it was the arrival six months' later of Emily Eden, Osborne's aunt, which may have been more decisive. Of all British amateur artists, Emily Eden was one of the most skilled and as she accompanied her brother, Lord Auckland the Governor-General, on his tours, she sketched people and places with relentless energy. Like others of the British, she found Sikhs irresistible and none was so charming as Sher Singh. 'Shere Singh came to my tent to sit for his picture (she wrote on 20 December, 1838). Such a gorgeous figure! . . . He made a very good picture.'[3] The drawing, later published in her book, *Portraits of the Princes and People of India*, was to prove one of her finest sketches—the great figure, sitting in indolent majesty, revealing a character that had clearly delighted in its own portrayal.[4]

This experience may well have had important consequences. We know from Emily Eden's sister, Fanny, that in 1838 Sher Singh was already 'fond of drawing'[5] and it is likely that until 1838 it was the work either of painters in Kangra or of Guler artists in the Plains that had aroused his interest. Yet of his keen aesthetic tastes there can be little doubt and, in 1842, when the Russian, Prince Soltykoff went to see him, it was the brilliance of the palace décor and Sher Singh's obvious love of sensuous effects that delighted and amazed him:

[1] *Ibid.*, 65. [2] *Ibid.*, vi. [3] Eden, *Up the Country*, 223. [4] Fig. 42.
[5] Fanny Eden, Journal, 8 December, 1838. India Office Library. MSS. Eur. C. 130.

'This morning, the King gave us a state audience. What a sight! I could scarcely believe my eyes. Everything glittered with precious stones and the brightest colours arranged in harmonious combinations. The green garden was decorated by a huge crowd of Sikhs in yellow, red, rose, white, gold, silver, green, lilac and azure, all armed and strikingly arrayed, some of them being in coats of mail. . . . In the midst of this bevy was the King, coming to meet us, a big stoutish man of forty, covered with the most beautiful jewels in the world. On his right arm was the Koh-i-Nur, the finest diamond that exists.'[1]

And of a second occasion, he wrote:

'The other day we were invited to pass the evening with the King whose palace is in a fortress at the other end of the city. The King received us in the open, in the midst of his warriors, in the moon-light in a vast courtyard, surrounded by vast, crenellated walls. There were thirty magnificent horses there, covered with precious stones and illuminated by torches and by a kind of Bengal fire which cast a blue light from the tops of the walls. I might mention that the Punjabis are famous for their fireworks. Seen thus the white horses, with their emerald ornaments, seemed like dream figures, while the black ones, with their ruby decorations, looked like spectres from the Inferno, in the dim torchlight.

The King, with the simple and unaffected air which distinguishes him, led us along some narrow corridors, and we soon found ourselves in another court, panelled with marble and hung with beautiful carpets. In the middle was a basin full of water-fowl and fine jets of water filled the air like diamond dust. Around it, thousands of illuminated globes of different colours gave a faint, soft light like that of dawn. As we advanced towards some splendid tents of shawls and gold brocade in the opposite corner of the court, enormous red curtains were drawn up slowly one after another, by means of cords like curtains of a theatre by Sikh warriors armed to the teeth, and as these curtains disappeared we were more and more overwhelmed by the splendour of a new hall which was disclosed to view, the walls and ceiling of which were decorated with green, white, and red crystals framed in gold and looking like a pavement of precious stones upon an enormous ladder. Thither we were conducted by the King, and on entering, we saw, spread out to view on brocade covered tables the royal arms; hundreds of swords, daggers, shields, cuirasses and helmets, all very richly decorated. . . .

'Then the girls arrived, some thirty in all, pretty but small and delicate, in splendid costumes with their little noses so loaded with jewels and their foreheads and eyebrows so gilded that one could hardly distinguish their features. Their feet and hands, adorned with rings and mirrors, were very pretty though dark. The

[1] Garrett, *The Punjab*, 96–97.

transparent veils that covered them were of gold, silver, or bright colours. Their short coats of velvet or other costly materials and their tight trousers of silk were very pleasing to the eye. These charming girls approached the King one by one and gave him one or two rupees. The King, who was in conversation with the ambassador, turned to them with an air of careless good humour. There is so much that is good natured and straightforward about him, that, although his figure is awkward, he is charming and one would say that, in spite of his nervous air, he possesses plenty of pluck in danger.

It seemed a curious household. The girls approached without any fear, most of them laughing, and looking about them. Then they sat down together on the ground between the tables. Suddenly a plaintive melody was heard, and two of them began a slow dance, while the others sat, looking like butterflies.'[1]

It was on this genial figure, already intrigued by Western drawing and keenly alive to sensuous effects, that a professional painter from Europe was now to impinge.

August Theodor Schoefft had been born in Budapest in 1809, a Hungarian by extraction, and had come to India in 1838. He was highly competent in oils and from the tone of advertisements in local newspapers, he appears to have had a quick success. Announcing on 2 August 1838 in the *Bombay Courier* his departure in September, he urged all who wished him to take their portraits to communicate with him quickly. A year later, in September 1839, he was in Madras where he received five thousand rupees for two full-length, life-size portraits. These were of the Nawab of Arcot and his uncle. From there he moved to Calcutta where once again he advertised his programme. On 13 June 1840, the *Calcutta Courier* announced: 'M. Schoefft who has resided amongst us for some months and acquired considerable reputation as an artist is, we understand, on the point of quitting Calcutta on a journey to Lahore. On his way thither, M. Schoefft proposes to halt at Moorshedabad, Monghyr, Patna, Dinapore, Benares, Allahabad, Lucknow, Cawnpore, Agra, Delhi, Meerut, Kurnaul etc. etc. and will, we believe, be happy to be employed by the residents at the several stations in every way in which his talents can be made available. It should be stated that M. Schoefft is not merely a portrait painter. He has much skill in painting historical subjects, landscapes, costumes, etc. works with astonishing quickness and is, we think, more reasonable in his charge than any artist who has preceded him.'[2] Late in 1840 or early in 1841, Schoefft reached Lahore.

What followed must be told in the words of Honigberger the German court

[1] *Ibid.*, 102–104.
[2] Foster, 'Some Foreign European Artists in India', *Bengal Past and Present*, XL, 79–98.

physician who entertained him and whose account, *Thirty-five years in the East*, is our main authority for Schoefft's stay:

'At this time the court happened to be at Umritsir, and I received an order from Sheer Sing to present myself at that place with my guest. On our arrival, it happened that one of the principal Sikh priests, named Baii Goormuck Sing, was present, and the maharajah desired Herr Schöfft to furnish him with a specimen of his abilities, by sketching a portrait of the baii; which he accordingly did, in pencil, and the likeness was a striking one. The result was, that the maharajah and several of the principal persons of the court sat to him for their portraits, and Herr Schöfft accordingly met with great respect and consideration.'

A promising beginning had been made and indeed the warmth of Sher Singh's reception must have surpassed all of Schoefft's expectations. Further commissions followed and soon there was a request for a view of Amritsar.

'In the centre of the city of Umritsir [Honigberger relates] is a gigantic reservoir of water, from the midst of which rises a magnificent temple, where the Grunth (the holy book of the Sikhs) is read day and night. Around this sheet of water are the houses of the maharajah, the ministers, sirdars, and other wealthy inhabitants. The square itself is called Durbar Saheb. At the time of Runjeet Sing and Sheer Sing, the scene which presented itself at this temple, when the court was at Umritsir, was of the most brilliant description, and at certain periods all the notabilities of the Punjab were to be seen collected together in all the splendour of oriental pageantry. During our stay at Umritsir it happened that the inhabitants gave an invitation to the court to visit the sacred temple at night time, when it was gorgeously illuminated; and Sheer Sing honoured me with his commands that we should accompany him, sending us a richly caparisoned elephant for our accommodation.

'Sheer Sing inquired of my friend, Herr Schöfft, if he could take for him a drawing of that brilliant scene. He answered in the affirmative, but proposed to the maharajah that it would be better if the scene was sketched under the effect of daylight instead of the imperfect one of the illumination. He was accordingly ordered to adopt the suggestion. On the following morning we went to the house of the Baii Gormuck Sing, who had promised to send a servant to point out to us the most elevated terrace in the square, from which Herr Schöfft could get a view of the temple and the surrounding buildings; on this place he prepared his atelier. He occupied the whole of the day in sketching the scene, and on the following day he also went there, but alone, to continue his work.'

And at this point drama intervened:

'Herr Schöfft [Honigberger explains] was a great smoker, and attracted attention in Umritsir from his scarcely ever being seen abroad without having a cigar in his mouth. Now smoking is considered by the Nahungs and the Sikhs as sinful, or rather criminal; more especially in or near such a holy place as their chief sanctuary; Herr Schöfft was aware of this, and therefore studiously avoided smoking whilst engaged in taking this sketch. It happened, however, that, as is customary with painters, he now and then in the course of the work placed one of his pencils in his mouth, in order to keep it separate from those in the left hand, whilst using another with the right. This was observed by those who stood watching his operations from beneath the terrace, and they imagined, in consequence, that he was smoking.'

No more dangerous misunderstanding could, in fact, have occurred and it is no surprise that events moved rapidly to a climax.

'The rumour first spread about in whispers one to another, and as the impression became confirmed, a general indignation manifested itself; and loud exclamations were soon heard, that the feringhee (frank) was committing sacrilege by smoking in their sacred place. The people speedily increased in numbers, and a clamorous mob soon surrounded the palace. The artist was at first unconscious of the cause of the gathering, but he soon became aware by their shouts and threats, that he was in some way the object of their fury, and that he was consequently in a dangerous position. He had no sooner, however, made up his mind that his best policy would be to effect his escape, if possible, unperceived, when some of the ringleaders of the mob, who had made their way through the palace, rushed upon the terrace, and attempted to seize him. Being a strong and vigorous man, he succeeded in wrenching himself from their grasp, and made his way to the staircase, which to his dismay he found crowded by the mob, who were making their way up. Knowing that his only chance lay in breaking through them as quickly as possible, he struck out right and left, and having the advantage of being always uppermost of those who attempted to stay his progress, he succeeded in reaching the bottom with some few bruises.

Here, however, the affair presented a still more formidable aspect; for no sooner had he reached the foot of the staircase, than he was seized by the collar and other parts of his coat by half-a-dozen of the mob, and saw at a little distance the glittering of several of their weapons. He gave himself up for lost, and in the energy of despair threw open his coat and taking advantage of a slight confusion at the moment (caused by a struggle to get possession of the gold watch which he had held in his hand, and had at the same instant relinquished to them), he slipped from the coat, which was held on all sides, and pushing away those in front of him,

46

he succeeded in reaching the street; here his nether garments fell, in some un-accountable manner about his feet, and he stumbled and fell into a miry puddle which was immediately before him; he instantly sprang to his feet, and rushed to the entrance of a dark stable close adjacent.'

Wretchedly naked, deprived both of coat and trousers, Schoefft was now in no condition to fight back. Only chance could save him and by some lucky accident he recognised an exit.

'The mob concluded they had now secured their prey, but they were mistaken; for Schöfft had, fortunately, whilst passing this stable on a previous occasion in my company, entered it, and noticed its back entrance, which led into the bazaar; through this back door he then gained the bazaar, and from thence (the mob all the way at his heels), reached the house of his protector, Baii Goormuck Sing. The door was immediately shut, and Schöfft was saved.

'He there met with a kind reception, and on cleansing himself from the mire and blood with which he was covered, it was found that he had not only received several contusions on the head from the iron knobs on the shields of the Nahungs, with which they had struck at him; but also a sword wound on the back, by which his braces had been cut through, which at once explained to him the cause of his fall into the mire at so critical a moment. The mob not evincing any inclination to disperse, the police interfered, and compelled them to retire.'[1]

This farcical incident might have ruined Schoefft's career. He had been treated as a foreigner who had seemingly insulted Sikh religion; he had cut a shameful figure as he fled with ignomiy through the streets; and his conduct could well have led to a demand for expulsion. But we must bear in mind the character of his patron. Sher Singh was brave and popular with the army. He was not a man to be trifled with and, above all, his interest in Western art had been aroused. So enthusiastic a protector was not to be easily deterred and as Schoefft recovered from the assault, he found the Maharaja avid to sponsor his painting. Schoefft himself wished to draw as many Sikhs as possible and throughout 1841, the year of his stay in Lahore, he sketched the principal characters at court and copied portraits of those who were recently dead. He learnt, in this way, how to paint famous figures such as Ranjit, Kharak and Nau Nihal and thus acquire material with which to reconstruct historical scenes.

These sketches and copies were to prove their value when, later in life, he worked at Vienna from 1844 to 1846, and held an exhibition there in 1855. They were not, however, of immediate importance and it was rather the large oils, painted both at

---

[1] Honigberger, *Thirty-five Years*, I, 171–175.

Lahore and afterwards, which illustrate the style which so impressed Sher Singh. We know from Soltykoff that in March, 1842, the palace treasures included

'five or six portraits in oils without frames, the work of Schoeft, the German painter who has returned to British India. There was also a portrait of the King covered with jewels and holding in his hand a scimitar straight and very broad at the point and a portrait of the chief minister, Raja Dhian Singh, a good looking man, on horseback and wearing that suit of armour which I have already described. The King who admires the armour wished to be painted in it also.'[1]

These portraits have unfortunately disappeared but a series of four oils formerly in the Princess Bamba Sutherland collection, and also by Schoefft, enable us to envisage what they were like.

The first,[2] perhaps a version of the ill-fated view of Amritsar, shows the golden temple in the centre, surrounded by its great tank. Ranjit Singh in yellow sits facing right while an attendant stands near him with the kind of long-poled umbrella, familiar to us from Guler standard sets. In the foreground, by some stroke of historical inaccuracy, the child Dalip is shown, sprawling on the ground playing with a hawk. Only three years old in 1839, the year of Ranjit's death, he could hardly have been as large as Schoefft depicts him but his babyish presence perhaps explains why Dalip or his daughter acquired the picture. Of greater interest is the fact that seated on Ranjit's left is Sher Singh himself, a clear tribute to his charm. The omnipresent chief minister, Dhian Singh, is studiously omitted and indeed the picture might almost be of Sher Singh himself, basking in the reflected glory of his great forebear.

The second picture[3] shows Sher Singh in council, his advisers ranged on either side; and a third[4] portrays him in bulky majesty, holding the kind of scimitar noted by Soltykoff.

It is the fourth picture,[5] a vast oil 120 by 192 inches in size, however, which reveals the full extent of Schoefft's powers. Dominating the exhibition in Vienna in 1855, it represents the Dasahra festival at the court of Ranjit Singh. Over sixty persons are included, almost all of them identified in a key plate attached to the catalogue. Ranjit, Kharak, Nau Nihal, Hira and Sher Singh are present—Ranjit being spelt in the German key as 'Renaschid Singh' and Sher Singh as 'Schir Singh'. Also present are the three Dogra brothers and Aziz-ud-din. Even the European adventurers—Allard, Avitabile, Ventura, Ffoulkes, Steinbach, Van Cortlandt, de la Roche, Mouton and Honigberger—are included. Indeed at first sight the picture appears to be a grandiose celebration of Ranjit Singh and all his court.

[1] Garrett, *The Punjab*, 103.   [2] Khan, *Princess Bamba Collection*, pl. 2.
[3] *Ibid.*, pl. 3.   [4] Fig. 43.   [5] Figs. 44, 45.

It is only when we review the composition and note the relative sizes of the figures that we see that this is not the case.

In this vast throng, the hero is not Ranjit but Sher Singh. Ranjit with flowing white beard is a tiny figure on a distant verandah, while Sher Singh, astride a richly caparisoned horse, dominates the left centre. In the right foreground is the body of a great stag, many times larger than the diminutive Ranjit, and although Sher Singh salutes the Maharaja with his left hand, the latter is so engrossed in examining a plateful of offerings that he does not notice him. The actual subject of the picture, in fact, is Sher Singh triumphantly returning from a hunt and in this huge picture not only does he hold the stage, but the court is shown as if acclaiming his prowess. Hunting, as we know, was one of Sher Singh's master passions and in grouping so great a concourse around him, Schoefft was not only exalting his royal patron but stressing his ruling interest.

Pictures of this kind were new to Sikh experience. Sensitive to detail and texture, to the play of light on bodily posture, concerned, above all, with achieving dramatic and realistic effects, Schoefft was nothing if not lively and natural. He strove to obtain individual impressions and then to interpret them through the chosen medium of oils. He painted people as he saw them and though his flair for composition ensured that distracting detail would be eliminated, his aim was to transmit a vivid sense of character. His figures appear sometimes full-face, three-quarter view or in profile, but whatever the angle, Schoefft is unvaryingly proficient. To Indian painters in Lahore, this portraiture was disturbingly novel. Not only did it represent a new view of Indian realism but the large dimensions of the pictures challenged the small, and almost private, scale of miniatures.

So keen an enjoyment of Western art could not but affect Indian painters and as we survey the period 1842 to 1850, we can discern three separate consequences. On the side of medium, Schoefft's influence was slight. Oils had little appeal and though in Travancore, the painter Ravi Varma was later to build up a wide reputation in this medium, painters in Lahore were unimpressed.

In contrast, the change in courtly attitude, the spectacle of a Sikh maharaja actively interested in painting, had far-reaching results. By 1837, Ranjit's early hostility to painting had slightly weakened and one or two artists were being casually employed. In January, 1838, for example, the Austrian, Baron Hugel, was interviewed by a painter who had been sent by Ranjit to copy a piece of his uniform. He had 'a portfolio filled with drawings, some very good'.[1] And, later the same year, Emily Eden had noticed an artist sketching her brother as he watched a review:

'The review was picturesque, but rather tiresome; however, I did not much

[1] Hugel, *Travels*, 355.

49

care, for I got a quiet corner from which I could sketch Runjeet. I was on his blind side but they said he found it out and begged I might not be interrupted. One of his native painters was sketching G., and if my drawing looked as odd to him as his did to me, he must have formed a mean idea of the arts in England. They put full eyes into a profile and give hardly any shade. They paint their own people with European complexions from coxcombry so that ours are a great puzzle to them, because we are so white. They had given G. light red hair.'[1]

There is no record of court painters in the employment of Kharak and Nau Nihal Singh but von Orlich, a German visitor to Sher Singh found one present in 1843:

'On occasions of this kind, [he wrote] it is customary for the Indian nobles to bring the artist attached to the court, to take the portraits of those present: the painter of Shere Singh was, therefore, incessantly occupied in sketching with a black lead pencil those likenesses which were afterwards to be copied in water colours, in order that they might adorn the walls of the royal palace; and some of them were admirably executed. I was among the honoured few and the artist was very particular in making a faithful representation of my uniform and my hat and feathers.'[2]

Such employment seems to have been perfunctory and conventional and it was rather Sher Singh's interest in the new, the foreign and the grand which affected the situation. Compared with Ranjit's furtive shrinking and secretive dislike, his enthusiasm for Schoefft's portraits was infectious. To enter the Punjab Plains was no longer to explore a region immune to art and although exact evidence is wanting, it is perhaps from the time of Sher Singh's rise to power that we must date the main arrival in Lahore of painters from Kangra and Delhi. Kangra painters were to make a brief but significant contribution in the years 1846 and 1847. Delhi painters were to usher in a new and final period.

It is in the field of style and taste, however, that Sher Singh's patronage of Schoefft was to leave its greatest mark. We have seen that in their standard portrait sets, Guler painters at Lahore had achieved a new Sikh style, a style that corresponded to certain aspects of Sikh character. This style was, in essence, an offshoot of painting in the Punjab Hills and like the parent style, it respected certain long-established conventions. It eschewed animated realism and relied rather on a more oblique approach. The sitter was presented as an image that might almost have been a diagram; the clean skin was painted with smooth clarity; clothes, limbs, turban, chair or shield were all recorded with grave and lucid calm. No shadows and but little shading tempered these ideal forms. Each head was shown

[1] Eden, *Up the Country*, 228.   [2] Von Orlich, *Travels*, I, 206–207.

50

in profile and neither full-face nor three-quarter view were attempted. It was as if each figure had been viewed from afar and then set down with stereotyped dignity.

Schoefft's pictures were the exact reverse and it is no surprise that, hanging on the walls of Sher Singh's palace, they should, unconsciously and indirectly, have deflated and superseded this early strand in Sikh painting. Their nearest equivalent was painting in Delhi—an art still miniature in scale but blending Mughal naturalism with Western realism. News of Schoefft's success may well have reached Delhi and although no drastic changes are, at first, apparent, it is the Anglo-Mughal style of Delhi which only a few years later becomes predominant. In the work of these later artists, not only is there a definite acceptance of Schoefft's ideas but a conscious borrowing from his work. Just as Mughal artists at Lucknow had succumbed to Tilly Kettle's portraits of their patron Suraj-ud-daulah, translating the British painter's poses and compositions into miniature terms,[1] Anglo-Mughal painters in Lahore modelled their renderings of Sher Singh on portraits by Schoefft.[2]

The second consequence was a brief experiment in large-scale portraits. In 1845, two years after Sher Singh's death, copies of Emily Eden's book *Portraits of the Princes and People of India* reached Lahore. This lavish portfolio of lithographs, based on drawings made in India, had much to interest the Sikhs. It included the masterly portrait of Sher Singh and tender studies of Ranjit, Hira and Pratap Singh. In vivid naturalism, her drawings were counterparts to Schoefft's portraits in oils. Yet in one respect, they were closer to Indian tradition. Schoefft's oils resembled murals in their great size and to painters of miniatures they could seemingly have had but little relevance. Emily Eden's drawings approached more closely to the miniature technique and hence could be studied with more advantage. There is no evidence that her portraits of Sher, Hira and Pratap Singh were copied by Indian artists, but her picture of Ranjit, sitting with one leg under him, a hand raised, his body slumped forward was too expressive to be ignored. In a picture of him by Guler artists in the Plains, the same pose is borrowed but is tactfully reversed. In place of showing his blind left eye, Ranjit is depicted facing right. In other particulars, the portrait is the same.[3]

It was their general largeness of effect, however, which may have had a fertile influence. Much smaller than Schoefft's oils, her figures were arrestingly big by miniature standards. In the drawing of Ranjit Singh, the head is one and a half inches square and the figure seven and a half inches tall. Hira Singh's head is two inches high by one and a half inches broad. Sher Singh's head is a little over one and a half inches square and his figure eight and three quarter inches high. Such

[1] Archer, *Indian Painting for the British*, 54–56.
[2] Figs., 92, 104.   [3] Figs. 25, 26.

enlargements, small by comparison with oils, were dramatic in the context of miniature painting. The subjects looked larger and by looking larger appeared greater.

Guler artists in the Punjab Plains may well have shrunk from adopting this fashion. Enlargement was against their tradition and it would also have compelled them to abandon standard tracings—the method used for making copies. Kangra artists, on the other hand, were newer to Lahore. They were already accustomed to somewhat larger sizes. A Kangra picture of a lady, perhaps 1825 in date, shows her with a head one and a quarter inches high and a full one inch broad.[1] Other Kangra portraits reveal the same enlarging trend. All that was needed was a new theme and in the sudden cult of Gulab Singh in 1846, Kangra artists in Lahore, spurred by Emily Eden's example, obtained the very subject they required.

(iii) THE CULT OF GULAB SINGH

During the last years of Ranjit Singh and the murderous anarchy that succeeded his death, one figure had stood out—Gulab Singh, ruler of Jammu and eldest of 'the three Dogra brothers'. To Cunningham, historian of the Sikhs, he was to seem in retrospect 'smooth and crafty'.[2] Vigne who had met him in 1835 had dismissed him as in origin 'only one of the better class of mounted sepahis' and had roundly declared: 'His career has been much stained by treachery and perfidy. He is now Rajah of Jumu, at the foot of the mountains; and the most powerful man in the Punjab. He occasionally commits acts of the greatest ferocity; such as skinning his prisoners alive.'[3] Emily Eden in December 1838 had found him the exact reverse of Sher Singh—'a horrid character', she had written.[4] Henry Lawrence, on the other hand, strongly approved of him and, earlier, Jacquemont had admired him almost as much as Ranjit Singh himself. In 1831, he had written home: 'I am sure I should not like the legitimate rajahs of Jammu, Kangra and other hill principalities which Ranjit has transferred to Gulab, as much as I do him. He is a lion in war, but anything but a rose-water dandy; he is a man of forty, remarkably handsome and with the simplest, most gentle and elegant manners.'[5] And in another letter, he described how Gulab had received him:

'I found the Rajah seated almost in the open air under a little tent on a little bed of flowers, in a garden lined on each side by soldiers and by servants seated on carpets. Gulab Singh came to meet me; we embraced and he made me sit with him

[1] Archer, *Kangra Painting*, pl. 8.   [2] Cunningham, *History*, 190.
[3] Vigne, *Personal Narrative*, 250–251.   [4] Eden, *Up the Country*, 135.   [5] Jacquemont, *Letters*, 179.

on a large velvet cushion embroidered with gold. My people had brought a chair, which was not used, as the Rajah courteously insisted that I should share his cushion. He is a man of about forty, of medium height and extremely good looking, a fine head covered with long curly hair, an aquiline nose, large dark oval eyes, a small mouth and well-chiselled lips. His figure suggested grace combined with energy and force. His costume was rich, though simple and soldierly; a little white turban of the finest muslin, carefully tied and brought down over the left ear; a close fitting coat of the same material and the enormous Sikh trousers which fall over the thighs in a number of folds and fit tight at the knees, which they half conceal. He had no jewels but a pair of earrings and a collar of magnificent pearls, but the hilt of his sabre was encrusted with emeralds, rubies and diamonds. On his back he carried a large shield of rhinoceros hide polished a dazzling black.'[1]

Fifteen years later, Hardinge, nephew of the Governor-General, was equally enthusiastic:

'Gulab Singh is about 50 years in age and not only noted for his political acumen, but for his physical activity and courage, which has never been disputed; his character also is free from those vices which have been attributed to his brothers, Rajahs Dhihan and Suchet Singh, and which pervade all orders of the Sikh nation, high and low. His features are regular, and the expression of his countenance more than usually mild, with an affectation of openness. Indeed, it has been remarked that a "man might almost take him for his grandmother", and the impression is certainly one which many who have conversed with him would form. He has remitted one fifth of the revenue paid by the Hill Chiefs in Kashmir, and, by abolishing the rite of Sati in the Valley of Kashmir, as well as by making lenient settlements, has taken steps to conciliate the feelings of the Kashmirians, who have been more or less oppressed by the successive governors appointed by the Lahore Durbar.'[2]

It was this figure who in 1846 was to become the centre of a popular cult.

Until the war of 1845, Gulab Singh had remained in careful isolation, exerting a powerful but invisible influence from his distant citadel. He had rarely attended Ranjit's court yet so important was his role that Guler artists in the Punjab Plains had included him in their standard portraits. They had gone even further, for at least one picture[3] reminds us of Gulab Singh's great-great-uncle, the famous patron of Jammu painting, Balvant Singh. This prince had caused his favourite artist, Nainsukh, to portray him in various poses—watching dancers, enjoying music,

[1] Garrett, *The Punjab*, 60–61.
[2] Hardinge, *Recollections*, Part II, plate 14.   [3] Fig. 37.

receiving a picture, doing *pūjā*[1]—and, in this picture, we see Gulab Singh, a man in his early forties, taking his bath before doing his *pūjā*. A priest waits to assist him and the various ingredients of worship are set out in the courtyard before him. The practice of bathing, doing *pūjā* and then eating alone was peculiar to Gulab Singh for Honigberger comments: 'The Rajas Dhyan Sing, Soochet Sing and Heera Sing were accustomed to take their repast from similar (leaf) cups and dishes, sitting with their retinue on white cloths, spread upon the ground. Every guest has one or more of these cups placed before him and they only employ their fingers in eating, as forks, knives or spoons are not used by the native inhabitants. The Maharajah Gholab Sing, however, does not dine in company but invariably takes his meals alone, in the kitchen where the dishes are prepared, having previously passed an hour or two in performing his ablutions and repeating his poojah.'[2] The habit had evidently caught the popular imagination for, in this picture, perhaps executed for the public at large, the artist has shown him in this attitude. No other Sikh minister was ever portrayed in such informal surroundings and we can only infer that already a mysterious aura was attaching to his presence.

By March, 1846, Gulab Singh was hero of the Punjab. He had rescued the Sikh State from the British and had preserved the child maharaja, Dalip Singh. He was by far the most powerful figure that the Sikhs possessed; an uncanny air of majesty surrounded him and indeed there appeared to be nothing that he could not do. Comparable, in fact, to Ranjit Singh himself, he was feared, admired and for a brief two years, was even loved. From Kangra artists in the Plains, his presence demanded ample treatment.

The 'Rothenstein' portrait[3] of Gulab Singh, now in the Victoria and Albert Museum, reveals this broad new style at perhaps its peak. Gulab Singh is seated on a terrace against a cushion, a black shield strapped to his back, his left hand clasping a sword, his right hand holding a sprig of roses. His figure is eight and a half inches high and three and a half inches broad. A great multi-coloured turban, in Sikh style, surmounts his head, his keen eyes shrewdly turned to the right as if to sense a lurking threat. The portrait is clearly in continuation of the Kangra style of about 1830 but possesses the masterful poise, solid firmness and greater depth of the Eden drawings. The great face, two and a quarter inches high by two and a half inches broad is slightly larger than any Eden head and the whole figure has an air of massive grandeur. The sitter is aged about fifty years and bearing in mind Gulab Singh's meteoric rise to popularity, we can plausibly date it to March or April 1846, the months when, following the first treaty of Lahore, his fame was at its height.

[1] Archer, *Indian Painting in the Punjab Hills*, figs. 35–39.
[2] Honigberger, *Thirtyfive Years*, I, 163–164.   [3] Fig. 50.

So grand a celebration of Gulab Singh was not confined to the hero himself but included members of his family. A second picture[1] in the same broad style shows him seated with his two dead sons—Udham and Sohan; and a third[2] in more conventional manner shows the same two sons seated opposite each other conversing. The eldest son, Udham, had died in 1840 in the same fall of masonry that had killed Nau Nihal Singh. The second, Sohan (or Randhir), had died in 1844 with Hira Singh. So strong, however, had popular interest become that despite their early deaths, pictures ennobling their faces and recalling Gulab Singh's bereavements were prepared. Yet other portraits[3] show Gulab Singh's third son, Ranbir, sitting with his father or instructing a secretary.

Such pictures contributed to his fame but perhaps his most striking memorial is a picture[4] of the Lahore darbar held on 26th December 1846. We have already seen that its prime purpose was to ratify the second treaty of Lahore by which a Regency Council of eight members was set up under Henry Lawrence. The young Maharaja Dalip Singh was therefore present, while, ranged in front of him, were Lord Hardinge, Governor-General, Gough, Commander-in-Chief, and Lawrence, the Resident. Beside Dalip was Currie, the Foreign Secretary, whose business it was to translate Hardinge's speech. These were the chief participants. In the picture, however, the assembly is divided into two opposing groups: on the left are the British with an Indian, perhaps a clerk, standing behind them; on the right are Dalip, Currie and eleven others. Of these figures, two in the foreground holding trays are clearly attendants carrying presents and seven of the remaining nine are perhaps intended to be seven of the eight members of the Regency Council. Of eleven figures nine can thus be accounted for and only two remain. Yet far from playing minor roles, it is these who dominate the scene. Seated to the fore, dwarfing not only the tiny Dalip but also the seven councillors, is Ranbir Singh, third and only surviving son of Gulab and present as proxy for his father. In the background between Ranbir and Hardinge, gazing steadily out at the viewer is the handsome Muslim, Sheikh Imam-ud-din, erstwhile Governor of Kashmir but now routed and deposed by Gulab Singh.

Here then is Gulab Singh triumphant. Absent from the picture, he is, none the less, its true subject. The darbar, in theory called to establish the Regency Council, in fact proclaimed Gulab Singh's friendship with the British, his new status as an independent power and his sovereignty over Jammu and Kashmir. In style, different from the 'Rothenstein' portrait yet blending and transforming certain Kangra idioms, the picture contrives to achieve the same result—the celebration of a man whose reputation had come to rival even that of Ranjit Singh.

Such a cult was short-lived. For two years Gulab Singh magnetised the Punjab,

[1]Fig. 55.   [2]Fig. 56.   [3]Figs. 57, 58.   [4]Figs. 59, 60.

providing in his realm of Jammu and Kashmir a distant reminder of Sikh achievement. Two years later, in 1849, the second Anglo-Sikh War found him neutral. By then, hero-worship of him in the Punjab had dwindled and only with the British did remnants of his greatness linger.

At Jammu, in 1847, Charles Hardinge, son of the Governor-General, had portrayed him mild and benevolent.[1] Eight years later, William Carpenter, a professional artist, met him in Kashmir. He was now alert and sprightly but in the portrait which Carpenter made,[2] we can sense the lively vigour and insidious charm which had mesmerised the Punjab in its critical years.

(iv) ECLIPSE AND NOSTALGIA

In October 1848, the British declared war and while, for a few months, the issue was uncertain, the battle of Gujarat in February 1849 extinguished Sikh hopes. There was now no question of reprieve and in March, the Punjab was annexed. At a darbar held in Lahore on 29 March 1849, a proclamation by Hardinge, the Governor-General, was read out. Its stern air of Victorian righteousness must have heartened the British party but, although its phrases are in fact the kind of remarks that victors normally address to the vanquished, there is something disquieting in its pompous tone of callous rightness. Fortunately, few of the Sikhs present at the darbar can have understood its contents and we can be sure that in translating it into Persian, the Foreign Secretary gave them only the mere gist. The proclamation ran:

'For many years during the time of Maharaja Ranjit Singh peace and friendship prevailed between the British nation and the Sikhs. When Ranjit Singh was dead and his wisdom no longer guided the Councils of the State, the sardars and the Khalsa army, without provocation and without cause, suddenly invaded the British territories. Their army was again and again defeated. They were driven with slaughter and in shame from the country they had invaded, and, at the gates of Lahore, the Maharaja Dulip Singh tendered to the Governor-General the submission of himself and his chiefs, and solicited the clemency of the British Government. The Governor-General extended the clemency of his Government to the State of Lahore, he generously spared the kingdom which he had acquired a just right to subvert, and, the Maharaja having been replaced on the throne, treaties of friendship were formed between the States. The British have faithfully kept their word, and have scrupulously observed every obligation which the treaties imposed

[1]Fig. 52.   [2]Fig. 53

56

upon them. But the Sikh people and their chiefs have, on their part, grossly and faithlessly violated the promises by which they were bound. Of their annual tribute no portion whatever has at any time been paid, and large loans advanced to them by the Government of India have never been paid. The control of the British Government to which they voluntarily submitted themselves, has been resisted by arms. Peace has been cast aside. British officers have been murdered when acting for the State; others engaged in a like employment have been thrown into captivity. Finally, the whole of the State and the whole Sikh people, joined by many of the sardars in the Panjab, who signed the treaties, and led by a member of the Regency itself, have risen in arms against us and have waged a fierce and bloody war for the proclaimed purpose of destroying the British and their power. The Government of India formerly declared that it required no further conquest, and it proved by its acts the sincerity of its professions.

The Government has no desire for conquest now, but it is bound in its duty to provide fully for its own security and to guard the interests of those committed to its charge. To that end, and as the only sure mode of protecting the State from the perpetual recurrence of unprovoked and wasting wars, the Governor-General is compelled to resolve upon the entire subjugation of a people whom their own Government has long been unable to control, and whom (as events have now shown) no punishment can deter from violence, no acts of friendship can conciliate to peace. Wherefore the Governor-General has declared and hereby proclaims that the Kingdom of the Panjab is at an end; and that all the territories of Maharaja Ranjit Singh are now and henceforth a portion of the British empire in India. His Highness the Maharaja shall be treated with consideration and with honour. The few chiefs who have not engaged in hostilities against the British shall retain their property and their rank. The British Government shall leave to all the people, whether Mussalmans or Hindus or Sikhs, the free exercise of their own religion, but it will not permit any man to interfere with others in the observance of such forms and customs as their respective religions may either enjoin or permit. The jagirs and all the property of sardars and others who have been in arms against the British shall be confiscated to the State. The defences of every fortified place in the Panjab which is not occupied by British troops shall be totally destroyed, and effectual measures shall be taken to deprive the people of the means of renewing either tumult or war. The Governor-General calls upon all the inhabitants of the Panjab, sardars and people, to submit themselves peaceably to the authority of the British Government which has hereby been proclaimed. Over those who shall live as obedient and peaceful subjects of the State, the British Government will rule with mildness and beneficence. But if resistance to constituted authority shall again be attempted, if violence and turbulence be renewed, the Governor-General warns the people of the Panjab that the time for leniency will then have passed away, and that their offence will be punished with prompt and most rigorous severity.'[1]

So strongly worded a document left little room for mediation. But we must remember how often Western individuals had warmed to the Sikhs. Jacquemont, Vigne, Osborne, Emily Eden, Henry Lawrence had greatly admired them and as the British fanned out over the Punjab—as soldiers, judges, administrators, doctors and engineers—they brought with them new but kindly ideas of government and order. In Guler and Kangra, Sikh rule had been mellowed by the warm personalities of the two Majithias—the father, Desa Singh; the son, Lehna Singh. In a similar way, foreign rule in the Punjab was softened by the strong regard in which the British held the Sikhs.

During this gradual coming to terms, British ideas affected almost every aspect of Punjabi life. Sikh religion was scrupulously respected but western ideas of government, law, education and industry were gradually imposed. There was no sinister after-thought in this matter. It reflected desire on the part of the British to give the Sikhs western 'benefits'. We may query their wisdom; but we cannot lightly scorn the motives of those whose evangelical upbringings drove them to mould the Punjab with such firm benevolence.

In such a situation, it is no surprise that British attitudes to painting slowly supplemented and superseded Indian. Artists at Lahore and Amritsar—immigrants to the Punjab Plains from Guler, Kangra and Delhi—had used gouache as their chief medium. The British preferred water-colour and as they settled down to live and rule, they induced Punjabi artists to adopt it. As early as 1838 or 1839, a British traveller in the Punjab had persuaded an Indian artist to portray the different peoples of Northern India, sketching them on British-supplied paper and binding them into an album.[2] Amongst these drawings, some were strongly Sikh in theme —portraits of rulers and pictures of the military. Their names were inscribed in Persian but the owner of the album had added his own notes: 'A Nahung or Akhalee', 'General Allard's Cavalry Punjaub 1838' and 'Lahore Life Guards, 1838'. Such drawings were comparable to those of Jivan Ram, the Indian painter who had travelled with Lord William Bentick's suite in 1831. He too had used pencil and water-colour and had painted exactly as his employer wished.

After 1850, the water-colour medium was more widely adopted; and subjects also were affected. The experience of ruling made some of the British curious. Castes and professions, architecture and heroes of the Sikh court aroused their

[1] Latif, *History*, 572–573.
[2] India Office Library, *Panjabi Characters*, Add. Or. 1347–1396.

58

interest and water-colour drawings were made to satisfy this need. As more and more British came to the Punjab, such pictures were hawked round British houses and *dak* bungalows. Artists would commission curiosity vendors to include their pictures amongst the vases, jewellery, ivory work and bric-à-brac that was offered to the sahibs. A volume of Sikh paintings, which appeared some years ago at Sotheby's, bore the inscription: 'Bought at Anarkulle, Lahore, April/62 for Rs 15 from a curiosity vendor. Dak Bungalow. G. R. Gibbs.' The artist or dealer had written: 'This book comprises all the Punjabees, workmen, the Rajah and many other things and this book is written in one year.' To this Mr Gibbs had added his own comments: 'The features of the men and women in these sketches are perhaps the best and truest part of them. There is a decided want of skill in drawing the drapery etc. but a good idea of wearing apparel is given. Very little knowledge of perspective shown. Though most of the men's legs appear not to belong to them; still a native can twist his legs in a very uncomfortable manner to all but himself.' As he spent hot and lonely evenings in the dak bungalow, Mr Gibbs had also added some facetious notes. 'Groom. Takes care of himself.' 'Chowkildar or watchman; sleeps, eats or coughs the whole night.'

Two other albums in the India Office Library entitled *Punjab Portraits, Buildings, Professions* have similar subjects. One bears a roman inscription in Sahib's Hindi: *Is ketabmen sab Panjabi chis hai. Raja log, naqsha, sab kam karne wala, tin kori panna hai, ekso bis taswir hai, sab sahiblog walait dikhlane ko lejate hain, yih kitab lahore men banti hai, qalim ka kam hai.* (In this book are all Punjabi things. Rajas, landscapes, all the trades. There are 60 pages, 120 pictures. All the sahibs take it to show in England. This book was made in Lahore. It is done with a pen.) Each portrait was inscribed with the name of its subject, and the books were thus a kind of directory of Punjabi life.[1]

Such books were products of private enterprise but in the sphere of public policy also, the British felt constrained to intervene. As they viewed the Punjab, ten years after their arrival, they were dismayed at the havoc caused by Western imports. They dimly saw that art was connected with industry and realised that unless firm action was taken the Punjabi craftsman would be ruined. The steps adopted follow a familiar pattern—enquiries by government servants, a survey of 'Punjab Manufactures', exhibitions, and lastly a report with recommendations. In some ways fortunately, in others less happily, the officer deputed for this work was B. H. Baden-Powell. His love for the Punjab was not in question but his knowledge and appreciation of Indian art were limited. It was rather in the mood of a strong but kindly father, chiding refractory children, that he assessed the Exhibition of 1864:

[1] India Office Library Add. Or. 1397–1451 and 1452–1511. Figs. 92–95

'In scarcely any part of India are the fine arts in so low a condition as in the Panjab. In Delhi, indeed, which is politically included in the province, the art of painting on ivory has for long been cultivated with great success, but in the Panjab proper there is, at present, little in painting, sculpture, or architecture worthy of notice. The reasons for this state of things are simple, and it is so desirable that they should be fully appreciated, that a few words in explanation of them may not be considered out of place in this report.

During the rule of the Muhammadan emperors, the Panjab was the battle-field of India. . . . There was no cultivation of the fine arts at that time, for the people were poor and it was all they could do to support and defend their families.

When the Moghal empire fell, the prospects of the fine arts did not improve. The condition of the Panjab between 1760 and 1810 resembled that of England during the reign of King John. In every direction rose forts of brick or mud, the homes of petty chiefs and barons, who with two or three hundred horsemen behind them ravaged the surrounding country and carried off the plunder to their strongholds. Those of the Sikh chiefs who were the most powerful were only the most successful robbers; any differences between them were only differences of degree.

At length Ranjit Singh rose to power on the ruins of the Sikh confederacies. But he had won his kingdom by the sword, and had no reverence for the brush or the chisel. His life was passed in incessant war to extend and consolidate his empire, and he had no time to devote to the fine arts. Like most of his nobles he was grossly illiterate, and could neither read nor write, and in his Court, in its most brilliant days, there were but three men who could be truly called educated. The ten years succeeding the death of Ranjit Singh were years of anarchy and revolution, and the Panjab first found rest when in 1849 it was annexed to the British empire.

It will not then be considered strange that the fine arts have not flourished in this province. They are the result of peace and civilisation, and it was not to be expected that they should arise in the midst of war and barbarism; but for the future there is good hope.

No one who has carefully examined the articles exhibited, not only in the Department of Fine Arts but also in that devoted to Manufactures, can fail to have been struck with the promise of future excellence which they display. The native of the Panjab possesses many of the qualities which ensure success in art. In common with the inhabitants of lower India, he has an instinctive appreciation of colour, and, though without any knowledge of the principles which should regulate its use, is often more happy in his combinations than the educated workman of Europe. His colour is often exaggerated but it is always warm, and rich and fearless. The native artist is also patient: for weeks and months he will work at his design, painfully elaborating the most minute details; no time is considered too long, no labour too intense to secure perfection in imitation or delicacy in execution. The greatest failing in native artists is their ignorance of perspective and drawing, and it is fortunate that this want is the most easy to supply. Nothing is required but schools of design and judicious instruction to effect a great change both in the fine arts themselves, and in art manufactures in the Panjab.'[1]

This passage cogently expresses what good Victorians seriously thought. We may deplore its naïve assumption of British superiority, its childish aesthetics, its over-simple standards. But we must realise that the modern movement in art had still to evolve. In the England of 1864 works by Constable and Turner had, admittedly, been painted and of all British painters these are most clearly the forerunners of certain types of modern art. But general British taste was still far from modern. We may deprecate Baden-Powell's attitudes and ideas but we can hardly blame him for being of his time. Moreover, in some respects, he was truly perceptive. 'For the future' he had said 'there is good hope'. He discerned 'promise of future excellence', 'instinctive appreciation of colour', a capacity for 'happy combinations' and in the last ten years these very qualities have characterised Punjabi contributions to modern Indian art.

The results of Baden-Powell's survey could have been easily predicted. They were, first, the establishment of the Mayo School of Art, Lahore, in 1875 and secondly, as a by-product, the introduction of new pictorial techniques. Certain artists, their names intriguingly Sikh, had already shown skill in water-colour. At the exhibition of arts and crafts held at Lahore in 1864, a painter from Kapurthala, Kishan Singh, exhibited an album of drawings of birds, figures and plants. Bishan Singh of Amritsar showed ten pictures including darbars of Ranjit Singh, Sher Singh and the Municipal Committee, Amritsar. 'The perspective of the buildings', the jury had noted 'is incorrect but the figure drawing is admirable. The colour is tasteful and rich and likenesses are good and the expression is varied and truthful'. Other pictures by him were in water-colour and illustrated the shawl trade and a carriage. His work was generally considered 'the most clever and truthful'.[2] Yet a third artist, Kapur Singh, is noted by Percy Brown as having 'painted a large number of figure subjects, miniature in size and showing a very fair knowledge of drawing with considerable action'.[3] The report is not entirely clear, but it would seem that most, if not all of these pictures, were in water-colour.

The new Art School, under Lockwood Kipling, principal, encouraged this medium and technique and we can gain an idea of the students' work from some drawings of utensils contributed by them to *The Journal of Indian Art* in 1884.

[1] Baden-Powell, *Punjab Manufactures*, 354.
[2] *Ibid.*, 355.   [3] Brown, *Indian Painting*, 62.

Technical skill in rendering appearances, firmness and precision of line, willing-ness to imbibe Western ideas of design, a flair for modernising form, colour and composition, a zest for Western subjects, these were the qualities that were most admired. Of Guler painting as it had developed at Lahore and Amritsar between 1835 and 1845, nothing was known; and even of Kangra and Guler—the greatest former centres of painting in the Punjab Hills—only the dimmest rumours re-mained. 'The artistic industries of Kangra' wrote Lockwood Kipling in 1887 'are now few and insignificant. Among native limners, *Kangra ki qalm* (the Kangra pencil) is a phrase occasionally heard and meant to distinguish the style or touch of a school of illumination and mythological picture painting that is supposed to have flourished there.'[1] In Guler and Kanga, painting was actually still persisting but in 1864 it was traditional work by Raja Sansar Chand's artists rather than contem-porary examples which had been exhibited. From 1875 to Indian independence in 1947, Punjabi artists were trained in British academic drawing, oblivious both of painting in the Punjab Hills and in the Plains.

It was rather in two different directions that painting of the Sikhs persisted and the stimulus given by Maharaja Sher Singh had its greatest effects. So long as Dalip Singh was technically on the throne his childish figure had aroused no public interest. Guler artists at Lahore and Amritsar were still producing standard por-traits but among them we find no sign of Dalip, his mother Rani Jindan, her brother Jawahir, her lover Lal Singh, Nur-ud-din the foreign secretary or Tej Singh the new commander-in-chief. A pathetic substitute for the great Ranjit, neither Dalip nor his circle had glamour. The child maharaja was over-shadowed first by his mother and then by the Regency Council under Henry Lawrence. Indeed to the Sikhs, at large, he was almost non-existent and it was only in a few British individuals that he seemingly aroused a lively concern.

In February, 1846, Hardinge, nephew of the Governor-General, drew him in Lahore and the picture[2] gives a vivid impression of the pathetic little boy, his face as blank as a puppet's. Almost three years later, when the second Anglo-Sikh war was over and the Sikh state had ended, Mrs Helen MacKenzie sketched his por-trait[3] and recorded her feelings. Wife of Colonel Colin MacKenzie, an army officer, she had moved from one cantonment to another, staying first at Ludhiana, then at Simla, later still at Lahore. From vantage points such as these, she had been a modest spectator *ab extra*. Like Lawrence she had sympathised with the Sikhs and with a sense of pitying dismay she watched Dalip, first smothered by the Regency Council and then removed.

The following extracts from her journal show his tutor, Dr Login, already installed. On the surface all is well but in a moment, the little boy will be hurried

[1] Kipling, *Journal of Indian Art*, II, No. 20, 40–41.   [2] Fig. 67.   [3] Fig. 66.

off and in place of youthful royalty—as appealing in its way as Sher Singh's child, Pratap Singh—the Sikhs will be left with a mass of blurred, distorted legends. Dalip is about to be exiled but in Helen MacKenzie's drawings and journal 'regardless of his doom the little victim plays'.

'*Wednesday, November 28th* (1849). James came with me on an elephant to Dr Login's apartments in the citadel to draw some Sikhs. I sketched six, several of them very fine-looking men. One old man had been keeper of the robes to Runjit for forty years. I drew him sitting, and then wanted a fine-looking younger man, who is Jemadar of Orderlies, to stand by him, but he said if he *stood* people would take him for the old man's servant. In vain I said he would be taken for his son. He was very unhappy until I offered to draw him on a separate sheet of paper, when he shouted and skipped for joy in so ludicrous a manner that James and I both burst out laughing.

After breakfast, Dr Login took us to visit the little Maharajah. He was in the Shish Mahal, or Glass Palace, a very lofty apartment, open on one side to the court, the walls and ceilings are covered with a sort of mosaic of little mirrors and colours. The back opens into his sleeping apartment, which is of the same description. Dhalip Sing is about eleven years old, with beautiful eyes and nose, but the lower part of the face is too full. He met us at the door and took Dr Login's hand: a gold chair was set for the little prince, and a silver one on his left for Dr Login. A box of toys had just arrived from Sir F. Currie and both the little Maharajah and his servants were anxiously waiting to see its contents, which consisted entirely of boxes of figures, some with and some without music, such as a blacksmith hammering, a cobbler drawing his thread, etc., very baby toys for a boy of eleven. We did not stay long, but returned home through the narrow streets of the city which are almost impassable except on an elephant.'

Friday, November 30th. The little Maharajah having expressed a wish that I should draw him, James accompanied me on an elephant at gun-fire. Dhalip Singh passed in an open carriage and four, with his hawk on his fist, escorted by some of Skinner's horse; so I took a sketch of the town, or rather of Runjit's Tomb and the Jamma Masjid. We saw the Commander-in-Chief and his staff come in, and then proceeded to the fort where we breakfasted with Dr Login, and then went to the little Maharajah, who was richly dressed in yellow velvet and silver, with a sort of crimson tunic underneath, and magnificent pearls round his throat. I took a sketch of him and several of his attendants; and he in return sent for two native artists, who made hideous representations of J. and me.'

Saturday, December 1st. James and C.[1] went to the Durbar; Sir H. Lawrence went to fetch the Maharajah, and Sir H. Elliot received him on alighting; and

[1] Mrs MacKenzie's husband, Colin.

the Governor-General met him at the door of the tent. Dhalip looked very handsome and royal. About fifty-three trays of presents were given to him, besides khillats or dresses of honour, and presents to all the people about him. Lord Dalhousie returned his visit in state a few days after; but it seems almost a pity that the Governor-General should have acted on the kindly impulse which prompted him to treat the little prince as a sovereign, for both he and his attendants will be proportionately disappointed at his being sent away to Fattinghar.'

Monday, December 3rd. Dined at the Governor-General's; the tents were exceedingly cold. There was a ball after dinner and we left early; everyone seems to know that we do not go to balls.[1] The Governor-General mentioned how much he had been struck with the regal manner of the little Maharajah. It is indeed most remarkable. At the Grand Durbar the other day, after a little whispered conversation with Dr Login, Dhalip Sing turned to Lord Dalhousie and said with childish simplicity in English, "I am very glad to see you here". In one sense the Governor-General was the last person whom the poor little prince should have rejoiced in seeing at Lahore, but as respects his future life and happiness, he had been his best friend. Dr Login mentioned that he was convinced that the little Maharajah fully enjoyed the feeling of personal security at present. He must remember the fate of his little predecessor, Purtab Sing, a son of Shir Sing's, who was murdered when about his own age. . . .'

Tuesday, December 4th. In the afternoon, C. accompanied Mrs McMurdo and me to take a second sketch of the little Maharajah in the dress he wore at the Durbar, as I thought Lord Dalhousie would like it better. He looked extremely handsome with a sirpesh, or aigrette of diamonds, and wreaths of pearls in his turban. His hawk is always in the hall, and when he drives out he carries it on his wrist; it is a mark of royalty.'

Wednesday, December 5th.—Drew all day, to finish the picture of the Maharajah and his attendants for the Governor-General.'[2]

Two months later, the masquerade was ended. Dalip was dispatched to Fatehgarh and all remnants of the great ideal—first defined by Guru Govind Singh and then so splendidly realised by Ranjit Singh—had vanished.

Yet, as happens not infrequently to public figures, the removal of Dalip was to have some strange results. Dim and unrecognised while in the Punjab, he underwent apotheosis in exile. As the Sikhs adjusted themselves to servile vistas, they experienced acute nostalgia for 'things past'. It was not only the grandeurs of Ranjit Singh that they viewed with 'ineffaceable regret'. Any member of the Sikh

[1] Mrs Mackenzie was a very strict evangelical Christian.
[2] MacKenzie, *Life in the Mission, the Camp and the Zenana,* III, 47–54.

royal family, any minister at the Sikh court, any foreigner who had defied the British, any matter that was truly Sikh acquired fresh value. The closing years of Sikh rule became as precious as those of Ranjit Singh, the child Dalip as real a symbol of Sikh power as the handsome Sher Singh. Four reigns blended into one. In the early eighteenth century, when Sikh power had collapsed, the first Sikh Guru—Nanak—had seemed as real as the last—Guru Govind Singh. They had even been portrayed encountering each other.[1] And in the Punjab under the British, a similar telescoping of characters now occurred.

The new situation demanded a new style and in the water-colour portraits on ivory in vogue at Delhi since 1830, the public at Lahore and Amritsar obtained the talismans it required. In 1839, Emily Eden had returned to Delhi, thrilled and delighted with the court and camp of Ranjit Singh. During her visit, she had drawn and sketched with tireless diligence and her portfolio was filled with portraits of the Sikhs. In Delhi, Mughal artists were producing standard sets of Mughal emperors and court beauties as well as individual portraits on ivory,[2] commissioned by the British. Their style was staidly Mughal but, egged on by their British patrons, they had blended photographic shading with careful realism. To Emily Eden, the chance of making a new experiment appealed. She would have her sketches 'translated' into ivory.

'I have had two Delhi miniature painters here (she recorded in 1839) translating two of my sketches into ivory, and I never saw anything so perfect as their copy of Runjeet Singh. Azim, the best painter, is almost a genius except that he knows no perspective, so he can only copy. He is quite mad about some of my sketches, and as all miniatures of well-known characters sell well, he has determined to get hold of my book. There is a foreshortened elephant with the Putteealah Rajah in the howdah, that particularly takes his fancy. However, I do not want them to be common, so I cut out of the book those that I wish to have copied, and I never saw a native so nearly in a passion as he was, because he was not allowed the whole book. Their miniatures are so soft and beautiful. F. had your likeness of my father copied.'[3]

This experiment may well have started a vogue but a second circumstance also helped to develop the new style. Attracted by Sher Singh's positive enjoyment of art, painters from Delhi must almost certainly have reached Lahore by 1842. Among them may have been a certain Hasan-al-din and at least four pictures either by himself or an assistant, reveal the same Anglo-Mughal style which ten years later was to prove so popular. The first picture[4] shows the court of Lahore when,

[1] Note XIII, p. 75.   [2] Archer, *Indian Painting for the British*, 67–70, figs. 33–35.
[3] Eden, *Up the Country*, 263.   [4] Fig. 62.

newly assembled in November 1843 after Sher Singh's death, it revealed to public gaze his young successor. Dalip is in the centre and we see him as child Maharaja, freshly haloed, patting a pet lap-dog and surrounded by fourteen of the grim and turbulent characters who were to mould his reign. The second[1] takes us to May 1845 when Jawahir Singh is now chief minister and two resolute supporters— Lal and Labh Singh—are there to aid him. The third[2] moves to November 1845. This is inscribed in Persian 'By Hasan-al-din painter' and we meet familiar faces which are soon to appear on ivories. The child Dalip is once again seated on a chair, gun in hand, the same lap-dog dozing at his feet. Dina Nath and Nur-ud-din —the one an expert on finance, the other on foreign affairs—are to the right; Tej Singh, commander-in-chief and Labh Singh, the tough army commander, are on the left. The same attendant who stood beside him in the picture of November 1843 is shown once more but this time standing with cloth and regal fly-whisk. The fourth picture[3] brings us nearer still. Henry Lawrence is now in charge and in place of Dalip, the British resident holds the stage, dictating comments to the ever-docile Dina Nath.

Pictures in this style are the models out of which portraits of the Sikhs were now to spring and from the eighteen-fifties onwards, standard portraits on ivory began to minister to Sikh pride. Certain characters—Jamadar Khushal Singh (Ranjit's earliest favourite), Jawahir Singh (Rani Jindan's brother), even the wily Aziz-ud-din (architect of Ranjit's foreign policy) had little popular appeal. They were either omitted or were very rarely portrayed. Some figures, on the other hand, played only minor parts but due to accidents of history they had caught the Sikh imagination. Rani Jindan herself was of small account but her banishment by the British had made her a martyr. She came to be viewed not as a meddlesome appendage of the child maharaja but as almost a national heroine. Her paramour, Lal Singh, had narrowly escaped the Sikh army's execration but when his quiet, behind-the-scene machinations almost succeeded in sabotaging the plan to sell Kashmir to Gulab Singh, he was seen in a different light. His trial by the British in November 1846 led to his expulsion from the Punjab and once again, trial and eviction by the conquerors gave him a special claim on Sikh gratitude. Mul Raj, Governor of Multan, was also magnified by events. Until 1848, he was little known but his share in murdering two British officers had led to the final catastrophe and made him famous. In a similar way, certain Sikh generals, of small account under Ranjit Singh, were gratefully remembered as enemies of the victors. Three Atariwalas— Sham, Chattar and Sher—were in this class. Sham Singh had led a suicidal charge at the battle of Sobraon, dying, full of years, for a cause whose wisdom he had, in fact, questioned. Chattar, the father, and Sher Singh Atariwala, the son, had fought

[1]Fig. 63.   [2]Fig. 61.   [3]Fig. 64.

66

the British in the second Sikh war. Both had been defeated and exiled but in the years succeeding the British triumph, it was their dour hostility rather than their abject failure which kindled Sikh homage. Even the vacillating Tej Singh—as dubious a figure as his Brahmin uncle, Khushal Singh—was loyally remembered as commander-in-chief in the first Anglo-Sikh war. Devious though his career may have been and unsuccessful some of his schemes, his defiance made him a potent mentor.

Such figures were fresh in public memory but as the Sikhs submitted themselves to British rule, it was the preceding half century as a whole that fired their imagination. Fighters of the British such as the Afghans Dost Muhammad and his family—characters the very opposite of Sikhs in real life—were recalled as valued allies. Though Muslims by religion, they had won Sikh respect by, on one occasion, routing British forces and their opposition to British aims had given them an air of almost brotherly identity. The outlaw, Phula Singh Akali, had enraged Ranjit Singh with his outbursts of impetuous fury but his feats of derring-do hinted at the wild guerilla tactics by which the early Sikhs had come to power. As the Sikhs watched the gradual collapse of their national ideal, they remembered his recourse to anarchy and gloried in the one outlet which circumstances had since denied them.

All these figures were portrayed on ivory but it was the court of Maharaja Ranjit Singh, his family, successors and intimates, which completed the series. The three Dogra brothers—formerly such vital components of Ranjit's 'public image'—had met successive fates. The youngest, the gay and fluttering Suchet Singh, had been killed by his nephew Hira Singh. Less significant than the others, he had dwindled in public esteem after the death of Ranjit in 1839 and although his portrait on ivory was duly made, it was rather to the eldest brother, Gulab Singh and the chief minister, Dhian Singh that the painters constantly returned. Dhian Singh's long and dutiful submission had made him almost as memorable as his master Ranjit for the spectacle of a Rajput noble so sedulously furthering Sikh aims had been part of Ranjit's spell. He had died with Sher Singh and even in death had suffered a Sikh fate. Gulab Singh, for his part, had ended by severing all connection with the Punjab but in retrospect his whole career, first as a commander in the Sikh army, then as administrator in Jammu and finally as its governor and independent ruler had been based on Sikh support. Other figures were added. Hira Singh had first impressed the public as Ranjit Singh's boy-favourite but had ended by becoming Dalip's chief minister. Sher Singh had been a late arrival on the scene but his portly figure, brandishing a great sword, seemed the very embodiment of Ranjit's own valour. The child Pratap, murdered before he could affect events, was a Sikh asset sadly wasted. Kharak and Nau Nihal Singh had also continued the line.

But it was the great Maharaja himself who claimed most homage. In his life-time and immediately after his death, the large right eye, flashing like the Koh-i-noor itself, had dimmed the blind left one and to Guler artists it had been a point of principle to portray him in profile facing right. In the ivory portraits which now sustained his legend, this practice was slowly abandoned. By the eighteen-fifties, Ranjit's greatness had far transcended his physical appearance. Indeed his facial blemishes may even have enhanced his personal mystique. He was therefore painted as much in three-quarter view as in profile, sometimes facing left and sometimes right.

Ivory portraits were symptomatic of the new era and from the eighteen-fifties on into the twentieth century, they continued to enthrall the public. But they were not the only direction in which Sikh feelings found vehement expression. Early in the nineteenth century, lithography had come to India, enabling books, news-papers and drawings to be rapidly copied. The process had reached the Punjab in the early fifties and by 1888 it was so widely employed that Lockwood Kipling could note in *The Journal of Indian Art*: 'Several of the smaller vernacular journals are lithographed and there is a considerable production of cheap story books with here and there a rude picture in outlines. A local 'Punch' prints curiously grotesque political and social cartoons. The subjects of these pictures are dictated by the editor with but little reference to their suitability for illustration and as the local Tenniel receives about fourpence in English money for drawing and lithographing each cartoon, the result in an artistic sense is more comic than was intended.'[1] Yet, more even than lithographs, woodcuts had become a mass medium. Printed in hundreds and sold in all the main bazaars, they served as popular accessories to portraits on ivory, vividly reminding Sikhs of their past glories. In certain cases, ivory portraits were used as models and the woodcut, brazenly coloured but care-fully outlined, assembled in row upon row the twelve figures who commanded most respect. The oval shape employed by ivories was retained and the woodcut served as a crude anthology of Sikh heroes, a kind of Gallup poll on popularity.[2] The same twelve figures were sometimes modelled on standard portraits in gouache or water-colour, the woodcuts once again revealing features familiar from long repetition.[3]

In these woodcuts of perhaps the year 1870, Ranjit, Sher and Dalip Singh remain unshaken—Sher Singh with his great sword and Dalip with his hawk or lap-dog flanking the great Maharaja. Rani Jindan is still as essential as her husband and son. Kharak and Nau Nihal, however, are both excluded. Gulab and Dhian Singh are present but not Suchet, Hira or Ranbir Singh. Chattar and Sher Singh Atariwala follow but the third Atariwala, Sham, is dropped as also is Tej Singh.

[1] Kipling, *Journal of Indian Art*, II, 60. [2] Figs. 108, 109. [3] Fig. 110.

Dina Nath and Mulraj remain but Nur-ud-din is missing. Finally come two figures still enigmatic and exotic—the Akali Phula Singh and the Afghan Dost Muhammad.

This choice of figures illustrates the complex nature of Sikh requirements and in another type of woodcut,[1] we find the same sort of celebration, though with somewhat different details. Maharaja Ranjit Singh is shown in darbar, royal, gigantic and with a huge halo. He presides over an assembly but, ignoring history, it includes Sher and Kharak Singh on the left and the three Dogra brothers and Tej Singh on the right. Below them are six further figures—among them, Dina Nath and, more incongruously, the Afghan Dost Muhammad. In the centre clambering towards Ranjit is the child Dalip. The 'magic circle' has at last been closed and with a sense of final abandonment, the Sikhs are groping for a new beginning.

It is perhaps this need for a fresh start which is crudely but vividly suggested by certain other woodcuts.[2] Besides idolising the recent dead, woodcuts returned to the sources of Sikh energy and power—the spiritual leaders who had founded their community, given it identity and cohesion and formulated the national ideal. The ten Gurus were therefore depicted sitting in the same kind of timeless conclave as Ranjit Singh and his successors. Sikh rites of baptism and the Golden Temple, Amritsar were also illustrated. In this way not only was the recent past extolled but the means to ultimate success was reaffirmed.

It was Guru Govind Singh, however, who provided the strongest clue to future action. In popular woodcuts, he and Guru Nanak vie with each other in general esteem—Guru Nanak appearing as a great father figure, venerable and benign, Guru Govind Singh as the bold fighter, the revolutionary enunciator of doctrine, the wise inventor of the 'five K's', the great exemplar whose life and death pointed to the future. Certain Sikh qualities—courage, heroism, energy and will-power— were conjured up by his image but his ultimate resolve was even more pertinent as a lesson. When war against the Mughals had failed, he had resorted to conciliation and it was in the Deccan, siding with the Mughal forces, that he had met his death. In 1849, the Sikhs were vanquished, their national ideal had collapsed but by co-operating with the new conquerors, the modernising British, it seemed that for a second time their goal might be attained.

This moral is hinted at in a woodcut of a starkly different kind.[3] Symbolic of the new Punjab, it shows a railway train in two sections standing in a station. The upper section is by a platform, the lower section has an engine about to start. Railways had reached the Punjab in the early eighteen-sixties and the Sikhs had been confronted by a new machine, as powerful in its way as the British government which had subdued them. At first, all trains were run and controlled by

[1]Fig. 111.   [2]Cat. No. 94.   [3]Fig. 112.

British drivers but presently Sikhs were actively associated with them. In the woodcut the passengers include both men and women, both Sikhs and British; and the same collaboration appears elsewhere. The driver and fireman are British or Anglo-Indian but the stationmaster, holding the vital tally, the clerk in the ticket office and the guard, waving a flag and setting the points, are all Sikhs. If we interpret the train as the Punjab, the meaning of the parable is only too clear.

As the nineteenth century merged with the twentieth, the Sikhs came increasingly to value modern forms of expression. They discarded the painting which had expressed the fugitive glories of the first Sikh state and it was rather in partnership with the West that they moved into the modern age. The symbol of that age is the Punjab's new capital, Chandigarh—the first great example of modern architecture in India and as vital a monument to Punjabi vigour as the Golden Temple, Amritsar, had been to Sikh fervour. In the nineteen-thirties, a Sikh painter, Amrita Sher-Gil, made a pioneer contribution to modern Indian art and in the nineteen-fifties and sixties, it was the Sikh writer and scholar, M. S. Randhawa, who inaugurated a new phase in Indian art-appreciation. Such achievements by modern Sikhs show how basic a revolution had been set in train by early Sikh painting. Serving as a stimulant to morale and a means to vicarious fulfilment, Sikh portraiture had, in effect, achieved one further and, perhaps an even more important, end. It had discovered art for the Sikhs and had nullified the charge that the Sikhs were a non-artistic people. Above all, this popular, rather than courtly, art had demonstrated that the people of India themselves must now evoke and sponsor modes of aesthetic expression. The patron must be the public at large, not the feudal great. The recognition of this truth has underlain all recent Indian art and its early discovery by the Sikhs is not the least of their contributions to Indian culture.

NOTES

The names and dates of the ten Sikh Gurus are as follows:

1. Nanak (founder and first Guru, 1469–1529)
2. Angad (second Guru, 1529–1552)
3. Amar Das (third Guru, 1552–1574)
4. Ram Das (fourth Guru, 1574–1581)
5. Arjun (fifth Guru, 1581–1606)
6. Har Govind (sixth Guru, 1606–1645)
7. Har Rai (seventh Guru, 1645–1661)
8. Har Kishan (eighth Guru, 1661–1664)
9. Tegh Bahadur (ninth Guru, 1664–1675)
10. Govind Singh (tenth Guru, 1675–1708)

Clear accounts of Sikh religion are given by Khushwant Singh, *The Sikhs* and *A History of the Sikhs*; for excerpts from the Granth and for Sikh hymns and prayers, see Khushwant Singh and others, *The Sacred Writings of the Sikhs*.

For contemporary references in the nineteenth century to this type of popular painting, see *Bibliography: Paintings of the Sikhs*, excerpts from Vigne (1842), Barr (1844), Hugel (1845), Helen MacKenzie (1853), Wolff (1860), Garrett (1935)—the latter quoting Jacquemont (1831).

Khan (*The Princess Bamba Collection*, 5) states that 'there are panels of wall paintings in the Samadhi of Maharaja Ranjit Singh; in the Haveli of Maharaja Nau Nihal Singh in Lahore and on the walls of the Mirs' Harem in the Hyderabad Fort. In the Lahore Fort, the Department of Archaeology has traced a number of wall paintings of the Sikh period which were concealed under lime plaster of the British Period.'

For a second series of Guru portraits, still in Guler style, though perhaps executed in the Punjab Plains in about 1830, see S. N. Gupta, 'The Sikh School of Painting', *Rupam* (1922), III, no. 12, 125–128. The four Gurus illustrated are Amar Das (3), Ram Das (4), Har Rai (7) and Har Kishan (8). It is noteworthy that Har Kishan is shown as distinctly older than in figure 5 and that Guru Har Rai appears nimbate with the same kind of state umbrella, favoured at the Sikh court and in paintings of the Sikhs. In general style, the series resembles figure 11 (Sikh sardar, perhaps the Governor Desa Singh Majithia, carousing with a Guler lady). The faces and expressions of the ladies and attendants, the carpet with parallel stripes, the scarlet screens and pale green and azure backgrounds are typical of painting in Guler of about the years 1815 to 1830. The fact that figure 11 was formerly in the Guler Raj collection reinforces the conclusion that it is a painting by a Guler artist at Guler.

A third series of Guru portraits is illustrated by figure 7 (Guru Govind Singh). Like series 2, it is either a product of Guler itself or is one of several versions based on Guler prototypes painted by Guler artists in the Plains. In this connection, compare the treatment of the puppy as in Gupta, *op. cit.*, plate 3 (Guru Har Rai).

Although alcohol was not forbidden to the Sikhs, Maharaja Ranjit Singh set a new fashion in hard drinking which was followed by many of his courtiers, including Desa Singh Majithia (pages 18–22, figure 11).

For Ranjit's own predilection for spirits, see figure 12, which shows him carousing with a Kangra lady (perhaps one of his Gaddan ranis from Kangra). Osborne, liveliest of all the early travellers, has the following entry in his journal for 2 July 1838:

'On my return home, I met the Maharajah taking his usual ride. He was very inquisitive as to where I had been, and I never saw him in so good a humour or such high spirits. After a good deal of gossip upon various subjects, he said, "You have never been at one of my drinking parties; it is bad work drinking now the weather is so hot; but as soon as we have a good rainy day, we will have one." I sincerely hope it will not rain at all during our stay, for, from all accounts, nothing can be such a nuisance as one of these parties. His wine is extracted from raisins, with a quantity of pearls ground to powder, and mixed with it, for no other reason (that I can hear) than to add to the expense of it. It is made for himself alone, and though he sometimes gives a few bottles to some of his favourite chiefs, it is very difficult to be procured, even at the enormous price of one gold mohur for a small bottle. It is as strong as aquafortis, and as at his parties he always helps you himself, it is no easy matter to avoid excess. He generally, on these occasions, has two or three Hebes in the shape of the prettiest of his Cachemirian girls to attend upon himself and guests, and gives way to every species of licentious debauchery. He fell violently in love with one of these fair cup-bearers about two years ago, and actually married her, after parading her on a pillion before himself on horseback, through the camp and city, for two or three days, to the great disgust of all his people. The only food allowed you at these drinking bouts are fat quails stuffed with all sorts of spices, and the only thing to allay your thirst, naturally consequent upon eating such heating food, is this abominable liquid fire. Runjeet himself laughs at our wines, and says that he drinks for excitement, and that the sooner that object is attained the better. Of all the wines we brought with us as a present to him from the governor-general, consisting of port, claret, hock, champagne, etc., the whiskey was the only thing he liked. During these potations he generally orders the attendance of all his dancing girls, whom he forces to drink his wine, and when he thinks them sufficiently excited, uses all his power to set them by the ears, the result of which is a general action, in the course of which they tear one another almost to pieces. They pull one another's nose and earrings by main force, and sometimes even more serious accidents occur; Runjeet sitting by encouraging them with the greatest delight, and exclaiming to his guests, "*Burra tomacha, burra tomacha*" (great fun).' (*Court and Camp*, 188–192.)

NOTE VI, P. 24

For detailed accounts of Sansar Chand's romance and subsequent marriage with Nokhu, a beauty from the Gaddi or shepherd caste, see M. S. Randhawa, 'Sujanpur Tira: the cradle of Kangra Art', *Marg* (1954), VII, no. 3, 35 and 'Maharaja Sansar Chand: the patron of Kangra painting', *Roopa Lekha* (1961), XXXII, no. 2, 22–23. Other references to the Gaddan or shepherd girl appear in J. C. French, *Himalayan Art* (London, 1931), 38, and Archer, *Kangra Painting* (London, 1952), 4. For a discussion of Nokhu's influence on Kangra painting and her poetic identification with Damayanti in the Nala Damayanti series of Kangra drawings, see A. C. Eastman, *The Nala Damayanti Drawings* (Boston, 1959) and Archer, 'Nala Damayanti Drawings', *Marg* (1959), XIII, no. 1, Supplement, 3–4.

NOTE VII, P. 27

At Maharaja Ranjit Singh's death on 27 June 1839, only one of the two Gaddan ranis from Kangra was surviving, the other having died some years earlier from tuberculosis. It was the surviving Gaddan rani who took the leading part at the funeral and led the other ranis and maids to commit *sati*. Like figure 13, figure 16 is in Kangra style.

NOTE VIII, P. 33

The persons in the Darbar scene (figure 15, Ranjit Singh with Astrologer and Pandits) are inscribed in Persian characters, from left to right: *rāja kalān dhiān singhjīv, shah zāda kharak singh bahādur, rāja adhirāj mahārāja sāhib chand gosāl ranjīt singh bahādur rāmapār, rāja hīrā singh, joshī kalān shankarnāth, pandit kalān maksūdan, rādhā kishan khalaf pandit kalān maksūdan, rāja gulāb singhjīv, rāja suchet singhjīv.*

Kalān means 'chief' or 'head', *joshī* 'astrologer', *khalaf* 'son of'.

For Joshi Shankar Nath, 'Native of Travancore', South India, and previous owner of five Sikh portraits (figures 28, 35 and 40) acquired by J. D. Sims in South India, *c*. 1844, and now in the Scott collection, London, see pages 33–34, 74, 130, 133, 168.

For examples of Jodhpur standard portraits of local rulers and nobles, see R. Skelton, *Indian Miniatures from the XVth to XIXth centuries* (Venice, 1961), plate 22.

Standard portrait sets from the Punjab Hills are illustrated in K. Khandalavala, *Pahari Miniature Painting* (Bombay, 1958) and M. S. Randhawa, *Basohli Painting* (Delhi, 1958).

For information concerning the 'Joshi Shankar Nath' portrait series, I am deeply indebted to Mr and Mrs T. W. F. Scott, my neighbours in Kensington from 1960 to 1961. Mrs Scott's great-great-uncle, James Duncan Sims, was a member of the Indian Civil Service from 1842 to 1875, serving in the Madras Presidency and early showing a special aptitude for the Telegu language. It was Sims who brought to England the 'Shankar Nath' series which in course of time passed by inheritance to Mrs Scott. We can reconstruct the circumstances in which Sims acquired the series from the following facts. A note, written in a thin and delicate hand, on the back of figure 40 (portrait of Sher Singh) records that the picture was 'Received from M. R. R. Sunkanada Johestree, a native of Travancore, for several years Chief Astrologer at the Court of Lahore, during Runjeet Sing, Cadagoo Sing and Shere Sing's reigns'. Travancore is in the Telegu-speaking country and two of the five portraits (figures 28 and 35) have inscriptions in Telegu written with a blunt nib in a thick and clumsy style. All five portraits have English inscriptions—some in the same clumsy hand as the inscriptions in Telegu (writer A), others in the thin and delicate style of the 'Sunkanada Johestree' note (writer B). It seems reasonable to assume that writer B is Sims and that, while learning Telegu in his early years in Madras—he was later appointed Examiner in this language—he met the much-travelled astrologer and obtained the series from him. In that case, writer A is almost certainly Joshi Shankar Nath himself. It is significant that writer A uses both Telegu and English but imparts only brief information; whereas writer B starts his notes where writer A leaves off, filling out his remarks in exactly the way in which a young Englishman, curious about the country and its people, might be expected to do.

Although no observations are dated, the form of phrasing on figure 35 (portrait of Dhian Singh, facing Kharak, Nau Nihal and Hira Singh) enables us to infer the year in which Sims wrote. Of Dhian Singh, he says: 'Raja Dana Singh or Deyan Sing, the Prime Minister of Runjeet Sing and afterwards of Shere Sing, along with whom he was assassinated by Adjeet Sing. His son, Hera Sing, is now Prime Minister of Dulheb Sing, a child of only 7 years of age now on the throne.' Since Dhian Singh and Sher Singh were murdered in September 1843, the inscription must obviously have been made after that date. Hira Singh, on the other hand, was killed in December 1844, yet when the note was written, he was still alive. At the same time, Dalip is recorded as being seven years old. Since he was born in 1837, sometime in 1844 must, therefore, be the date on which Sims obtained the portraits and wrote his remarks.

For examples illustrating the use of the halo in Mughal and Rajasthani painting and its absence from painting in the Punjab Hills, contrast the following portraits:

I. Mughal (with halo)

Archer, *Indian Miniatures* (New York, London, 1960), plates 28, 30.

R. Ettinghausen, *Paintings of the Sultans and Emperors of India* (Delhi, 1961), plates 11–14.

S. C. Welch, *The Art of Mughal India* (New York, 1963), plates 29, 30, 42, 43, 58, 59, 77.

II. Rajasthani (with halo)

Archer, *Indian Painting* (London, 1956), plates 10, 12.

Archer, *Indian Miniatures*, plates 54, 55, 61, 81.

Archer, *Indian Painting in Bundi and Kotah* (London, 1959), figures 22, 29, 36, 37, 40, 41, 45, 48, 51, 53, 54.

S. E. Lee, *Rajput Painting* (New York, 1960), plates 38, 48.

Skelton, *Indian Miniatures*, plates 12, 23.

III. Punjab Hills (without halo)

Archer, *Indian Miniatures*, plates 63, 71, 80, 82, 83.

Lee, *Rajput Painting*, plates 65, 67, 70, 71.

Skelton, *Indian Miniatures*, plates 37, 38, 51–53, 55, 57, 61, 71, 76, 79.

Note: The one exception referred to in the text (page 38) shows Raja Balvant Singh, nimbate, slaying a lion (Skelton, plate 75). In all other known portraits of this prince, the halo is wanting.

NOTE XII, P. 38

The comparative rarity of royal umbrellas in Mughal painting is illustrated by the fact that of the works cited in Note XI, only one contains an example. Welch (*The Art of Mughal India*, plate 42) shows the Emperor Shah Jahan on horseback, attended by Dara Shukoh, who holds above him an umbrella with straight stick.

For examples of royal umbrellas, with bent handles, see Skelton, *Indian Miniatures*, plate 50 (Punjab Hills) and Archer, *Indian Painting in Bundi and Kotah*, figure 48 (Rajasthan).

NOTE XIII, P. 65

The nine Gurus who succeeded Nanak, the first Guru, are regarded as his reincarnations. This idea is expressed by painting the first and the tenth Gurus together. These, though not contemporaries, are regarded as one person.

GENERAL BIBLIOGRAPHY

ABDUL ALI. F. M. 'Notes on the Life and Times of Ranjit Singh', *Bengal Past and Present* (January–March 1926), XXXI, 42–65.

AITCHISON, C. U. *A Collection of Treaties, Engagements and Sunnuds relating to India and neighbouring countries* (Calcutta, 1909), VIII.

ALI, S. *The Sikhs and Afghans in connection with India and Persia* (London, 1847).

ALLAN, J., HAIG, T. W. and DODWELL, H. H. *The Cambridge Shorter History of India* (Cambridge, 1934).

ARCHER, J. C. *The Sikhs* (Princeton, 1946).

BADEN-POWELL, B. H. *Handbook of the Manufactures and Arts of the Punjab* (Lahore, 1872).

BARNES, G. C. and LYALL, J. B. *Report of the Land Revenue Settlement of the Kangra District, Punjab* (Lahore, 1889).

BARR, W. *Journal of a March from Delhi to Peshawur and from thence to Cabul, including travels in the Punjab* (London, 1844).

BROWNE, F. *A History of the Origin and Progress of the Sicks* (London, 1788).

BURNES, A. *Travels into Bokhara* (London, 1834).

CUNNINGHAM, J. D. *A History of the Sikhs* (London, 1849).

DUNBAR, JANET. *Golden Interlude* (London, 1955).

DUNLOP, J. *Mooltan, a Series of Sketches during and after the Siege* (London, 1849).

EDEN, EMILY. *Portraits of the Princes and People of India* (London, 1844).
        Letters from India (London, 1872).
        Up the Country (London, 1866; reissued, 1937, ed. E. Thompson).

FANE, H. E. *Five Years in India* (London, 1842).

FORSTER, G. *A Journey from Bengal to England* (London, 1798).

GARRETT, H. L. O. (ed.) *The Punjab a Hundred Years Ago as described by V. Jacquemont (1831) & A. Soltykoff (1842)* (Lahore, 1935).

GORDON, J. H. *The Sikhs* (London, 1904).

GRIFFIN, L. *Ranjit Singh* (Oxford, 1892).

GRIFFIN, L. and MASSY, C. F. *Chiefs and Families of Note in the Punjab* (Lahore, 1909).

GREY, C. (ed. GARRETT, H. L. O.). *European Adventurers of Northern India, 1785–1849* (Lahore, 1929).

GUPTA, H. R. *History of the Sikhs 1739–1768* (Calcutta, 1939).
       Studies in later Mughal History of the Punjab 1707–1793 (Lahore, 1944).
       History of the Sikhs 1769–1799 (Trans-Sutlej Sikhs) (Lahore, 1944).

HARDINGE, C. *Recollections of India* (London, 1847).

HONIGBERGER, J. M. *Thirty-five Years in the East* (London, 1852).

HUGEL, C. *Travels in Kashmir and the Panjab, containing a particular account of the government and character of the Sikhs* (London, 1845).

HUTCHISON, J. and VOGEL, J. P. *History of the Panjab Hill States* (Lahore, 1933).

JACQUEMONT, V. *Letters from India, 1829–1832* (London, 1834; reissued 1936, ed. Catherine A. Phillips).

KEENE, H. G. *Hindustan under Free Lances, 1770–1820* (London, 1907).

LATIF, S. M. *History of the Panjab* (Calcutta, 1891).

LAWRENCE, H. M. L. *Some Passages in the Life of an Adventurer in the Punjaub* (Delhi, 1842).

MACAULIFFE, M. A. *A Lecture on how the Sikhs became a militant race* (Simla, 1903).
       The Sikh Religion: its Gurus, Sacred Writings and Authors (Oxford, 1909).

MACKENZIE, HELEN (MRS COLIN). *Life in the Mission, the Camp and the Zenana: or Six Years in India* (London, 1853).

MALCOLM, J. 'Sketch of the Sikhs', *Asiatick Researches* (1810), XI, 197–292.

MARSHMAN, J. C. *The History of India* (Serampore, 1867).

MASSON, C. *Narrative of various Journeys in Balochistan, Afghanistan, and the Panjab* (London, 1842).

MCGREGOR, W. L. *The History of the Sikhs* (London, 1846).

MOORCROFT, W. and TREBECK, G. (ed. WILSON, H. H.). *Travels in the Himalayan Province of Hindustan and the Panjab* (London, 1837).

MURRAY, W. *History of the Punjab* (London, 1846).

ORLICH, L. VON. *Travels in India, including Sinde and the Panjab* (London, 1845).

OSBORNE, W. G. *The Court and Camp of Runjeet Sing* (London, 1840).

PANIKKAR, K. M. *The Founding of the Kashmir State* (London, 2nd edition 1953).

PRINSEP, H. T. *Origin of the Sikh Power in the Punjab and Political Life of Muha-Raja Runjeet Singh* (Calcutta, 1834).

ROBERTS, P. E. *History of British India under the Company and the Crown* (Oxford, 1921).

ROSE, H. A. *A Glossary of the Tribes and Castes of the Punjab* (Lahore, 1919).

SINGH, KHUSHWANT. *The Sikhs* (London, 1953).
> *Ranjit Singh* (London, 1962).
> *A History of the Sikhs, 1469–1839* (Princeton, 1963).

SINGH, KHUSHWANT, and OTHERS. *The Sacred Writings of the Sikhs* (London, 1960).

SINHA, N. K. *Ranjit Singh* (Calcutta, 1933).
> *Rise of the Sikh Power* (Calcutta, 1936).

SMYTH, G. C. *A History of the Reigning Family of Lahore* (Calcutta, 1847).

SOLTYKOFF, A. *Indian Scenes and Characters* (London, 1859).

SPEAR, P. (ed.). *The Oxford History of India* (Oxford, third edition, 1958).

STEINBACH, LIEUT.-COL. *The Punjaub; being a brief Account of the History of the Sikhs* (London, 1845).

THACKWELL, E. J. *Narrative of the Second Seikh War, in 1848–49* (London, 1851).

VIGNE, G. T. *A Personal Narrative of a Visit to Ghuzni, Kabul, and Afghanistan* (London, 1840).
> *Travels in Kashmir, Ladak, Iskardo* (London, 1842).

WOLFF, J. *Travels and Adventures* (London, 1860).

WOODCOCK, G. 'The Army of the Pure', *History Today* (September 1962), 603–613.

BIBLIOGRAPHY: PAINTINGS OF THE SIKHS

PHASE ONE 1830–1870:
RECORDS AND FIRST IMPRESSIONS BY EARLY TRAVELLERS

1834 JACQUEMONT, V. *Letters from India, 1829–1832* (London, 1834; reissued 1936, ed. Catherine A. Phillips).

A candid but warmly sympathetic account of Maharaja Ranjit Singh and of life at his court. No references to painters.

All page references in the text are to the 1936 edition.

1840 OSBORNE, W. G. *The Court and Camp of Runjeet Sing* (London, 1840).

Journal of a visit to Ranjit Singh and his court, May 1838, by a nephew of the Governor-General, Lord Auckland. No references to painters.

Contains 16 lithographs from original sketches made by the author of persons and places in the Punjab, May 1838 (including Maharaja Ranjit Singh with the boy-favourite, Hira Singh, seated beside him and the chief minister, Dhian Singh, standing on his left; 'Adeenanuggur', 'Sher Sing', 'Faqueer Uzeezoodeen', 'Ajit Sing', 'Maharajah Runjeet Sing', 'Akalees').

1840 VIGNE, G. T. *A Personal Narrative of a Visit to Ghuzni, Kabul, and Afghanistan* (London, 1840).

A vivid description of travels in northern India by a British geographer, bent on drawing and sketching people and scenery, 1832–1839. Recounts his meetings with Ranjit Singh, 1835 and 1836, and his drawing of 'a large showy grey horse that was sent to me to be drawn as Leili', Ranjit Singh's favourite mare (265). Records (257) the drawing-rooms of the European adventurer, General Ventura, at Anarkali, 'the blossom of the pomegranate', a suburb of Lahore: 'The ceilings and wainscots were entirely covered with paintings and glass mirrors in gilt frames, *à l'orient.*'

No references to painters.

Gives the following account (274) of his first, abortive attempts to sketch Ranjit Singh:

'By persevering in my request, Runjit at length allowed me to attempt his portrait in full durbar. When I first asked him I was at Lahore, in company with Baron Hugel. He coloured, smiled, and replied, "To-morrow, at Amritsir!" which was only an oriental mode of refusing, as he had no idea of going to Amritsir. I again respectfully urged the request, "No! No!" he said, "I am an old man. Take his picture," pointing to Heera Sing; "He is young and handsome." This, however, I never did, as it would have looked too much like flattery to his master. Had I been obsequious enough to have given Runjit two eyes, he would probably have made no objection; and when he did sit to me, he was constantly turning away, so as to conceal his blind side.'

For a lithographed portrait of Ranjit by Vigne, see present figure 68.

1842 VIGNE, G. T. *Travels in Kashmir, Ladak, Iskardo* (London, 1842), 2 vols.
Supplement to a *Personal Narrative*. Reproduces as frontispiece (II) his own drawing of Maharaja Sher Singh (present figure 39).
Describes mural paintings at Wazirabad (I, 236–237):

'Vuzirbad is the neatest looking place in the Panjab. Its streets and bazaar are laid out at right-angles, and the houses and shops have an appearance of room and comfort much superior to that of a merely native town. It is entered by a handsome gateway, over which is the house of M. Avitabile, a Neopolitan officer in the service of Runjit, who, in common with his other European officers, has ever made himself conspicuous by his attention and hospitality to Europeans who have visited the Panjab. M. Avitabile had the management of the revenue arising from the country around Vuzirbad; and the thriving state and appearance of the town are chiefly owing to his exertions. On the northern side of it is a garden and three houses; two belonging to the late Maharajah, and the other to the minister, Rajah Dhihan Singh. They are very neat buildings, partly Saracenic, and the rest *ad libitum*; generally rectangular in shape, and surmounted with a terrace. From one of them there rises a square tower, fifty or sixty feet in height. The greater part is painted with Hindu mythological devices, intermixed with horses and other animals, and wreaths and bouquets of flowers, on a white ground. The broad walks in the garden, as well as the garden itself, are also laid out with very good effect; but being nearly new, it could not boast of any great show of either fruits or flowers'.

1842 MASSON, C. *Narrative of various Journeys in Balochistan, Afghanistan, and the Panjab* (London, 1842), 3 vols.

Describes Avitabile's house with murals at Lahore (I, 414):

'To the east of the city (Lahore) are the cantonments of the troops, commanded by M. Avitabile and Court, with the residencies of these officers. The mansion of the former, a Neapolitan, is painted in a singular and grotesque fashion.'

1844 BARR, W. *Journal of a March from Delhi to Peshawur and from thence to Cabul, including travels in the Punjab* (London, 1844).

Journal of a young lieutenant in the Bengal Horse Artillery deputed to accompany Colonel C. M. Wade on his mission to Afghanistan, January to December 1839.

No references to miniature paintings.

Gives the fullest and most detailed accounts by any traveller of murals on various buildings in the Punjab.

1. *The royal palace, Lahore*

'The gateway, which consists of a tolerably lofty archway with a tower at each side, is covered from its summit to its base with paintings, the greater number taken from the history of Crishna as related in the Prem Sagur, though a few describe the habits and peculiarities of the wandering fakeer. The figures are almost all about one-third the size of life, but with proportions as ludicrous and absurd as they can well be. In some the eye occupies nearly the whole side of a face, and in others the head appears as massive as the body. Here fakeers may be seen with their hands clasped above their heads, and with finger-nails two or three inches long; there are others standing on one foot, their bodies besmeared with ashes, and their long lank hair streaming over their shoulders in the most offensive state of filth. Crishna's exploits occasionally partake of the ludicrous and disgusting. In one compartment he is portrayed with a milkmaid shampooing his great toe; in another, he is perched up in a tree, from the branches of which depend various articles of dress he has stolen from some fair damsels who are refreshing themselves in a limpid stream below, and whose head and hands, clasped in a supplicatory manner, appear above water beseeching him to return their apparel, but to no purpose, as he is only laughing at their distress. In a third, he is dashing out the brains of a man with his club; and in a fourth, tearing out the entrails of a prostrate foe with the most brutal ferocity. Having satisfied our curiosity at these wonderful (!) embellishments, we passed beneath the archway and came to the inner gate of the palace; but here we were stopped by a sentry, who forbade our further progress. We remarked, however, that it is enriched with paintings of a similar character to those on the first, and though no doubt considered in good taste by the Punjabees, to Englishmen they have a most ridiculous appearance.' (69–71).

On another occasion:

'Passing through another gateway decorated with paintings of figures, wild animals, etc., fashioned in the most grotesque style, we were conducted into a large rectangular court, in which the Hall of Audience is situated. . . . The throne from whence the emperors, in former days, were wont to administer justice, projects from the centre of one of the longer sides, and is raised several feet above the ground. . . . We were admitted through a low archway beneath the throne to a small court, and close to a building which contains the regal entrance to the hall of justice. The exterior of this is covered with paintings in oil of a very extravagent description, and evidently of late construction, as one subject represents the interview of the Maharajah with Lord William Bentinck at Roopur. The parties are supposed by the artist to be assembled in the audience tent, the Sikhs being arranged on one side and the British on the other. The two great potentates occupy the centre of the scene, and Lady William, accoutred in white trousers, boots, and gold straps, is seated a few paces behind her husband. An uglier set of vagabonds than the man of daubs has made of our countrymen cannot well be conceived; though the people who accompanied us regarded them as likenesses, and were eager to point out "Macnaghten Sahib", the "Bakhshee Sahib", and others, who have only to *see* their portraits to be grateful. Another picture represents the Maharajah in the presence of Baba Nanuk, the founder of the Sikh sect: the holy father being most splendidly robed in a suit of embroidered gold, and sitting; whilst his disciple, who has done so much to extend the domains of his followers, is dressed in bright green silk, and standing, with his hands joined in a supplicatory manner. Behind the Baba, keeping guard, is an Akalli with a drawn sword, and with but very little covering. A third represents a similar scene, with the single exception of Runjeet Singh being in a still more humiliating position—on his knees. A few drawings of flowers, which separate these compartments one from another, are extremely well done, and true to nature.

On leaving the picture-gallery, as we dubbed this remarkable building, we were conducted to the king's garden, around which is a handsome stone balustrade.' (99–102)

2. *Allard's house, Anarkali (a suburb of Lahore)*

Visited in February 1839, when Allard had just died.

'Anarcolly, which is in the centre of the Lahore cantonments, was the joint property and built by the Generals Allard and Ventura. On their first entering the Maharajah's service they lived together in a large adjoining mosque or tomb, where the family of the latter, with about forty or fifty female slaves, have resided without once moving out of doors since the General took his departure for France, now two years ago. He is, however, daily expected here, as he arrived some months ago at Bombay, and the intelligence of his friend's death will no doubt hasten his movements. In the room where we dined there was a portrait of General Allard, which bespeaks him to have been a handsome and benevolent man, possessing much firmness and decision of character, tempered with mildness. He wore, at the time it was taken, a uniform similar to that of our horse-artillery, and was decorated with two orders, one, the "Legion of Honour", the other the "Bright Star of the Punjab", lately instituted by Runjeet Singh. Another picture of the General and his family, taken by a French artist when he returned home some three or four years ago, was pointed out to us, and though not finished, being merely the design from which a larger drawing was made, the group is well arranged, and the pretty faces of his Cashmerian wife and his children, who were dressed in the costume of their mother's country, drew forth the admiration of us all. Adjoining the dining-room is another of some dimensions, lined from top to bottom with looking-glass, and which, when illuminated, must have a brilliant effect, as it looked extremely pretty and dazzling even with the two candles that were brought in with us. With the exception of wanting the bath and fountains, it reminded me much of the "Sheeshah Khanuh" in the palace at Agra. We were subsequently shown into what may in truth be termed "the Painted Chamber", as it is adorned with pictures of battles in which the two Generals were engaged, and executed on the chunam walls by native artists. The perspective of these scenes is most ridiculous; and at the siege of Moultan the cannons are turned up on end to enable the gunners to load them, the figures overtop the fortification, and the cavalry seem to be manoeuvering in the air; and absurdities of a similar nature are perpetrated throughout them all, and no doubt afford much amusement to their gallant owners, whose policy has led them this far to assimilate their dwellings with those of the native population; for it can hardly be supposed their taste is so far vitiated as to regard these embellishments as ornamental.' (77–80)

Note: Allard entered Ranjit Singh's service in May 1822. The date of the murals must be about 1830.

3. *Allard's garden house, beyond Anarkali*

'[Due to a downpour] our camp this morning presents a most miserable appearance . . . we saw there was no possibility of getting anything cooked for ourselves and a kettle of water being with difficulty heated we were fain to content ourselves with a biscuit and a cup of tea for breakfast, a meal we soon found to be quite insufficient for three hungry men; we therefore, as soon as it was fine, and a few nags that had been standing nearly up to their knees in water had been removed to more elevated and drier spots, rode over to Anarcolly, as we knew there must be something in the larder there. Two of us, however, arrived rather late for the matin spread, but an early tiffin being ordered, we in the mean time, with Mons. Benet, the Maharajah's doctor, as our "cicerone", went to Allard's country-seat, where his body is at present lying in state.

'Crossing the parade ground, we entered on a road that winds through a very pretty grove of date-trees, celebrated for their exquisite fruit; and at the termination of this, on the right-hand side, the late general's retreat is situated. A large garden surrounds it, but is not laid out with any particular taste; and the residence itself, two stories high, is built in a half European and half Native style of architecture; the whole, inside and out, being embellished with paintings of dragoons, lancers, and foot-soldiers, nearly half as large as life.' (81–83)

4. *Fort of Hari Singh Nalwa, Gujranwala*

'In the evening, we walked to the fort and entered it by a large and new, though not quite finished gateway, called the "Nuobut Khaneh", or place where the state drums play. After passing through a second gateway, which brought us to a garden, our attention was immediately arrested by a ridiculous picture representing the battle of Jamrood, in which Harri Singh lost his life. It is painted on the back of an apartment fitted up with receptacles for lamps to illuminate the fountains in its interior, and is about twelve feet long by six feet in height. It is divided into two compartments, the left side being devoted to the exploits of Harri Singh's army, the other to those of Akbar Khan, his antagonist's. The two upper rows tell of the advance of cavalry regiments on either side; the next two, of the formidable array of jinjalls carried on camels' backs, preceded by a few horsemen, who have already come into action; the fifth, which is the centre one, displays the valiant Harri Singh sumptuously clothed, and seated on an elephant, with an attendant behind holding a "chattah" over his head, the renowned Akbar Khan being opposite to him, similarly mounted and similarly attended. Below these, are other squadrons of cavalry and camel sowars, of both nations, facing each other; and the concluding line is occupied by a detachment of Sikh infantry marching in regular order to the sound of martial music, with a gun in front blowing a party of Affghans into eternity. The whole skill of the artist seems concentrated on this spot; for independent of the grape-shot, which appear in multitude as the stars of the firmament, he portrays with dignified ease and simplicity the muscular power of an Affghan, who is lifting his wounded comrade from the ground with one hand, and that too with so little apparent exertion as to be seemingly a matter of ordinary occurrence with him. The same display of strength is exhibited among the cavalry in one of the upper rows, where a Sikh, with one stroke of his scimitar, has severed a horse into two equal portions, which, strange to say, in spite of the dismemberment, are capable of retaining the uprightness of their position; and another, of the same nation, has, by a clean sweep of his sabre, cut off the head of an Affghan, which is being returned with the velocity of a bullet into the ranks of his wondering countrymen, whose heads and arms are flying off in every direction, and are parted with by their owners with all possible indifference and utter disregard of their value, whilst the Sikhs are unscathed! Nor ought the dignified complacency and perfect good humour visible in the countenances of the two chiefs, opposed to each other in deadly conflict, to be overlooked; and it would be well if more civilised generals were to display equal urbanity of manner and coolness of demeanour when brought in such close contact on similar occasions, and take example from their behaviour, as depicted by the artist, whose skill is only equalled by his impartiality; inasmuch as, though it is a notorious fact that the Sikhs in the end were defeated, it is not so well known that *all* the wounded and slain were on the side of the *victors*. Such, however, we found it to be in this panorama; and it need not be added, that we derived much amusement from the representation of the battle of Jamrood, in which the really gallant Harri Singh closed his career some two or three years ago; the Sikhs at first, from their numbers and better discipline, gaining the day, but who, instead of following up the victory, were observed by the Affghans to disperse in search of plunder; on which they again returned to the charge, took their enemies by surprise, drove them off the field, and re-captured some ordnance which had been taken from them. Harri Singh, indeed, refused to quit his ground, and rallying around him a few horsemen, with hardy spirits like his own, he dashed into the midst of his foes and fell covered with wounds. He was one of the best of Runjeet Singh's generals, and had risen with his master's fortune. His body was burnt not far from the spot where he met his death, and the ashes collected and transmitted to Gujranwala, where they are deposited beneath a plain but neat tomb in the gardens surrounding his residence.' (130–134)

Of a visit the following day:

'Morning, however, dawned before the camels returned, and as the carts were not forthcoming for some hours after, our march was postponed till the afternoon, and I took advantage of the delay to pay Harri Singh's villa another visit, in hopes of seeing the upper apartment. Nor was I disappointed; and the harmonious manner in which the gilding and colours are blended, the elegant arrangements of the ornaments on the ceiling, and the richness of the chamber throughout, deserved the encomiums we had heard lavished on it. In recesses formed beneath a series of Saracenic arches, are a number of glazed paintings on a small scale, and, omitting the perspective, by no means badly executed. Some of these related to their gods, others to the haram, and the latter, as may be supposed, were by no means most decorous in their description. As several of them have been entirely removed, and many glasses of others are cracked, we asked our guide for an explanation; and he replied that the apartment belonged exclusively to the fair daughters of Eve, who on one occasion had quarrelled amongst themselves, and to settle their differences had resorted to the feminine weapon of slippers, which they heroically flung at each other's heads, and thus caused the destruction apparent in the late Sirdar's property.' (137–138)

Note: For a reference to Hari Singh Nalwa's collection of miniature paintings, see Hugel, *Travels*, 254.

5. *Summer house by the tombs of Ranjit Singh's parents, Gujranwala*

'On our return to camp, a respectable and intelligent Sikh offered his services to pilot us to the "Sirkari Bagh", where the remains of Runjeet Singh's father and mother are interred. As it still wanted some time before we should march, Rattray and I accepted them, and on our way thither found our guide particularly inquisitive as to the strength of our army; whether we thought it was capable of contending with the Maharajah's; the number of our guns, and other questions of a similar tendency. We were hardly repaid for our walk, as there is nothing particular about the tombs of Runjeet's ancestors, which are close together, and under separate roofs; but a large and circular, though unfinished building stands near them, and is interesting, as our informant told us the Maharajah is having it erected for his own mausoleum, and that at his death he will be buried here: it is, however, for so great a man, a poor monument when compared with the Taj Mahal at Agra, or even Jehanguire's tomb at Shahdera. A "baraderie", or summer-house, covered with paintings in bad taste, and but indifferently executed, is erected in the centre of the garden, which is large, but very inferior to Harri Singh's, though it can boast of a few good trees.' (138–139)

6. *Town gateways, Wazirabad*

'Before, however, we reached Wuzeerabad, the villages had become numerous, the jungle was cleared away, and fields of young corn threw a cheerful aspect round the neighbourhood. We passed beneath a lately-constructed and lofty gateway, covered, as usual, with grotesque paintings of all descriptions, the figures being nearly as large as life. The street we traversed was broad, clean, and possessed of some good houses, and is, I should say, a mile, or not far short of it, in extent. A similarly decorated gateway brought us out of the town, and another adjacent to it, under which we also passed, is even more highly embellished—the pictures being stuck as close to one another as they can be put.' (140–141)

Note: For other descriptions of murals at Wazirabad, compare Vigne, *Travels*, I, 236–237 and Hugel, *Travels*, 250.

7. *Shooting-box of Ranjit Singh, Gujarat*

'We walked in the evening to a building a short distance from our camp, and which, though unfinished, is evidently intended for a shooting box, as the majority of the pictures with which it is embellished are representations of sporting feats; such as cock-fighting, hunting, wrestling, etc.; and are the only drawings on such subjects that I have yet met with in the Punjab.' (147)

1844 EDEN, EMILY. *Portraits of the Princes and People of India* (London, 1844).
A large album of lithographs, reproducing, with comments, a series of original drawings made by Emily Eden during her travels in India with her brother, the Governor-General, Lord Auckland. Includes the following drawings made in the Punjab, December 1838: 'Two Sikh attendants of Kurrack Sing', 'Prince Ajeet Sing, nephew of Ranjit Sing', 'Maharaja Ranjit Sing' (present figure 26), 'Prince Pertab Sing', 'Heera Sing' (present figure 49), 'The Jamadar who had the care of Ranjeet Sing's stud', 'The Raja of Patiala', 'Sher Sing' (present figure 42), 'The Jewels of Ranjeet Sing' and 'Sikh Head-dress'.

1845 HUGEL, BARON C. *Travels in Kashmir and the Panjab, containing a particular account of the government and character of the Sikhs* (London, 1845).

A diffuse, and caustic account of travels in northern India by a sour-minded Austrian who knew Vigne and visited Ranjit Singh and his court. Perhaps the least genial and entertaining of the early travellers.

Describes a visit to the country house of Ranjit Singh at Wazirabad, with its accompanying murals (250):

'It seemed like a dream when I found myself really seated in this vehicle, and drawn by four horses to Wazirabad. There the Maha Raja has built a palace in the midst of a lovely garden, which is a singular edifice, both in its exterior form and its internal decorations. It has two stories, and in the centre is a sort of tower which divides the wings, while the outside walls, as well as the apartments within, are adorned with fresco paintings illustrative of the religion of the Sikhs. Among them are the portraits of the ten Gurus from Nanak the first to Govind the last, the size of life; the chief painter of Ranjit's court is certainly not a Raphael.'

Note: For other descriptions of murals at Wazirabad, compare Vigne, *Travels*, I, 236–237 and Barr, *Journal*, 140–141.

Includes the following description of murals in General Ventura's house at Anarkali, January 1836 (283–284):

'General Ventura's house, built by himself and though of no great size, combines the splendour of the East with the comforts of a European residence. On the walls of the entrance hall, before the range of pillars on the first story, was portrayed the reception of the two French officers at the court of Ranjit Singh, consisting of many thousand figures. The second room is adorned with a profusion of small mirrors in gilt frames, which have an excellent effect; the third is a large hall, extending the entire width of the house, and terminating in the sleeping apartments.'

And of similar murals in the neighbouring house belonging to General Allard (311):

'In General Allard's garden, built by himself, is a pretty little building. The eagle and Napoleon's flag are displayed on every wall, and here and there are figures representing the soldiers who served under him. In the upper story are a few rooms, adorned with mirrors, and set apart for the females of his family.'

Describes Vigne's efforts to sketch Ranjit Singh, January 1836 (352–353): 'Vigne had long wished to take the Maha Raja's portrait, and I told him when first we came here, that it would be best to choose a day when we visited him, and then to request permission to sketch him while we conversed. He was of opinion that it would be better to ask permission through the fakir; and the natural result of this was, that nothing more was heard of it. He now felt mortified at the idea of leaving Lahore without succeeding in his wish; and at the moment when the Maha Raja got to the palankeen, he begged Henderson to ask leave for him to take his likeness. Henderson had declined, as being too late to ask the favour, but Vigne exclaiming, "Maha Raja," and Ranjit turning round, Henderson was obliged to speak out. Ranjit thought for a moment, and then asked him how many days he required. "Half an hour only, before I set off to-morrow."—"That is too short a time. Go to Amritsir, and take it there." "How is that possible?" said Vigne.—"The Governor General has my portrait, and nobody wishes for it. If you wish to take one, bring me first as an evidence of your skill a likeness of the King of England." Then turning round to us, he said, "Remember that you have always a friend in the Panjab." I was too much moved to make any reply.'

Contains one reference only to a court artist of Ranjit Singh, 25 January 1836, (355):

'One of the commissions with which the Maharaja charged the Fakir Sahib was to ask for a piece of my uniform. I offered him the whole of it but this he would not accept. He sent an artist at day break this morning to paint it and in writing requested that I would send him a dozen ells of the same stuff or one complete uniform. The artist had a portfolio filled with drawings, some very good. Vigne's was among them and the artist had been directed to paint a fine Govind Singh on the flag. I was surprised to see how accurately and with what facility he had executed his task.'

Was impressed by Hari Singh Nalwa, a commander-in-chief of Ranjit Singh's army and while staying with him at Guseraoli (between Wazirabad and Lahore), was shown some drawings (254):

'Hari Singh's manner and conversation are very frank and affable; and having acquainted myself beforehand with the history of this most distinguished member of Ranjit's court, I surprised him by my knowledge whence he had gained the appellation of Nalwa, and of his having cloven the head of a tiger who had already seized him as its prey. He told the Diwan to bring some drawings, and gave me his portrait, in the act of killing the beast.'

Note: For references to murals and some glazed miniatures in Hari Singh Nalwa's house at Gujranwala, see Barr, *Journal*, 130–134, 137–138.

1845 ORLICH, L. von. *Travels in India, including Sinde and the Punjab* (London, 1845).
    A vivid account, in the form of letters, by a young German soldier, attached to the British army in India but denied active service due to the abrupt ending of the British campaign in Sind, 1842. Availed of his arrival in India to visit, amongst

others, the Sikh court of Maharaja Sher Singh. Period of travels: August 1842 to June 1843.

Alludes to a portrait of Ranjit Singh (204) intended to be given by Sher Singh through his son Prince Pratap Singh to Lord Ellenborough at camp Ferozpur, January 1843:

'We were then conducted into the large tent where champagne, madeira, and the fruits of Cabul and Kashmir were placed in silver vessels upon a long table. The Prince and Dheean Singh did the honours of the table to admiration; they helped their guests to wine and requested some of them to accept the silver goblets and vessels in token of remembrance. A present intended for the Queen of England was next exhibited: it was a perfectly beautiful green Kashmir tent, embroidered with silk, containing a silver bed and morning dresses for ladies, with pearls, jewels and other ornaments while the floor was covered with the finest Kashmir shawls. But the Prince seemed to think a great deal more of a wretched portrait of Runjeet Singh, daubed on paper with water-colours, which was to accompany the present.'

Describes an interview with Sher Singh and the latter's employment of a court painter (206–207, quoted page 50).

1846 MCGREGOR, W. L. *The History of the Sikhs* (London, 1846).
A vivid account of Sikh history by a British officer serving in the first Anglo-Sikh war.

No references to painters; but includes titled lithographs based on individual portraits in gouache by Indian artists in the Punjab Plains.

Persons portrayed: Ranjit Singh, Kharak, Nau Nihal, Dhian, Gulab and Suchet Singh and, in a group, Jawahir, Lal and Labh Singh (present figure 63).

1847 HARDINGE, C. *Recollections of India* (London, 1847).
A series of 26 tinted lithographs in 2 parts based on original drawings by Hardinge made in India between 1844 and 1847 while A.D.C. to his father, the Governor-General, Lord Hardinge. Includes the following titles:

Part I
1. Panjab. The Maharajah Dhulip Sing (present figure 67).
7. Panjab. Battle of Ferozeshah.
8. Panjab. Outpost of Rhodawala.
9. Panjab. Entry into Lahore. From the parade ground.
10. 11. Scenes in Lahore.
12. Panjab. Sikh soldiers receiving their pay at the Royal Durbar, Lahore.
13. Panjab. Rajah Lal Sing.

Part II

14. Kashmir. Gulab Sing (present figure 52).
19. Alpine Panjab. Hill Fort of Gulab Sing.
26. Sheikh Imam-ud-Din, Runjur Sing, Dina Nath.

1852 HONIGBERGER, J. M. *Thirty-five Years in the East* (London, 1852).

Reminiscences by a German physician who lived at Lahore, 1835–1850 and attended Maharajas Ranjit, Kharak, Sher and Dalip Singh.

Host to the Hungarian oil-painter, August Theodor Schoefft, resident at Lahore and painter to Sher Singh, 1841.

Describes Schoefft's experiences in Lahore and misadventure while sketching the tank at Amritsar (171–175, partly quoted pages 45–47).

Reproduces titled lithographs based on individual portraits in gouache or water-colour by Indian painters of Lahore or Amritsar, *c*. 1850, of the following Sikh characters: Maharajas Ranjit, Kharak, Nau Nihal and Sher Singh (92); Chand Kaur (Rani Jindan), Dalip, Jawahir and Lal Singh (108); Gulab, Dhian, Suchet and Hira Singh (114); Tej Singh, Dina Nath, Nur-ud-din, Dost Muhammad (118).

1853 MACKENZIE, HELEN (Mrs Colin). *Life in the Mission, the Camp and the Zenana: or Six Years in India* (London, 1853), 3 vols.

Describes the events of 1846 to 1852 from the point of view of a strait-laced, Victorian-minded lady of strong evangelical views, married to a serving soldier of similar convictions.

An ardent sympathiser with the Sikhs.

Describes visits to Dalip Singh, the presence with him of two painters and her experiences of drawing his portrait (III, 47–55 quoted in part pages 62–64) as also that of Chattar Singh Atariwala (III, 56–58).

Has the following account of murals at Ram Bagh, Amritsar (III, 58–59):

'I started about half-past eight in my palki for Amritsar and arrived about sunrise next morning at the Ram Bagh, Ranjit Sing's residence, where Mr McLeod, the Assistant Commissioner, now lives. . . . After breakfast our kind host took me into a tower from which I sketched the gateway. The walls of the small room in which we sat were covered with curious paintings of scenes from the Hindu Mythology. After tiffin Mr McLeod drove me through the town. It is by far the cleanest town I have seen in India; has been newly paved and supports an establishment of bhistis, sweepers and watchmen. . . . It is a most picturesque place with narrow streets, beautifully carved houses, the upper stories projecting over the lower ones and many of them adorned with curious paintings. I saw one house with a row of peacocks, the size of life, supporting the balcony. In Lahore a row of geese perform a similar office, so well carved and painted and in such natural attitudes (one of them stretching out its neck as if hissing at passers-by) that we at first took them for live birds.'

1854 MACKENZIE, HELEN (Mrs Colin). *Illustrations of the Mission, the Camp and the Zenana* (London, 1854).

20 lithographs from her own original drawings of people in various parts of India. Includes portraits of 'Maharaja Dhalip Sing' (plate 6, present figure 66), 'A Sikh Orderley and Gardiner' (plate 9) and 'A Group of Afghans, Sikhs and others' (plate 10)—the latter including a portrait of Chattar Singh Atariwala.

1859 SOLTYKOFF, A. *Indian Scenes and Characters* (London, 1859).

A series of 16 lithographs based on original drawings by Prince Alexis Soltykoff, a Russian visitor to the Punjab, 1842 and 1843. Plates 8 and 9—'Cavalcade of Sikh Chieftains' and 'Sikh Chieftains'—give vivid impressions of Sikh horsemen.

1860 WOLFF, J. *Travels and Adventures* (London, 1860), 2 vols.

Resided with the Italian adventurer, Avitabile, Governor of Wazirabad, 1832. Has the following note on murals (II, 61):

'He had kept the streets of the city clean and had got a beautiful carriage made for himself and a fine palace. He was a cheerful, clever man, full of fun. He told Wolff at once that he would show him his guardian angels and took him up to his bedroom, the walls of which were covered with pictures of dancing-girls. . . .'

1866 EDEN, EMILY. *Up the Country* (London, 1866; reissued London, 1937, ed. E. Thompson).

A tart, witty and vivacious account of travels in India by the sister of the Governor-General, Lord Auckland and an inveterate pursuer of 'the picturesque'. Gives first-hand impressions of characters at the court of Ranjit Singh, based on a visit in December 1838.

One of the most accomplished amateur artists in India in the early nineteenth century.

Alludes to a court painter sketching Lord Auckland and stresses Ranjit Singh's antipathy to being drawn from the left side (288, quoted pages 49–50).

Expresses the following candid opinion of Ranjit's character and appearance (208–209):

'Another of Runjeet's topics was his constant praise of drinking, and he said he understood that there were books which contained objections to drunkenness, and he thought it better that there should be no books at all, than that they should contain such foolish notions. He is a very drunken old profligate, neither more nor less. Still he has made himself a great king; he has conquered a great many powerful enemies; he is remarkably just in his government; he has disciplined a large army; he hardly ever takes away life, which is wonderful in a despot; and he is excessively beloved by his people.

'I certainly should not guess any part of this from looking at him.'

All page references here and in the text to the 1937 edition.

PHASE TWO 1870–1900:
OFFICIAL SURVEYS, OPINIONS AND REPORTS

1872 BADEN-POWELL, B. H. *Handbook of the Manufactures and Arts of the Punjab* (Lahore, 1872).

A survey of art-manufactures (arts and crafts) in the Punjab, based on an exhibition held at Lahore in 1864.

Diagnoses the economic and aesthetic crisis confronting Punjabi craftsmen and proposes a typically Victorian solution (354–355, quoted pages 60–61).

Names 3 Punjabi painters and lists their work (351–352, quoted page 61).

Gives the following opinion (351–352) of Punjabi painters on ivory:

'There are one or two native artists at Lahore but their works are not of sufficient merit to be described. Oval pictures of Sikh chiefs and ladies are executed by these people but so inferior to the Delhi work as to merit no place in the collection.'

1887 KIPLING, J. L. 'The Industries of the Punjab', *The Journal of Indian Art* (October 1887), II, no. 20, 27–42.

Describes various Punjabi crafts and has the celebrated reference to Kangra painting: 'Among native limners, *Kangra ki qalm* (the Kangra pencil) is a phrase occasionally heard and meant to distinguish the style or touch of a school of illumination and mythological picture painting that is supposed to have flourished here.' (40–41, quoted page 62).

1888 KIPLING, J. L. 'The Industries of the Punjab: the Lahore Division', *The Journal of Indian Art* (July 1888), II, no. 23, 60.

Describes lithography in the Punjab (quoted page 68).

1892 GRIFFIN, LEPEL. *Ranjit Singh* (Oxford, 1892).

An encomium of the great Maharaja written with admiring enthusiasm. Indispensable for understanding how late Victorians regarded the greatest of the Sikh rulers.

Has the following paragraph on ivory portraits of Ranjit Singh (89):

'No traveller can have visited the Punjab without becoming familiar with the features of the great Maharaja. Although half a century has passed since his death, his name is still a house-hold word in the province; his portrait is still preserved in castle and in cottage. It is a favourite subject with the ivory painters of Amritsar and Delhi, by whom the Maharaja is ordinarily represented in middle or old age, and it is rare to find one of him in youth or in the prime of life. The fine arts were not much patronised in early days at the Court of Lahore. Late in life Ranjit Singh did not make a pleasing picture, though his appearance was striking and memorable. Hard work, the exposure of numerous campaigns, drunkenness and debauchery aged him before his time, and left him at fifty a worn-out, broken-down, old man.'

PHASE THREE 1900–1965:
ART-HISTORIANS AND CRITICS

1908 HAVELL, E. B. *Indian Sculpture and Painting* (London, 1908).

A glowing appreciation of Sikh-inspired painting by the most eloquent British writer on Indian art in the early twentieth century.

Points out that such painting was a popular, not a courtly art, that it reached a wider and a different public from that of most previous Indian miniatures and at a time when British rule and Victorian standards were nullifying Indian painting, it was a new and valid form of Indian national expression (230–232).

Describes in detail a picture 'The Music Party' (plate 69), later attributed by Coomaraswamy to 'the Sikh school'. The picture portrays Mian Jai Singh, younger brother of Raja Shamsher Singh of Guler, listening to musicians. The chief characters wear Sikh costume and the picture, in Guler style of about 1840, illustrates Sikh cultural influences in the Punjab Hill state of Guler.

Of this picture, Havell says (228–229): 'Like the pure melody of an old folk-song, it is a true creation of national sentiment, of the poetic impulse which flows spontaneously from the heart of a people inspired by the joy of life and love of beauty. In the previous illustrations we have seen how an Indian artist shows "the gloom of gloom"; here we have the "sunshine of sunshine", given with the same pure delight with which the lark trills his song of joy in the high heavens on a summer morning. The figures in the picture are by no means attractive types or very deeply studied as to character; but their glowing draperies and the gay colours of the musical

93

instruments, together with the pearly whiteness of the marble and the bright hues of the flowers, serve the purpose of the artist—to express the beauty and gladness of the radiant Indian sunlight.'

1911 VOGEL, J. P. 'Historical Notes on the Lahore Fort', *Journal of the Panjab Historical Society* (1911), I, 51–53.

Describes murals of the Sikh period in the Lahore Fort and records the painting of a flower on one of the arched panels of the back walls of the Shah Burj by the child Maharaja, Dalip Singh. Dalip is supposed to have pointed this flower out to Fakir Qamru-d-din and to have said 'Hazrat, ever remember that this flower was painted by me'.

1911 SMITH, V. A. *A History of Fine Art in India and Ceylon* (Oxford, 1911).

Describes and illustrates two pictures (figures 223 and 224) by the Punjabi painter, Kapur Singh of Amritsar.

It is remarkable that in this pioneer survey of Indian painting, Smith should have found room for two pictures which by Sikh standards are little better than rubbish.

1912 PRAKASH, SUNGA. 'Indian Art', *Empire Magazine* (London, January 1912).

Said by Coomaraswamy (*Rajput Painting*) to contain a reference to Sikh painting.

1916 COOMARASWAMY, A. K. *Rajput Painting* (Oxford, 1916), I, 25, II, plates 75B and 76.

The first attempt to define painting of the Sikhs in detail and to assess it in the context of painting in the Punjab Hills and Plains.

Errs in dating its commencement to as early as 1750 and its end to 1850.

Gives the following somewhat restrained account (I, 25):

'Towards the middle of the 18th century the Sikh power began to be consolidated in the districts of Amritsar and Jalandhar, and to be established in some parts of the hills in the early part of the 19th; and there exists a corresponding group of paintings, ranging from about A.D. 1750 to 1850, which may be described as of the Sikh school. A majority of these are portraits or portrait groups. A fine example expressive of the true Sikh dignity, is reproduced on plate 76. Many of the Kangra Sikh paintings are most easily to be recognised by the fact that in them the faces of young men are unshaven, a peculiarity that never appears in Pahari art executed for Hindu patrons; an example of this Kangra Sikh style of the early 19th century is reproduced by Mr Havell, *Indian Sculpture and Painting*, plate 69. The Sikh art is also to be recognised in various rather crude "portraits" of the Gurus, which are still produced in Amritsar, and better, in some half-obliterated fragments of wall-painting, about a century old, within the precincts of the Golden Temple at Amritsar. Most likely the Sikhs gave occasional patronage also to similar work in Kashmir, where I have found little trace of any older or purer tradition. It may be mentioned also that some copies of the "Granth Sahib" or Sikh scriptures are magnificent examples of austere calligraphy; and I have seen one fairly well illustrated, said to have been prepared in Kashmir. On the whole we may say of Sikh painting that while a few very distinguished examples are to be found, the greater part, compared with what has gone before, whether Rajput or Mughal, is decadent.'

Of the two 'Sikh' pictures reproduced, one (plate 75B) shows Guru Nanak and his minstrel Mardana seated with five others (Sikh, Punjab Plains, c. 1840) but captioned by Coomaraswamy: 'Kabir instructing a group of Hindu and Musulman ascetics. Sikh, late 18th century'; the other (plate 76) shows a group of Pahari Rajputs (Kangra, c. 1780), captioned: 'A Sikh Assembly. Sikh, 18th century', and claimed to be 'expressive of the true Sikh dignity'.

1917 BROWN, PERCY. *Indian Painting* (Calcutta, 1917).
    The second attempt to view Sikh painting in its historical context as part of Indian painting as a whole.

    'In the nineteenth century, Pahari artists extended the sphere of their activity, and it is noticeable that a considerable number of their pictures . . . found their way to the large cities of Hindustan. The Sikh court at Lahore and Amritsar, ruled over by the Maharajah Ranjit Singh (1803–1839) also gave it some encouragement as there are numerous paintings of Sikh notabilities forthcoming, painted in the Kangra *Kalm*.' (53–54).
    'In the Punjab, at Lahore and Amritsar, the productions of several Sikh painters found favour at the end of the nineteenth century, their work having a strange mixture of the East and West. One, Kapur Singh, painted a large number of figure subjects, miniature in size, and showing a very fair knowledge of drawing with considerable action.' (56)

1922 GUPTA, S. N. *Catalogue of Paintings in the Central Museum, Lahore* (Calcutta, 1922), 37–54, plates 19 and 20.
    Lists and describes a series of 54 portrait sketches (D1 to D54) of Sikhs and other characters of the Sikh period; 13 portraits of the ten Gurus (F 37 to F 49) and 3 water-colour studies of birds (L 79 to L 81) by the late nineteenth-century artist Kapur Singh. Plate 19 illustrates a Guler drawing, c. 1825 of Guru Nanak preaching and plate 20 a sketch of Ranjit Singh executed at Lahore or Amritsar in the period 1835–1845.

Although each portrait is confidently identified and is accompanied by a useful biographical note, no actual evidence for identification is cited.

1922 GUPTA, S. N. 'The Sikh School of Painting', *Rupam* (1922) III, no. 12, 125–128.

Reconstructs and judges the history of Sikh painting from the point of view of a Bengali Assistant Principal of the Mayo School of Art (later, Curator, Central Museum, Lahore) and a member of the neo-Bengal school of revivalist Indian painting.

Reproduces (plate 1) portrait sketches of Ranjit Singh (also reproduced *Catalogue, Lahore Museum*) and of figures said to be Diwan Bhawani Das (banker of Ranjit Singh), Fateh Singh Ahluwalia, Jassa Singh Ramgarhia and one Sikh, unidentified; and (plate 2) William Moorcroft, Herbert Edwardes and Sher Singh (present figure 38). Chairs in Sikh style with characteristic looped arms. Plate 2 also reproduces a Guler sketch of Guru Nanak, *c.* 1820. Plate 3 reproduces 4 portraits of Gurus Amar Das, Har Kishan, Har Rai and Ram Das. (Guler, *c.* 1820, from a different but comparable series to present figures 2–6.) Plate 4 reproduces 2 murals, provenance unspecified.

On the 'dead blank' of the arts in the Punjab Plains, Gupta writes (126): 'There are hardly any indications to show the actual condition of pictorial art in the Punjab plains immediately preceding the Sikh period. While the natural isolation of the hills and the patronage of almost all the hill chiefs helped the indigenous art to sustain and flourish, the helpless condition of the plains only led to the destruction of all that was necessary for the existence of art.'

Advances the theory that the new wealth and power of Maharaja Ranjit Singh attracted artists of Kangra and other Hill States whose power was fast waning and that it was these hill artists 'whose works executed under the patronage of the Sikh rulers came under the Sikh school proper'.

Assumes degeneration of style and attributes it to loss of 'surroundings associated with their hereditary art' and to contact with Europeanised Delhi miniatures on paper and ivory.

Alleges that none of the Sikh rulers had 'any serious experience of aesthetic emotions nor the artistic training to realise what the loss of indigenous art traditions meant.'

Indicts the Sikh school in the following stern terms (128):

'Taking all these into consideration it appears wonderful how under such indifferent and chaotic conditions and within such a short period the Sikh school produced such innumerable works. That none of them come in the front rank of Indian paintings is a national misfortune for which both the artists and their patrons are responsible. Under different restful conditions and under the guidance of patrons of understanding this school may have proved itself worthy of the notable house of

Kangra from which it descended; by the glamour of new influences, it lost its own individuality and produced a feeble expression of hybrid art but attracted as it was by the glamour of new and alien influences, it soon lost its own individuality in its attempts at imitation and left an object lesson, the repetition of which is to be avoided in the interest of national aesthetic development.'

1925 HEATH, L. *Examples of Indian Art at the British Empire Exhibition 1924* (London, 1925), plate 10.

Plate 10, captioned 'Seated portrait of a Raja. Unidentified (lent by Prof. W. Rothenstein)'. has the following curious comment: 'The evidence of the hairdressing, the folds of the turban, its pattern and the ornament, point to this being the portrait of a Rajput Prince. From the style and character and the flesh colour it is not a Hill painting but a Rajput painting, possibly of Lucknow about the late seventeenth century or early eighteenth century.'

The sitter is, in fact, Raja Gulab Singh (1792–1851) eldest of the three Dogra brothers and leading associate of Ranjit Singh's court. The portrait, now in the Victoria and Albert Museum (the 'Rothenstein' Gulab Singh) should, more properly, be regarded as 'Sikh, Lahore, *c.* 1846.' (cat. no. 25, figure 50).

1926 KRISHNA, R. 'Some Fresco Paintings in the Lahore fort', *Rupam* (1926), nos. 27 and 28, 86–88, figures 1–6.

Reproduces copies of murals (*c.* 1840–1850) on chiefly Krishna subjects executed on the verandah of the Shish Mahal in Ranjit Singh's palace, Lahore. Notes that other buildings in Lahore with Sikh affiliations (tomb of Ranjit Singh, Dharmsala of Bhai Vasti Ram) have similar murals.

Suggests that the painting of murals illustrating Krishna, Rama and the ten Gurus was a common Punjabi practice.

1926 COOMARASWAMY, A. K. *Catalogue of the Indian Collections in the Museum of Fine Arts, Boston, V, Rajput Painting* (Boston, 1926), 17–19, plates 133 and 134.

Includes a brief reassessment of Sikh painting (18–19).

Reproduces (plate 123) an inscribed portrait of Raja Suchet Singh dated 1839 but mistranslates the subject as 'Sri Chet Singh'. Plate 124 ('Sikh Assembly') shows Pahari Rajputs, not Sikhs; as also does plate 125 (no. 530). Plate 125 (no. 518) is not 'Maharaja Ranjit Singh?', but a different Sikh altogether.

1929 STCHOUKINE, I. *La Peinture Indienne* (Paris, 1929), 63, plate 91.

'Les peintres de Lahore, capitale des Sikhs, subissent l'influence de leurs collègues de Kangra. Leurs œuvres, empreintes d'une rudesse martiale, ne sont pas dépourvues du charme qui réside dans leur force et leur expression. Les Sikhs empruntent á l'école moghole son gout du portrait.' (63)

Plate 91, captioned 'Sikh nobles, Sikh school, end of eighteenth century' is a portrait of Raja Ranbir Singh of Jammu, seated with a secretary; Sikh, Punjab Plains, c. 1846.

1930 FOSTER, W. 'Some Foreign European Artists in India', *Bengal Past and Present* (July–December, 1930), XL, 79–98.

The prime source for the life, career and work of the Hungarian painter in oils, Theodor August Schoefft, painter of Maharaja Sher Singh and resident in Lahore, 1841.

1930 SMITH, V. A. *A History of Fine Art in India and Ceylon* (second edition, revised by K. de B. Codrington, Oxford, 1930).

Wisely discards Smith's previous and wholly unfortunate choice of illustrations of Punjabi painting.

Makes no further reference to painting of the Sikhs.

1931 FRENCH, J. C. *Himalayan Art* (Oxford, 1931), 74–76, 81, 88–93.

Discusses Sikh influence in the Punjab Hills and refers to 'Sikh' murals in 'Kangra Valley style' in Ventura's house at Lahore.

1933 GOETZ, H. 'Some Court Portraits of the Pahari school in Dutch collections', *Journal of the Indian Society of Oriental Art* (1933), I, no. 2, 121–123, figure 5.

Reproduces a picture of a Sikh sardar in a garden (Sikh, Punjab Plains, c. 1835–1840). Inscribed with Hindi poem and artist's name, Chajju.

1935 GARRETT, H. L. O. (ed.). *The Punjab a Hundred Years Ago, as described by V. Jacquemont; (1831) and A. Soltykoff (1842)* (Lahore, 1935).

Jacquemont's journal refers to murals as follows:

'There is more movement and more life in Amritsar than in any town in British India. . . . The richer bankers and merchants have houses three or four storeys high, the front being whitened and covered with coarse mythological pictures.' (26) Notes that the rooms in Allard and Ventura's house (Anarkali, Lahore) 'are magnificently decorated; the walls and ceilings are covered with inset glass, brightly gilded or adorned with pictures, arabesques etc.' (34)

Soltykoff describes visits to the palace of Maharaja Sher Singh (96–98, 100–104, quoted in part pages 45–47) and has the following reference (96) to a court painting of Ranjit Singh: 'The late maharaja Ranjit Singh had once given him (Mr Clerk) a magnificent sword and his portrait adorned with precious stones, but even these he had been obliged to send in.'

1936 ARNOLD, T. W. and WILKINSON, J. V. S. *The Library of A. Chester Beatty: a catalogue of the Indian miniatures* (London, 1936), I, 49; III, plate 92.
Reproduces a portrait of Jamadar Khushal Singh, inscribed with name at base in pencil.

1947 GOETZ, H. 'Indian Painting in the Muslim Period', *Journal of the Indian Society of Oriental Art* (1947), XV, no. 1, 40.

'Sikh Painting: In this late form "Kangra" painting was taken over by the Sikhs, at that time rather vulgar upstarts, boisterous, realistic, puritan. There was no room for Rajput romanticism and mystic symbolism. Like the early Mughals they appreciated a realistic portrait, enjoyed a foul zenana jest or could use a few religious pictures where Hindu mythology had intruded into the Sikh cult. Later they began to appreciate the whole range of Kangra themes, like the Hindus living under that rule. But (by) then the Sikh kingdom was already disintegrating and Indian painting everywhere declining fast.'

1950 GRAY, B. 'Painting', *Art of India and Pakistan* (ed. L. Ashton, London, 1950), 103, 134.
Claims that 'the effect of the Sikh conquest of Kangra, Guler, Nurpur and Kulu was to spread the Kangra style more widely and even to carry it to Lahore their capital and Srinagar. But it took the heart out of it, so that after 1820 there is a slow but steady decline.'
Catalogues no. 572, page 134 (the 'Rothenstein' portrait of Gulab Singh) as 'Kharak Singh; Lahore, about 1840.'

1951 ARCHER, W. G. 'Sir William Rothenstein and Indian Art', *Art and Letters* (1951), XXV, no. 1, 8–9, plate 7.
Reproduces (plate 7) the now famous 'Rothenstein' portrait of Gulab Singh (present cat. no. 25, figure 50), but, following Gray, misidentifies the subject as Kharak Singh.

1952 ARCHER, W. G. *Indian Painting in the Punjab Hills* (London, 1952), 69–70.

Employs the term 'Jammu-Sikh' to describe a type of portraiture at Kangra (1775–1820), and suggests that Jammu artists may have been induced to go to Kangra on account of Sikh connections with these states.

1952 ARCHER, W. G. *Kangra Painting* (London 1952), 24.

'Of greater significance as a social symptom is the phase of Kangra painting connected with the Sikhs. As was natural in a people with no traditional art of their own, the Sikhs had avidly adopted whatever art-forms were current in the areas they ravaged. They were thus, unconsciously, the "art-carriers" of the Punjab Hills. From about 1810 onwards, certain Kangra painters seem to have adjusted their subjects to Sikh requirements and thus a second provincial Kangra school was established, its chief centres being Lahore and Amritsar. Most of its products, however, have a garish brightness which makes them a travesty of Kangra painting proper.'

1953 RANDHAWA, M. S. 'Guler: the birthplace of Kangra art', *Marg* (1953), VI, no. 4, 30–42, figures 13, 15–17.

A pioneer contribution.

Discusses for the first time Sikh influences in Guler painting, *c.* 1810–1890.

Illustrates portraits of the Guler prince, Mian Jai Singh, in Sikh dress.

1953 SINGH, KHUSHWANT. *The Sikhs* (London, 1953), 81.

Reproduces 2 nineteenth-century murals from the domes of a gurdwara and the Sikh temple of Tarn-Taran.

1954 ANAND, MULK RAJ. 'Painting under the Sikhs', *Marg* (1954), VII, no. 2, 23–32, 8 figures.

A first attempt to assess the painting of the Sikhs from a sociological angle.

Figure 1 (page 23), captioned 'Dhyan Singh with two nobles, perhaps his sons', is Gulab Singh with his sons, Udham and Sohan. Figure 2 (page 24), captioned 'A prince said to be Dhalip Singh' is more probably Hira Singh. Figure 8 (page 30), captioned 'The Signature of the treaty of Lahore, 1846' is the darbar held to ratify the second treaty of Lahore, 26 December 1846.

1954 RANDHAWA, M. S. 'Sujanpur Tira: the cradle of Kangra art', *Marg* (1954), VII
no. 3, 21–36.
Discusses Sikh influence in Kangra painting following the death of Raja Sansar
Chand, 1823.

'As the Katoch kingdom lost its independence, some of the artists migrated to
Lahore and Amritsar and enjoyed the patronage of the Sikh Rajas and sardars. Thus
we find the Rajput-inspired art of Kangra Valley evolving into the Sikh-inspired art
of the Punjab Plains.'

1955 ARCHER, MILDRED and W. G. *Indian Painting for the British* (London, 1955), 66–68.
Discusses the development at Delhi of water-colour painting on ivory and the
growth of an Anglo-Mughal (Indian-British) style of painting (later adopted by the
Sikhs, see present pages 65–68).
Refers to a visit to the Punjab by Lord Bentinck and to sketching by Emily Eden,
sister of Lord Auckland.

1955 RANDHAWA, M. S. 'Some Nurpur Paintings', *Marg* (1955), VIII, no. 3, 20–25,
figures 1 and 2.
Discusses Sikh influences in Nurpur painting, *c.* 1815–1850.
Reproduces a portrait of Raja Bir Singh (1789–1846) of Nurpur in Sikh dress.

1955 DUNBAR, JANET, *Golden Interlude* (London, 1955).
An account of travels in the Punjab in 1838 by Fanny Eden (sister of Emily Eden
and Lord Auckland), based on her manuscript journal, preserved in the India Office
Library (MSS. Eur. C. 130). Reproduces 28 of her original sketches, many of them
of Sikh characters.

1957 ANAND, MULK RAJ. 'Specimens of Paintings under the Sikhs, *Marg* (1957), X,
no. 2, 37–44, 8 figures.
Text and captions as in 1954 but with 4 new illustrations including a portrait of
Maharaja Sher Singh.

1957 SINGH, BHAI GIAN. 'The Techniques of the Fresco Painting', *Marg* (1957), X,
no. 2, 27–29, 3 figures.
Describes the technique of Sikh murals in the Golden Temple, Amritsar. Illustrates 3 murals from the Baba-atal Temple, Amritsar.

1958 KHANDALAVALA, K. *Pahari Miniature Painting* (Bombay, 1958), 240, 242–244.

Reviews and assesses previously published material on Sikh painting.

Comes to the conclusion that 'all the might of Ranjit Singh's sword could not enable him and his parvenu court to create a school of painting even faintly comparable to the schools of Basohli, Guler, Jammu and Kangra'.

Stigmatises certain Sikh paintings as 'lifeless, second-rate' 'of no particular merit', 'listless', 'pompous, gaudy and petrified'.

Reproduces the 'Rothenstein' Gulab Singh (cat. no. 25) and the Boston portrait of Suchet Singh.

1959 ARCHER, W. G. *India and Modern Art* (London, 1959), 80–99 frontispiece, figures 23, 24, 26–29.

Discusses and illustrates the modern painting of the Sikh woman artist, Amrita Sher-Gil.

1960 ARCHER, W. G. *Indian Miniatures* (New York, London, 1960).

Reproduces and comments on the 'Rothenstein' portrait of Gulab Singh (cat. no. 25).

1961 RANDHAWA, M. S. 'Paintings from Arki', *Roopa Lekha* (1961), XXXII, no. 1, 5–26.

Discusses and illustrates Sikh influences in Arki painting, *c.* 1840–1880.

1961 RAWSON, P. *Indian Painting* (Paris, London, 1961), 144, 147 (colour plate).

Reproduces in colour the 'Rothenstein' portrait of Gulab Singh (cat. no. 25). Describes it as 'a superb example of Sikh portraiture'.

1961 KHAN, F. A. *The Princess Bamba Collection* (Karachi, 1961).

Catalogues a collection of 18 oils, 14 water-colours and 22 paintings on ivory, formerly owned by Princess Bamba Sutherland, eldest daughter of Dalip Singh and acquired by the Pakistan Government after her death in 1957.

The oils and water-colours are the work of European painters: Schoefft, Leslie Poole Smith, Goldingham, Blakeney Ward, P. C. French, Paillet and Winterhalter.

Reproduces four oil paintings by Schoefft: 'Maharaja Ranjit Singh at Amritsar' (colour), 'Maharaja Sher Singh in Council' (colour), 'Maharaja Sher Singh, seated,' (present figure 43), and 'The Dasahra Festival at the Court of Lahore' (present figures 44, 45).

1963 LAWRENCE, G. *Indian Art: paintings of the Himalayan States* (Paris, London, 1963), plate 15 (colour).

Reproduces in colour and discusses the 'Rothenstein' Gulab Singh portrait (cat. no. 25).

1963 BARRETT, D. *Painting of India* (London, 1963), 192.

Claims that 'by 1800 the spirit which had sustained Hill painting for over a century was spent. Patronised by Sikhs and others, the Kangra style took another long century to die.'

BIOGRAPHICAL NOTES

AJIT SINGH SANDHAWALIA. From the same family as Chand Kaur, wife of Maharaja Kharak Singh. With Attar and Lehna Singh Sandhawalia conspired against Maharaja Sher Singh and himself shot him, 15 September 1843. Became chief minister of Dalip Singh, but, a few days later, was killed at instance of Hira Singh (q.v.).

Inscribed portraits:
(1) Fig. 83. Victoria and Albert Museum, I.S. 171–1953 (sketch).
(2) Osborne, W. G., *The Court and Camp of Runjeet Sing* (London, 1840), 70.
    Lithograph from an original drawing by Osborne, May 1838.

AZIZ-UD-DIN (Fakir). Muslim. Born about 1780. Elder brother of Nur-ud-din. Joined Ranjit Singh as court physician, 1799. Specialised in foreign affairs and in relations with the British. Confidential secretary to Maharaja Ranjit Singh. Remained influential until death of Sher Singh, September 1843. Died 1845.

Inscribed portrait:
(1) Osborne, W. G., *The Court and Camp of Runjeet Sing* (London, 1840), 69.
    Lithograph after an original drawing by Osborne, 1838.

CHAND KAUR (1) Member of Sandhawalia misl and wife of Kharak Singh (q.v.).
            (2) Also an alias for Rani Jindan (q.v.) widow of Maharaja Ranjit Singh.

CHATTAR SINGH ATARIWALA. Father of Sher Singh Atariwala. Commander-in-Chief, Sikh army, second Anglo-Sikh War, 1848–1849. With his son, defeated by the British at battle of Gujarat, February 1849. Surrendered and later exiled from Punjab.

Inscribed portraits:
(1) Fig. 99. Victoria and Albert Museum, 03592 I.S. (ivory).
(2) Victoria and Albert Museum, I.S. 156–1954 (ivory).

(3) Fig. 110. Victoria and Albert Museum, I.M. 2/47–1917 (woodcut).
(4) Fig. 109. Victoria and Albert Museum, I.M. 2/119–1917 (woodcut).
(5) Fig. 108. Victoria and Albert Museum, I.M. 2/56–1917 (woodcut).

CHET SINGH. Chief Minister to Kharak Singh. Murdered October 1389.

Inscribed portrait:
(1) India Office Library, *Panjabi Characters*. Add. Or. 1389 (water-colour).

DALIP SINGH. Born 1837. Accepted son of Ranjit Singh by Rani Jindan. Succeeded when six years old to Sikh throne, September 1843. Supported by Hira Singh (killed December 1844), later by Jawahir Singh (Rani Jindan's brother, executed September 1845). After first Anglo-Sikh War (December 1845 to March 1846), put under a Council of Regency. Deposed, December 1849. Given pension, with Sir John Login as guardian and tutor. Exiled from Punjab, 1850. Became a Christian, 1853. Went to England, 1854. Received by Queen Victoria. K.C.S.I., 1861. G.C.S.I., 1866. Abjured Christianity and re-embraced Sikhism, 1886. Died Paris, 1893.

Inscribed portraits:
(1) Fig. 96. Victoria and Albert Museum, I.S. 143–1954 (ivory).
(2) Victoria and Albert Museum, 03598 I.S. (ivory).
(3) Fig. 109. Victoria and Albert Museum, I.M. 2/119–1917 (woodcut).
(4) Fig. 110. Victoria and Albert Museum, I.M. 2/47–1917 (woodcut).
(5) Fig. 108. Victoria and Albert Museum, I.M. 2/56–1917 (woodcut).
(6) India Office Library, *Punjab Portraits*. Add. Or. 1399b (water-colour).
(7) India Office Library, *Punjab Portraits*. Add. Or. 1453 (water-colour).
(8) Fig. 67. Hardinge, C. S. *Recollections of India* (London, 1847), part I, pl. 26.
(9) Fig. 66. Mackenzie, Helen C. (Mrs Colin), *Illustrations of the Mission, the Camp and the Zenana* (London, 1854), pl. 6.
(10) Honigberger, J. M., *Thirty-five Years in the East* (London, 1852), 108.

DHIAN SINGH. Dogra Rajput. Second son of Mian Kishor Singh, grandson of Zorawar Singh, great-grandson of Surat Singh (brother of Raja Ranjit Dev, ruled 1735–1781, of Jammu). Born 1796. Entered Ranjit Singh's army, 1812. Favourite and court chamberlain, 1818. Raja, 1822. Chief Minister of Ranjit Singh, 1828–1839, and of Nau Nihal Singh, 1839–1840. Served Sher Singh. Murdered, September 1843. Father of Ranjit Singh's boy-favourite, Hira Singh. Younger brother of Gulab, elder brother of Suchet Singh.

Inscribed portraits:
(1) Fig. 24. Victoria and Albert Museum, I.S. 116–1953 (gouache).
(2) Fig. 30. Victoria and Albert Museum, I.S. 117–1953 (gouache).
(3) Fig. 33. Victoria and Albert Museum, I.M. 59–1936 (gouache).
(4) Victoria and Albert Museum, I.S. 165–1954 (ivory).

(5) Victoria and Albert Museum, 03604 I.S. (ivory).
(6) Fig. 109. Victoria and Albert Museum, 2/119–1917 (woodcut).
(7) Fig. 110. Victoria and Albert Museum, 2/47–1917 (woodcut).
(8) Fig. 108. Victoria and Albert Museum, 2/56–1917 (woodcut).
(9) India Office Library. Add. Or. 709 (gouache).
(10) India Office Library, *Panjabi Characters*, Add. Or. 1390 (water-colour).
(11) India Office Library, *Punjab Portraits*, Add. Or. 1400b (water-colour).
(12) Fig. 35. Mr and Mrs T. W. F. Scott collection, London (gouache).
(13) Fig. 15. Chester Beatty Library, Dublin, 195 (gouache).
(14) Osborne, W. G., *The Court and Camp of Runjeet Sing* (London, 1840), 73.
(15) Honigberger, J. M., *Thirty-five Years in the East* (London, 1852), 114.

DINA NATH. Joined Ranjit Singh's state office, 1818. Received royal seal, 1826. Became head of civil and finance office, 1834. Diwan, 1838. Remained finance minister under Maharajas Kharak, Nau Nihal, Sher and Dalip Singh, 1839–1849. Signed first treaty of Lahore with British, 9 March 1846. Member of Council of Regency, 1846. Raja, 1847. Collaborated with British after second Anglo-Sikh War, 1849. Died 1857.

Inscribed portraits:
(1) Fig. 81. Victoria and Albert Museum, I.S. 174–1953 (sketch).
(2) Victoria and Albert Museum, I.S. 161–1954 (ivory).
(3) Victoria and Albert Museum, 03594 (ivory).
(4) Fig. 109. Victoria and Albert Museum, I.M. 2/119–1917 (woodcut).
(5) Fig. 110. Victoria and Albert Museum, I.M. 2/47–1917 (woodcut).
(6) Fig. 108. Victoria and Albert Museum, I.M. 2/56–1917 (woodcut).
(7) India Office Library, *Punjab Portraits*, Add. Or. 1404b (water-colour).
(8) India Office Library, *Punjab Portraits*, Add. Or. 1457 (water-colour).
(9) Fig. 64. India Office Library (photo from gouache).
(10) Hardinge, C. S., *Recollections of India* (London, 1847), part II, pl. 26.
(11) Honigberger, J. M., *Thirty-five Years in the East* (London, 1852), 118.

DOST MUHAMMAD KHAN. Afghan. Ruler of Kabul and Ghazni from 1826 and Amir of Afghanistan 1836–1840 and 1841–1863.

Inscribed portraits:
(1) Victoria and Albert Museum, I.S. 147–1954 (ivory).
(2) Fig. 109. Victoria and Albert Museum, I.M. 2/119–1917 (woodcut).
(3) Fig. 108. Victoria and Albert Museum, I.M. 2/47–1917 (woodcut).
(4) India Office Library, *Punjab Portraits*, Add. Or. 1406a (water-colour).
(5) India Office Library, *Punjab Portraits*, Add. Or. 1460 (water-colour).
(6) Vigne, G. T., *A Personal Narrative of a visit to Ghuzni, Kabul and Afghanistan* (London, 1840), frontispiece.

(7) Eden, Emily, *Portraits of the Princes and People of India* (London, 1844), pl. 1.

(8) Honigberger, J. M., *Thirty-five Years in the East* (London, 1852), 118.

GULAB SINGH. Dogra Rajput. Elder brother of Dhian Singh. Born, 1792. Entered Ranjit Singh's army, 1809. Obtained Jammu as fief, 1820. Raja, 1822. Semi-independent Governor of Jammu Hills, 1825–1846. Chief Minister to Dalip Singh, January to March, 1846. Negotiated first treaty of Lahore with British, 8 March 1846. Obtained Kashmir and was recognised by the British as independent Raja of Jammu and Kashmir (treaty of Amritsar, 16 March 1846). Died 1857. Sons (1) Udham, (2) Sohan, (3) Ranbir Singh.

Inscribed portraits:

(1) Fig. 53. Victoria and Albert Museum, I.S. 153–1882 (water-colour by William Carpenter).

(2) Fig. 107. Victoria and Albert Museum, I.S. 149–1954 (ivory).

(3) Victoria and Albert Museum, 03603 I.S. (ivory).

(4) Fig. 110. Victoria and Albert Museum, I.M. 2/47–1917 (woodcut).

(5) Fig. 109. Victoria and Albert Museum, I.M. 2/119–1917 (woodcut).

(6) Fig. 108. Victoria and Albert Museum, I.M. 2/56–1917 (woodcut).

(7) Fig. 34. India Office Library, Add. Or. 707 (gouache).

(8) India Office Library, *Punjab Portraits*, Add. Or. 1401b (water-colour).

(9) India Office Library, *Punjab Portraits*, Add. Or. 1461 (water-colour).

(10) McGregor, W. L., *The History of the Sikhs* (London, 1846), II, 41.

(11) Fig. 52. Hardinge, C. S., *Recollections of India* (London, 1847), part II, pl. 14.

(12) Honigberger, J. M., *Thirty-five Years in the East* (London, 1852), 114.

HIRA SINGH. Dogra Rajput. Son of Dhian Singh. Born *c.* 1816. Boy favourite of Maharaja Ranjit Singh. Raja, 1828. Married daughter of Ludar Chand of Kangra, 1829. Avenged his father's murder and put Dalip Singh on throne, September 1843. Chief Minister to Dalip Singh. Killed, December 1844.

Inscribed portraits:

(1) Fig. 19. Victoria and Albert Museum, I.S. 114–1953 (gouache).

(2) Fig. 20. Victoria and Albert Museum, I.S. 115–1953 (gouache).

(3) Fig. 29. Victoria and Albert Museum, I.M. 60–1936 (gouache).

(4) India Office Library, *Punjab Portraits*, Add. Or. 1400a (water-colour).

(5) Fig. 35. Mr and Mrs T. W. F. Scott collection, London (gouache).

(6) Osborne, W. G., *The Court and Camp of Runjeet Sing* (London, 1840), 73.

(7) Fig. 49. Eden, Emily, *Portraits of the Princes and Peoples of India* (London, 1844), pl. 7.

(8) Honigberger, J. M., *Thirty-five Years in the East* (London, 1852), 114.

IMAM-UD-DIN, SHEIKH. Sikh Governor of Kashmir. At the instigation of Lal Singh (q.v.), resisted Gulab Singh's absorption of the state in 1846, following the Treaty of Amritsar, 16 March 1846. Quelled by Sikh, British and Jammu forces. Attended trial of Lal

Singh at Lahore, December 1846 and the Darbar celebrating the Second Treaty of Lahore (16 December 1846), held at Lahore on 26 December 1846.

Inscribed portrait:
(1) Hardinge, C. S., *Recollections of India* (London, 1847), part II, pl. 26.

JAWAHIR SINGH. Brother of Rani Jindan. Intrigued against Hira Singh. Imprisoned, November 1843–February 1844. Killed Hira Singh and became Chief Minister in Rani Jindan's regency, December 1844. Executed by the Sikh army, 21 September 1845.

Inscribed portraits:
(1) Fig. 63. McGregor, W. L., *The History of the Sikhs* (London, 1846), II, frontispiece, third figure from left.
(2) Honigberger, J. M., *Thirty-five Years in the East* (London, 1852), 108.

JINDAN, RANI. Acknowledged wife of Maharaja Ranjit Singh and accepted mother of Maharaja Dalip Singh. Head of Lahore court and regent, September 1843 to December 1846. Sister of Jawahir Singh. Exiled by British, August 1847. Died in London, 1863.

Inscribed portraits:
(1) Fig. 97. Victoria and Albert Museum, 03597 I.S. (ivory).
(2) Fig. 110. Victoria and Albert Museum, I.M. 2/47–1917 (woodcut).
(3) Fig. 109. Victoria and Albert Museum, I.M. 2/119–1917 (woodcut).
(4) Fig. 108. Victoria and Albert Museum, I.M. 2/56–1917 (woodcut).
(5) India Office Library, *Punjab Portraits*, Add. Or. 1455 (water-colour).
(6) India Office Library, *Punjab Portraits*, Add. Or. 1399b (water-colour).
(7) Honigberger, J. M., *Thirty-five Years in the East* (London, 1852), 108.

JOSHI SHANKAR NATH. Born Travancore. Chief Astrologer to Maharajas Ranjit, Nau Nihal and Sher Singh. Returned to South India, 1843.

Inscribed portrait:
(1) Fig. 15. Chester Beatty Library, Dublin, 195.

KHARAK SINGH. Born 1802. Son of Maharaja Ranjit Singh by Rani Raj Kaur. Married Chand Kaur, 1812. A son, Nau Nihal Singh. Succeeded as Maharaja with Chet Singh as Chief Minister, June 1839. Chet Singh murdered, October 1839. Kharak Singh deposed by Nau Nihal, October 1839. Died, November 1840.
(1) Fig. 21. Victoria and Albert Museum, I.S. 113–1953 (gouache).
(2) Fig. 22. Victoria and Albert Museum, I.S. 338–1951 (gouache).
(3) Fig. 31. Victoria and Albert Museum, I.M. 57–1936 (gouache).
(4) Victoria and Albert Museum, I.S. 157–1954 (ivory).
(5) Victoria and Albert Museum, 03601 I.S. (ivory).
(6) India Office Library, *Panjabi Characters*, Add. Or. 1389 (water-colour).

(7) India Office Library, *Punjab Portraits*, Add. Or. 1397b (water-colour).
(8) Fig. 35. Mr and Mrs T. W. F. Scott collection, London (gouache).
(9) McGregor, W. L., *The History of the Sikhs* (London, 1846), II, 4.
(10) Honigberger, J. M., *Thirty-five Years in the East* (London, 1852), 92.

KHUSHAL SINGH (JAMADAR). Born 1790. Son of a Brahmin shop-keeper. Came to Lahore to seek his fortune, 1807. Joined Ranjit Singh's bodyguard. Favourite. Promoted Chamberlain, 1811. Embraced Sikhism and took the name Khushal Singh. Superseded by Dhian Singh, 1818, but remained member of Ranjit Singh's inner council. Governor of Multan. Supervised revenue collections in Kangra Hills. Died, 1839.

Inscribed portraits:
(1) India Office Library, *Panjabi Characters*, Add. Or. 1386 (water-colour).
(2) Arnold, T. W. and Wilkinson, J. V. S., *The Library of Chester Beatty: a catalogue of the Indian Miniatures* (London, 1936), I, 49, III, pl. 92 (gouache).

LABH SINGH. Army commander under Maharajas Ranjit, Kharak, Sher and Dalip Singh.

Inscribed portrait:
(1) Fig. 63. McGregor, W. L., *The History of the Sikhs* (London, 1846), II, frontispiece (figure on extreme left).

LAL SINGH. Brahmin. Favourite and lover of Rani Jindan. Appointed Chief Minister, Lahore, December 1845. Replaced by Gulab Singh but later (March 1846) re-appointed. Instigated Sheikh Imam-ud-din, Sikh Governor of Kashmir, not to surrender Kashmir to Gulab Singh. Arrested and tried by the British, December 1846. Exiled to Banaras.

Inscribed portraits:
(1) Fig. 102. Victoria and Albert Museum, 03608 I.S. (ivory).
(2) Fig. 63. Reproducing McGregor, W. L., *The History of the Sikhs* (London, 1846), II, frontispiece, second figure from left.
(3) Hardinge, C. S., *Recollections of India* (London, 1847), part I, pl. 13.
(4) Honigberger, J. M., *Thirty-five years in the East* (London, 1852), 108.

MUL RAJ. Brahmin. Governor of Multan, September 1844. An incident (the murder of two British officers at Multan, April 1848) contributed to the second Anglo-Sikh war (October 1848 to March 1849). Mulraj captured by British, January 1849. Died, *c.* 1850.

Inscribed portraits:
(1) Fig. 105. Victoria and Albert Museum, I.S. 142–1954 (ivory).
(2) Victoria and Albert Museum, 03590 I.S. (ivory).
(3) Fig. 110. Victoria and Albert Museum, I.M. 2/47–1917 (woodcut).

(4) Fig. 109. Victoria and Albert Museum, I.M. 2/119–1917 (woodcut).
(5) Fig. 108. Victoria and Albert Museum, I.M. 2/56–1917 (woodcut).
(6) India Office Library, *Punjab Portraits*, Add. Or. 1404a (water-colour).

NAU NIHAL SINGH. Born, 1821. Only son of Kharak Singh. Married, March 1837. Superseded his father as Maharaja, October 1839. Killed at Lahore by a fall of masonry from a gateway on returning from his father's funeral, 5 November 1840.

Inscribed portraits:
(1) Fig. 24. Victoria and Albert Museum, I.S. 116–1953 (gouache).
(2) Fig. 32. Victoria and Albert Museum, I.M. 58–1936 (gouache).
(3) Victoria and Albert Museum, I.S. 146–1954 (ivory).
(4) Victoria and Albert Museum, 03600 I.S. (ivory).
(5) India Office Library, *Panjabi Characters*, Add. Or. 1388.
(6) Indian Office Library, *Punjab Portraits*, Add. Or. 1398b (water-colour).
(7) Fig. 35. Mr and Mrs T. W. F. Scott collection, London (gouache).
(8) McGregor, W. L., *The History of the Sikhs* (London, 1846), II, 6.
(9) Honigberger, J. M., *Thirty-five Years in the East* (London, 1852), 92.

NUR-UD-DIN. Younger brother of 'Fakir' Aziz-ud-din. Appointed Ranjit Singh's personal physician, 1801. Courtier and adviser to Dalip Singh. Member, Council of Regency, 1846.

Inscribed portraits:
(1) Fig. 101. Victoria and Albert Museum, 03596 (ivory).
(2) Honigberger, J. M., *Thirty-five Years in the East* (London, 1852), 118.

PHULA SINGH AKALI. Member of the ascetic sect, Akalis, distinguished by their fanatical heroism and blue garments (originally prescribed by Guru Govind Singh). Armed guardians of the Golden Temple, Amritsar. Wore round their turbans steel quoits. Phula Singh himself a wild rebel and outlaw with legendary reputation. Feared and revered. Defied Ranjit Singh. Headed a mob which attacked Metcalfe at Amritsar, 1809. Led an irregular attack on Multan, 1816. Killed in battle at Naushera, 1823.

Inscribed portraits:
(1) Fig. 103. Victoria and Albert Museum, 03589 I.S. (ivory).
(2) Fig. 109. Victoria and Albert Museum, I.M. 2/119–1917 (woodcut).
(3) Fig. 110. Victoria and Albert Museum, I.M. 2/47–1917 (woodcut).
(4) Fig. 108. Victoria and Albert Museum, I.M. 2/56–1917 (woodcut).

PRATAP SINGH. Son of Maharaja Sher Singh. Born, 1831. Murdered by Lehna Singh Sandhawalia, September 1843.

Inscribed portraits:
(1) Fig. 100. Victoria and Albert Museum, I.S. 144–1954 (ivory).
(2) Eden, Emily, *Portraits of the Princes and Peoples of India*, pl. 19.

RANBIR SINGH. Date of birth (1829, Panikkar) uncertain. Third son of Maharaja Gulab Singh of Jammu. Died, 1885.

Inscribed portraits:
(1) Fig. 54. Victoria and Albert Museum, I.S. 154–1882 (water-colour by William Carpenter).
(2) Fig. 95. India Office Library, *Punjab Portraits*, Add. Or. 1402b (water-colour).

RANDHIR SINGH (alias of Sohan Singh, q.v.).

RANJIT SINGH. Born 1780. Maharaja of Punjab 1799. Died 27 June 1839.

Inscribed portraits:
(1) Fig. 14. Victoria and Albert Museum, I.S. 480–1950 (gouache).
(2) Fig. 17. Victoria and Albert Museum, I.S. 111–1953 (gouache).
(3) Fig. 18. Victoria and Albert Museum, I.S. 112–1953 (gouache).
(4) Fig. 19. Victoria and Albert Museum, I.S. 114–1953 (gouache).
(5) Fig. 27. Victoria and Albert Museum, I.M. 56–1936 (gouache).
(6) Victoria and Albert Museum, 03599 I.S. (ivory).
(7) Victoria and Albert Museum, I.S. 167–1954 (ivory).
(8) Victoria and Albert Museum, I.S. 148–1954 (ivory).
(9) Fig. 108. Victoria and Albert Museum, I.M. 2/56–1917 (woodcut).
(10) Fig. 110. Victoria and Albert Museum, 2/47–1917 (woodcut).
(11) Fig. 109. Victoria and Albert Museum, 2/119–1917 (woodcut).
(12) Fig. 69. Victoria and Albert Museum, 03530 I.S. (glass).
(13) India Office Library, *Panjabi Characters*, Add. Or. 1390 (water-colour).
(14) India Office Library, *Punjab Portraits*, Add. Or. 1397a (water-colour).
(15) India Office Library, *Punjab Portraits*, Add. Or. 1452 (water-colour).
(16) Fig. 28. Mr and Mrs T. W. F. Scott collection, London (gouache).
(17) Fig. 15. Chester Beatty Library, Dublin, 195 (gouache).
(18) Fig. 68. Commonwealth Relations Office, London. Lithograph from an original drawing by G. T. Vigne.
(19) Osborne, W. G., *The Court and Camp of Runjeet Sing* (London, 1840), 73, 109.
(20) McGregor, W. L., *The History of the Sikhs* (London, 1846), I, frontispiece.
(21) Fig. 26. Eden, Emily, *Portraits of the Princes and People of India* (London, 1844), pl. 13.
(22) Honigberger, J. M., *Thirty-five Years in the East* (London, 1852), 92.
(23) Fig. 45. Sikh Museum, Lahore, Pakistan: oil by Theodor August Schoefft.

SHAM SINGH ATARIWALA. Sikh general. Killed at battle of Sobraon, February 1846.

Inscribed portraits:

(1) Victoria and Albert Museum, I.S. 151–1954 (ivory).
(2) Victoria and Albert Museum, 03591 (ivory).
(3) Fig. 94. India Office Library, *Punjab Portraits*, Add. Or. 1403a (water-colour).

SHER SINGH. Accepted son of Ranjit Singh by Mehtab Kaur. Born, 1807. Sikh governor of Kangra state, 1830–1831. Sometime governor of Kashmir and Peshawar. Succeeded Nau Nihal Singh as Maharaja, 18 January 1841. Retained Dhian Singh as Chief Minister. Murdered along with his son, Pratap Singh and Dhian Singh, September 1843.

Inscribed portraits:

(1) Fig. 104. Victoria and Albert Museum, I.S. 162–1954 (ivory).
(2) Fig. 110. Victoria and Albert Museum, I.M. 2/47–1917 (woodcut).
(3) Fig. 109. Victoria and Albert Museum, I.M. 2/119–1917 (woodcut).
(4) Fig. 108. Victoria and Albert Museum, I.M. 2/56–1917 (woodcut).
(5) Fig. 92. India Office Library, *Punjab Portraits*, Add. Or. 1398a (water-colour).
(6) India Office Library, *Punjab Portraits*, Add. Or. 1454 (water-colour).
(7) Fig. 40. Mr and Mrs T. W. F. Scott collection, London (gouache).
(8) Fig. 38. Punjab Museum, Chandigarh (gouache).
(9) Osborne, W. G., *The Court and Camp of Runjeet Sing* (London, 1840), 64.
(10) Fig. 39. Vigne, G. T., *Travels in Kashmir, Ladak*, etc. (London, 1842), frontispiece.
(11) Fig. 42, Eden, Emily, *Portraits of the Princes and People of India* (London, 1844), pl. 2.
(12) Honigberger, J. M., *Thirty-five Years in the East* (London, 1852), 92.
(13) Fig. 44, 45. Sikh Museum, Lahore, Pakistan: oil by Theodor August Schoefft 'The Dasahra Festival at the Court of Lahore'.
(14) Fig. 43. Sikh Museum, Lahore, Pakistan: oil by Theodor August Schoefft 'Maharaja Sher Singh'.

SHER SINGH ATARIWALA. Son of Chattar Singh Atariwala. Sikh general. Sided with British against Mul Raj at Multan, 1848, but later defeated, joining his father as commander-in-chief, second Anglo-Sikh war. Fought in battle of Chilianwala, January 1849. With his father defeated by British in battle of Gujarat, February 1849. Surrendered and exiled from Punjab.

Inscribed portraits:

(1) Victoria and Albert Museum, 03593 I.S. (ivory).
(2) Victoria and Albert Museum, I.S. 145–1954 (ivory).
(3) Fig. 110. Victoria and Albert Museum, I.M. 2/47–1917 (woodcut).
(4) Fig. 109. Victoria and Albert Museum, I.M. 2/119–1917 (woodcut).
(5) Fig. 108. Victoria and Albert Museum, I.M. 2/56–1917 (woodcut).
(6) Fig. 93. India Office Library, *Punjab Portraits*, Add. Or. 1404b (water-colour).

SOHAN (RANDHIR) SINGH. Second son of Maharaja Gulab Singh of Jammu. Killed with Hira Singh and Pandit Jalla, December 1844.

Inscribed portrait:
(1) Fig. 56. India Office Library, Add. Or. 708.

SUCHET SINGH. Dogra Rajput. Youngest brother of Gulab Singh and Dhian Singh. Born, 1801. Entered Ranjit Singh's army, 1812. Raja, 1822. Obtained eastern half of Jammu hills as fief. Murdered at Lahore, March 1844.

Inscribed portraits:
(1) Fig. 106. Victoria and Albert Museum, 03605 I.S. (ivory).
(2) India Office Library, *Panjabi Characters*, Add. Or. 1387 (water-colour).
(3) India Office Library, *Punjab Portraits*, Add. Or. 1401 (water-colour).
(4) Fig. 15. Chester Beatty Library, Dublin, 195 (gouache).
(5) McGregor, W. L., *The History of the Sikhs* (London, 1846), II, 26.
(6) Honigberger, J. M., *Thirty-five Years in the East* (London, 1852), 114.

TEJ SINGH. Originally Tej Ram (a Brahmin). Nephew of Jamadar Khushal Singh. Embraced Sikhism, 1816. Commander-in-Chief, Sikh army, 1845. With Lal Singh and three others signed first treaty of Lahore on behalf of Sikh darbar, 8 March 1846. Member Regency Council of Maharaja Dalip Singh, 16 December 1846.

Inscribed portraits:
(1) Fig. 98. Victoria and Albert Museum, 03595 (ivory).
(2) Victoria and Albert Museum, I.S. 51–1882 (water-colour by William Carpenter).
(3) India Office Library, *Punjab Portraits*, Add. Or. 1405a (water-colour).
(4) Honigberger, J. M., *Thirty-five Years in the East* (London, 1852), 118.

UDHAM SINGH. First son of Maharaja Gulab Singh of Jammu. Died with Nau Nihal Singh from fall of an archway when returning from funeral of Kharak Singh, November 1840.

Inscribed portrait:
(1) Fig. 56. India Office Library, Add. Or. 708 (gouache).

Catalogue of
Sikh Paintings
in the
Victoria and Albert Museum

I GOUACHES

1. *Frontispiece.* Maharaja Ranjit Singh (1780–1837) on horseback with armed escort. Sikh, Punjab Plains, *c.* 1835–1840.

Size: 308 × 226 mm; with border 398 × 280 mm.

Dark blue margin with Guler-Kangra floral scrolls in gold, white rules; border pink, flecked with red. At the top a blank perhaps intended for a superscription.

Victoria and Albert Museum, I.S. 282–1955.

Given by Mrs L. M. Rivett-Carnac on behalf of the Van Cortlandt family. Said, by family tradition, to have been one of a pair of portraits made for Ranjit Singh by his court artist and presented by Ranjit Singh to Mrs Rivett-Carnac's grandfather, Colonel Henry Charles Van Cortlandt, the other copy being kept by the Maharaja. Van Cortlandt (1814–1888) entered Ranjit Singh's service in 1832 and, after the first Anglo-Sikh War (1845–1846) commanded Sikh detachments under the British.

Description: Maharaja Ranjit Singh with gold halo, bestrides a white stallion, heavily bejewelled and with golden saddle-cloth. He wears a pink and green coat edged with grey and a yellow vest, turban and trousers. He holds the reins lightly in his right hand and raises a pink flower in his left hand. An attendant follows shading him with a yellow umbrella edged with grey. Thirteen other followers, some in red and blue army tunics, escort him, five of them carrying guns wrapped in cloth covers, four of them knobbed staffs and one a lance. Background a dark green hillside, bedecked with flowering plants in red, pink, blue and yellow and rimmed with pink contours, dotted with lines of black trees. Sky deep blue.

Comment: In style, a slightly crude derivative from later Guler painting—the rimmed hillsides, however, preserving an early idiom (see Archer, *Indian Painting from the Punjab Hills* (London, 1952), pls. 23, 26, 29). The hillside with its clumps of flowering trees can be paralleled in N. C. Mehta, *Studies in Indian Painting* (Bombay, 1926), pl. 55, 'The Glory of Spring'—a picture which is perhaps assignable to the 1820–1830 period at Tehri Garhwal. For the tunics of the soldiers, compare no. 19.

Since the portrait is larger than those in standard portrait sets, it may well have been intended for presentation purposes. If this is the case, it must rank as the only portrait so far known which can plausibly be connected with a court artist.

In contrast to most portraits of Ranjit Singh, where the beard and moustaches are already white, the right eye-brow is black and the moustaches and upper part of the beard are grey. No firm inferences can be drawn from this circumstance, however, and it would seem prima facie unlikely that a young European adventurer would be 'presented' with a special portrait except after several years' service and then perhaps only in exceptional circumstances. If the family tradition is accepted, it would suggest that the picture was painted between 1835 and 1838.

Of Van Cortlandt's early years with Ranjit Singh, nothing significant has so far been recorded (see Grey, *European Adventurers in Northern India*, 303–307).

Like other studies of Ranjit Singh, the present portrait is clearly an idealised rendering, stressing qualities such as majesty of presence, dignified serenity and grave and earnest demeanour rather than the athletic energy and lively gusto which endeared him to his times. The following extracts from Burnes, Jacquemont, Osborne and the modern Sikh historian, Khushwant Singh, give us something of his vital flavour.

Comments on character:

BURNES

'Nature has, indeed, been sparing in her gifts to this personage; and there must be a mighty contrast between his mind and body. He has lost an eye, is pitted by the small pox, and his stature does not certainly exceed five feet three inches. He is entirely free from pomp and show, yet the studied respect of his Court is remarkable; not an individual spoke without a sign, though the throng was more like a bazar than the Court of the first native Prince in these times.'[1]

'A conversation could not, of course, conclude without his favourite topic of wine; and, as he first sat down, he remarked that the site of his tent was an agreeable one for a drinking party, since it commanded a fine view of the surrounding country. He enquired of the doctors, whether wine was best

[1] Burnes, *Travels into Bokhara*, III, 154–155. Lieutenant Alexander Burnes visited the Punjab in 1831–1832.

before or after food; and laughed heartily at an answer from myself, when I recommended both.'[1]

JACQUEMONT

'The biography of Ranjit Singh might possibly be amusing but it abounds in facts impossible to write down in the vernacular, which would require to be put in Latin notes. Yet in spite of all that is reprehensible in Ranjit, do love him a little for my sake.'[2]

'I have spent a couple of hours on several occasions conversing with Ranjit *de omni re scibili et quibusdam aliis*. His conversation is a nightmare. He is almost the first inquisitive Indian I have seen, but his curiosity makes up for the apathy of his whole nation. He asked me a hundred thousand questions about India, the English, Europe, Bonaparte, this world in general and the other one, hell and Paradise, the soul, God, the devil, and a thousand things besides. Like all persons of quality in the East he is a *malade imaginaire*, and since he has a large band of the loveliest girls of Kashmir and sufficient means to pay for a better dinner than anybody else in this country, he is particularly annoyed at not being able to drink like a fish without getting drunk, or eat like an elephant without choking. Women no longer give him any more pleasure than the flowers in his garden, and for good reasons, and that is the most cruel of his ills. He had the decency to refer to those functions of whose weakness he complains as his digestion. But I knew what the word stomach signified in the mouth of the King at Lahore, and we discussed his malady exhaustively, though in veiled terms.'[3]

'This model Asiatic king is no saint: far from it. He cares nothing for law or good faith, unless it is to his interest to be just or faithful; but he is not cruel. He orders very great criminals to have their noses and ears cut off, or a hand, but he never takes life. He has a passion for horses which amounts almost to a mania; he has waged the most costly and bloody wars for the purpose of seizing a horse in some neighbouring State which they had refused to give or sell him. He is extremely brave, a quality rather rare among Eastern princes, and though he has always been successful in his military campaigns, it has been by treaties and cunning negotiations that he has made himself absolute king of the whole Punjab, Kashmir, etc., and is better obeyed by his subjects than the Mogul emperors were at the height of their power. A professing Sikh, though

[1] *Ibid.*, I, 21.

[2] Jacquemont, *Letters from India, 1829–1832*, 1936 edition, 280–281. Jacquemont, a French botanist, stayed at the Court of Ranjit Singh 1830–1831.

[3] *Ibid.*, 171.

in reality a sceptic, he goes to Amritsar every year to perform his devotions, and, oddly enough, visits the tombs of various Moslem saints as well; yet these pilgrimages do not upset any of his more strait-laced co-religionists.'[1]

'One knows that Orientals are debauched; but they have some shame about it. Ranjit's excesses are shameless. The fact that this greybeard has had and has a number of catamites is nothing shocking in this country; but, apart from this, he has always consorted publicly with the women of the bazaar, whose patron and protector he is. At the great festivals there are hundreds of them at Lahore and Amritsar, whom he makes dress up in the most ridiculous way, ride on horses and follow him; on such occasions they form his bodyguard. He always has some of them in his camp, and they follow him everywhere riding upon his elephants. One of his pastimes when he has nothing better to do is to watch their flirtations with the young men of his court.'[2]

OSBORNE

'A tolerably correct notion of the character of Runjeet Sing may be gathered from this sketch and still more from the Journal which it introduces. Brought up but not educated in the idleness and debauchery of a zenana, by the pernicious influence of which it is marvellous that the stoutest mind should not be emasculated, he appears from the moment he assumed the reins of government to have evinced a vigour of understanding on which his habitual excesses, prematurely fatal as they proved to his bodily powers, produced no sensible effect.

His was one of that order of minds which is destined by nature to win their way to distinction and achieve greatness. His courage was of that cool and calculating sort, which courted no unnecessary danger, and shunned none which his purposes made it expedient to encounter; and he always observed a just proportion between his efforts and his objects. Gifted with an intuitive perception of character, and a comprehensive knowledge of human nature, it was by the overruling influence of a superior mind, that he contrived gradually, almost insensibly, and with little resistance, not only to reduce the proud and high-spirited chiefs of his nation to the condition of subjects, but to render them the devoted adherents of his person, and the firm supporters of his throne.

With an accurate and retentive memory, and with great fertility both of invention and resources, he was an excellent man of business without being able to write or even to read. As insensible to remorse and pity as indisposed to cruelty and the shedding of blood, he cared neither for the happiness or

[1] Ibid., 173.   [2] Garrett, The Punjab one hundred years ago: Jacquemont's Journal, 54-55.

lives of others, except as far as either might be concerned in the obstruction or advancement of his projects, from the steady pursuit of which no consideration ever diverted him. His success, and especially the consolidation of his power, are in great measure attributable to the soundness of his views, and the practicable nature of his plans. He never exhausted his strength in wild and hazardous enterprises, but restraining his ambition within the limits of a reasonable probability, they were not only so well timed and skilfully arranged as generally to ensure success, but failure (in the rare instances when they did fail) never seriously shook his stability, or impaired his resources.

He seems to have had a lively, fanciful, and ingenious mind, but the ceremonious forms of Indian etiquette and the figurative and hyperbolical style of Oriental intercourse, are not favourable to the development of social qualities. Runjeet, however, had a natural shrewdness, sprightliness and vivacity, worthy of a more civilized and intellectual state. He was a devout believer in the doctrines, and a punctual observer of the ceremonies, of his religion. The Grunth, the sacred book of the Sikhs, was constantly read to him, and he must have been familiar with the moral precepts it inculcated. But—

> Let observation with extensive view
> Survey mankind from China to Peru,

and the same invariable inconsistency will be found between professed belief and habitual conduct: nothing could be more different than the precepts of Nanac and the practices of Runjeet. By the former were enjoined, devotion to God, and peace towards men. The life of Runjeet was an incessant career of war and strife and he indulged without remorse or shame in sensualities of the most revolting description. Nor did the excesses over which he was at no pains to throw a decent veil either detract from his dignity or diminish the respect of his subjects; so depraved was the taste and so low the state of moral sentiment in the Punjab. It is no impeachment of the sagacity of Runjeet that he was a believer in omens and charms, in witchcraft and in spells. Such superstitions only proves that early impressions were not eradicated and that his mind did not make a miraculous spring beyond the bounds of his country and his age.'[1]

KHUSHWANT SINGH

'In the history of the Punjab, no man has excited the imagination of the people as much as Ranjit Singh.

Despite his slight stature and spare frame, Ranjit Singh was wiry, as if made of whipcord. He was a superb horseman and, since horses were the ruling

[1] Osborne, *Court and Camp*, xxxviii–xliii. Osborne, nephew and A.D.C. to the Governor-General, Lord Auckland visited Ranjit Singh in May, 1838, prior to a second visit with Auckland in December 1838.

passion of his life, he often spent as much as ten hours of the day in the saddle. Although of excellent constitution, he was a hypochondriac. He consulted physicians every other day and insisted on their prescribing drugs (in later years, laudanum) for his imaginary ailments. But this obsession with illness did not produce a fear of death. He was a man of courage who led his men in battle and faced danger without concern for his own life. This quality earned for him the title, "The Lion of the Punjab".

Although ugly himself, Ranjit Singh was a lover of beautiful things. He surrounded himself with handsome men and beautiful women. He wore the plainest of clothes (saffron-coloured cashmere in winter and plain white muslin in summer) but he insisted that courtiers and visitors wear their regalia and jewellery in the Durbar. He maintained a bevy of Kashmiri girls who dressed as soldiers and rode out with him on ceremonial occasions. His appreciation of beauty was not confined to human beings. He loved the open country and spent his morning hours riding out to the river or to some garden. Whenever dark monsoon clouds appeared in the sky or it started to rain he stopped work and gave himself up to merrymaking. The sight of the new moon moved him to rapturous delight and he would order a gun salute to honour its appearance. The Mughal garden at Shalamar (which he renamed Salabagh, the lover's garden) was his favourite haunt, where he relaxed amid the playing fountains, drank goblets of heady wine, and listened to his favourite flautist, Attar Khan, or watched the nautch. Ranjit Singh was a bon vivant who did not find it difficult to combine the lust for living with the lust for power. It would seem that Kipling wrote the following lines for Ranjit Singh:

Four things greater than all things are:
Women and Horses and Power and War.

An anecdote told in Punjabi circles to this day relates a dialogue between Ranjit Singh and his Muslim wife, Mohran. She commented on the Maharajah's ugliness and asked "Where were you when God was distributing good looks?"

"When you were occupied with your looks, I was busy seeking power", answered the monarch.

Ranjit Singh did not receive any education, and remained unlettered to the last. But he respected men of learning and, like the illiterate Akbar, made up the deficiency by seeking the company of scholars and satisfied his craving for knowledge by badgering them with questions.

He had the same capacity for work as he had for enjoying life. When the feasts were over and the dancers' bell silent, he retired to his bedchamber and spent many hours dictating his correspondence to relays of scribes who were always in attendance.

Ranjit Singh had the virtues and vices of Punjabi character. He was simple in his habits, utterly outspoken and warm and generous towards people he liked. Although he became a king, he did not lose the common touch or sympathy with the peasant folk from whom he had sprung. He also had the peasant's shrewdness and cunning, and once his suspicion was aroused he considered no trick unfair to outwit an adversary. But he never held a grudge for very long. He forgave people who had wronged him and rehabilitated enemies he had vanquished. He hated inflicting punishment: never in his entire life did he sentence a man to death—not even an Akali fanatic who tried to assassinate him.

Ranjit Singh summed up his own achievements in the following words: "My kingdom is a great kingdom: it was small, it is now large; it was scattered, broken, and divided; it is now consolidated; it must increase in prosperity, and descend undivided to my posterity. The maxims of Taimur have guided me: what he professed and ordered I have done. By counsel and providence, combined with valour, I have conquered; and by generosity, discipline, and policy, I have regulated and consolidated my government. I have rewarded the bold, and encouraged merit wherever it was not to be found: on the field of battle, I exalted the valiant; with my troops I have shared all dangers, all fatigues. Both on the field and in the cabinet I shut partiality from my soul, and closed my eyes to personal comfort; with the robe of empire, I put on the mantle of care; I fed faqirs and holy men, and gained their prayers; the guilty as the innocent I spared; and those whose hands were raised against my self have met my clemency; Sri Purakhji [God] has therefore been merciful to his servant, and increased his power, so that his territory now extends to the borders of China and the limits of the Afghans, with all Multan, and the rich possesions beyond the Sutlej."'[1]

2. *Fig. 9*. Raja Dhian Singh (1796–1843) on a hawking expedition. Sikh, Punjab Plains. *c*. 1830–1835.

Size: 228 × 250 mm; with border 286 × 320 mm.

Margin dark blue with gold floral scrolls and black rules, pink border, flecked with red.

Uninscribed.

Victoria and Albert Museum, F. B. P. Lory collection, I.S. 124–1960.

[1] Khushwant Singh, *History*, I, 291–296. A view of Ranjit Singh's character and achievements, as a modern Sikh historian would regard it.

Description: Raja Dhian Singh, Chief Minister of Maharaja Ranjit Singh, in mauve vest and yellow turban and trousers, is on a hawking expedition. A mauve umbrella with blue and yellow rims is carried above him. He rides a roan stallion and is attended by a posse of fourteen footmen, armed with swords, lances and guns. Three riders follow him; the nearest, a youth, carries a falcon, two others wield lances. Dhian Singh and a footman carry hawks. Two hounds, one white, the other black, gambol beside them. Turbans red, mauve, blue and green. Costumes chiefly white. Background pale green with faint streaks of red at the top and a band of pale blue sky with white blobs as clouds.

Comment: In style closely related to Guler painting of the 1820 to 1830 period. The execution, while delicate and sensitive, however, already shows a tendency to greater simplification. Contrast, in this connection, the Guler portrait of Mian Amar Singh 'Darhiwala' (figure 8). This and the dark blue border and special type of floral scroll suggest the hand of a Guler painter perhaps only recently arrived in the Punjab Plains.

For the identity of the chief personage, Dhian Singh, see inscribed portraits (figures 24, 30, 33 and 35). The trim features and shorter cut of beard suggest a man in his mid-thirties, and, if the portrait is contemporary, this would make its date nearer to 1830 than 1835.

Comments on character:

VIGNE

'Raja Dhihan Sing, the prime minister, was originally little more than a common suwar. His handsome appearance, his skill in martial exercises and his address in the hunting-field procured him the especial favour of Runjit; who eventually created him the Rajah Rajghan or Rajah of Rajahs. He filled his office with ability and distinction; and perhaps, notwithstanding a studied but dignified insolence of demeanour, he was one of the best men and the finest fellow in the Punjab, which is not, however, saying much for him. He really was attached to Runjit; but his pretended attempt to throw himself upon his funeral pyre was nothing but a masterly piece of humbug.'[1]

EMILY EDEN

'Uncommonly good looking'[2]

[1] Vigne, *Personal Narrative*, 249–250.   [2] Eden, *Up the Country*, 199.

Related Examples:

(*1*) *Fig. 7.* Guru Govind Singh (tenth Guru, 1675–1708), nimbate, on horse-back holding a falcon and accompanied by two hounds. Behind him an attendant holds a state umbrella. In the sky a winged angel with Guler-style dress and features, waving a yak's tail fly-whisk and peacock-feather fan. Guler, or perhaps Punjab Plains, *c.* 1830. Maharaja of Tehri Garhwal collection, Narendranagar, U.P.

Comment: Includes the early Guler idiom of fanged and jagged hillsides. Crinkly clouds as in no. 2. For the gambolling puppy compare Gupta, *op. cit.*, pl. 3 (Guru Har Rai).

(*2*) *Fig. 8.* Mian Amar Singh 'Darhiwala', travelling with escort, hounds, and falcon. In the background, a mule loaded with a bed and baggage. Guler, *c.* 1825. Punjab Museum, Guler Raj collection, Chandigarh.

Comment: With its lithe and rhythmical postures, typical of Guler-style painting from which no. 2 may be presumed to derive. No state umbrella. For horse and hound, compare no. 2, especially the dark hound in bottom right-hand corner.

Note: Mian Amar Singh 'Darhiwala' was son of Kishan Singh, a nephew of Wazir Dhian Singh of Kotla. Dhian Singh, an ex-Wazir of Guler, seized Kotla from Guler and made it into a separate state. It was re-annexed by the Sikhs under Desa Singh Majithia in 1811. Amar Singh's magnificent beard is said to have so delighted Ranjit Singh that he awarded him a monthly stipend for especially tending it.

3. *Fig. 65.* A youth with attendant. Sikh, Punjab Plains, *c.* 1832–1835.
Size: 210 × 163 mm; with border 290 × 245 mm.
Margin dark blue with white rules and Guler-Kangra type floral scroll in gold and slate-blue; border pink, flecked with red.
Victoria and Albert Museum, J. C. French collection, I.S. 193–1955.
Obtained by French in Amritsar.

Description: A youth, in Sikh turban and costume, sits in a gold chair on a white terrace, facing a boy attendant who stands before him with hands pressed together. He holds a pink flower. Fountains spurt below them. Both are dressed in yellow. Background bluish grey with streaks of white and dark blue at the top. Beyond the terrace are three frail trees with pink and yellow flowers.

Comment: Although the seated youth does not resemble very closely the young Hira Singh of no. 7, he is not unlike the boy riding with Dhian Singh in no. 2 and may therefore be intended to be Ranjit's young favourite. The fact that he is seated on a gold chair suggests that his position is far from ordinary. In style close to no. 2 and perhaps for that reason of about the same date.

4. *Fig. 14.* Maharaja Ranjit Singh (1780–1839) on horseback. Sikh, Punjab Plains, *c.* 1835–1840.

Size: 211 × 141 mm; with border 280 × 215 mm.

Margin dark blue with white rules and Guler-Kangra type floral scroll in white and gold; border pink, flecked with red, red rules.

Inscribed on reverse in English: *Runjeet Singh. The Lion of the Punjaub.*

Victoria and Albert Museum, D. J. Elliott collection, I.S. 480–1950.

Description: Ranjit Singh dressed entirely in yellow, a black shield strapped to his back, bestrides a white stallion, whose fetlocks are stained crimson. He faces right. An attendant in red turban and wrap, white vest and blue shorts, supports a gold umbrella over him. Green stippled foreground. Pale bluish white background with streaks of blue and white at the top.

Comment: In design and posture similar to no. 5. The inscription may or may not antedate Ranjit Singh's death.

Yellow dress was worn on the occasion of the Spring festival of Basant— one of the few Punjabi festivals, which Muslims, Hindus and Sikhs celebrated in common, when everyone wore yellow to resemble the mustard flower. For this festival Ranjit Singh usually went to Lahore, visited the tomb of Madho Lal Hussain and began the morning by listening to a recitation of the Granth.

Burnes who was with Ranjit in 1832 witnessed the celebrations and described the sight as follows: 'The troops of the Punjab were drawn out, forming a street of about two miles long, which it took upwards of thirty-five minutes to traverse. The army consisted entirely of regular troops—cavalry, infantry, and artillery; and the whole corps was uniformly dressed in yellow, which was the gala costume of this Carnival. The Maharaja passed down the line, and received the salute of his forces. Our road lay entirely through the ruins of old Lahore, over irregular ground, which gave the line a waving appearance that greatly heightened the beauty of the scene. At the end of this magnificent array stood the royal tents, lined with yellow silk. Among them was a canopy, valued at a lac of rupees, covered with pearls, and having a border of precious stones.

126

Nothing can be imagined more grand. At one end Runjeet took his seat, and heard the Grunth, or sacred volume of the Seiks, for about ten minutes. He made a present to the priest; and the holy book was borne away wrapped in ten different covers, the outside one of which, in honour of the day, was of yellow velvet. Flowers and fruits were then placed before his Highness; and every kind of shrub or tree that produced a yellow flower must have been shorn of its beauties on this day.'[1]

5. *Fig. 17.* Maharaja Ranjit Singh (1780–1839) on horseback. Sikh, Punjab Plains, *c.* 1838–1840.

Size: 205 × 129 mm; with border 265 × 189 mm.

Dark blue margin with white oval-and-stroke pattern; border pink, flecked with red.

Inscribed on the flap in English: *Maharaja Runjeet Singh.*

Formerly in the collection of Lord Auckland (Governor-General of India 1836–1842) and brought by him to England in 1842. Given to the Victoria and Albert Museum by Auckland's great-nephew, O. E. Dickinson. From the same collection as nos. 6–11.

Victoria and Albert Museum, I.S. 111–1953.

Description: Ranjit Singh, nimbate, in dark green coat and trousers and yellow turban bestrides a white stallion with red saddle-cloth edged with gold. He faces right. An attendant in green turban and yellow dress holds a red umbrella, flecked with gold, above him. Stippled green foreground with tufted plants. Background pale blue with suggestions of white.

Comment: Auckland visited the court of Maharaja Ranjit Singh at Lahore in December 1838 and was accompanied by his sisters, Emily and Fanny Eden and nephew, William Osborne. For accounts of the visit, see Emily Eden, *Up the Country* and Janet Dunbar, *Golden Interlude*—the latter drawing upon Fanny Eden's unpublished journal in the India Office Library, *MSS. Eur.C.130 I–IV.*

While it is possible that nos. 5–9 and 11 had already been painted by the time of Auckland's visit, no. 10 which shows Nau Nihal Singh seated on a chair with Dhian Singh on the ground before him can hardly be earlier than October 1839 in which month Nau Nihal replaced his father, Kharak, as Maharaja.

Since all seven pictures are inscribed on their flaps in the same English hand and are in substantially the same style, they were doubtless painted at

[1] Burnes, *Travels*, I, 27.

127

about the same time and acquired together. Their date would probably not be earlier than about 1838 nor perhaps much later than the end of 1840, Nau Nihal Singh having died in November 1840. We can conjecture that, aware of the keen interest in the Sikh court aroused in Lord Auckland and his sisters by their visit, an English resident or traveller at Lahore or Amritsar acquired these seven pictures, wrote the names of the subjects on their flaps and presented them to the Governor-General.

6. *Fig. 18*. Maharaja Ranjit Singh (1780–1839) on horseback. Sikh, Punjab Plains, *c*. 1838–1840.

Size: 209 × 134 mm; with borders 274 × 205 mm.

Dark blue margin with Guler-Kangra type floral scroll in white and gold, red rules; pink border, flecked with red.

Inscribed on back of flap in English (same hand as no. 5): *Maharaja Runjeet Sing*: and in *nāgarī* characters, enclosed in a red cartouche, *srī ranjīt sīngh*.

Formerly in the collection of Lord Auckland (Governor-General of India 1836–1842) and brought by him to England in 1842. Given to the Victoria and Albert Museum by Auckland's great nephew, O. E. Dickinson. From the same collection as nos. 5, 7, 8, 9, 10 and 11.

Victoria and Albert Museum, I.S. 112–1953.

Description: Ranjit Singh, nimbate, in green turban, trousers and long green coat, bestrides a white stallion with crimson saddle-cloth, edged with gold. He faces right. An attendant in dark blue *dhoti*, pink vest, red wrap and yellow turban, holds above him a yellow umbrella edged with green and crimson. Pale green foreground with tufted plants. Background pale blue with faint streaks of red as in no. 2. Hints of white cloud.

Comment: In style, typical of work by Guler artists at Lahore or Amritsar after their adjustment to Sikh conditions in the Punjab Plains.

On the role of Amritsar in Punjabi life, Khushwant Singh writes: 'The Punjab's second largest city, Amritsar, was commercially more important than Lahore. It was the chief trading centre of Northern India where caravans brought goods from Central Asia and exchanged them for the products of India. In its narrow, winding streets were business houses trading in all conceivable kinds of goods: silks, muslins, spices, tea, hides, matchlocks and other kinds of armaments. Because of the rich merchants, subsidiary trades such as those of gold and silversmiths had grown up. Besides its riches, Amritsar had sanctity in the eyes of the Sikhs. It was founded by the fourth Guru, Ram Das, and it was here that the fifth Guru, Arjun, had compiled their scripture, the "Adi Granth", and built the temple in the centre of the sacred pool. Twice a year at least, all Sikhs, who could, came to Amritsar to bathe in the pool and make their offerings at the shrine. As far as the Sikhs were concerned, Amritsar was the most important city in the world.'[1]

For this reason, while not excluding Lahore, Amritsar was probably the chief centre for painting of the Sikhs.

7. *Fig. 19*. Maharaja Ranjit Singh (1780–1839) seated with Hira Singh (*c.* 1816–1844). Sikh, Punjab Plains. *c.* 1838–1840.

Size: 201 × 139 mm; with borders 283 × 222 mm.

Dark blue margin with Guler-Kangra type floral scroll in white and gold; border pale pink dotted with red strokes.

Inscribed on flap in English (same hand as in no. 5): *Maharaja Ranjit Singh & Raja Heera Singh.*

Formerly in the collection of Lord Auckland (Governor-General of India 1836–1842) and brought by him to England in 1842. Given to the Victoria and Albert Museum by Auckland's great-nephew, O. E. Dickinson. From the same collection as nos. 5, 6, 8, 9, 10 and 11.

Victoria and Albert Museum, I.S. 114–1953.

Description: Ranjit Singh, nimbate, in yellow turban, white vest and dark green trousers sits in a gold chair. His legs are tucked under him on the seat. He faces right. Around him is a terrace with white balustrade. Seated before him in a chair, is the boy favourite, Hira Singh, in white dress, crimson coat and yellow turban and trousers. His right leg is drawn up on the chair. Dark red carpet with floral patterns in white, blue and green. Pale green background with, to the left, a frail tree with pink flowers. At the top an orange blind rimmed with dark green.

Comment: Ranjit Singh's face is identical with that in no. 6, suggesting that, despite the somewhat more elaborate setting, the picture is from the same workshop. For Ranjit's practice of sitting on a throne and chairs either cross-legged or with one leg tucked under him, see figures 25, 26 and 28.

Portraits for comparison:

(1) *Fig. 28*. Maharaja Ranjit Singh on a gold throne. Sikh, Punjab Plains, *c.* 1840.

[1] K. Singh, *Ranjit Singh*, 54.

Inscribed on reverse in *nāgarī* and Telegu characters; and in English in two hands:

Maha Raja Runjeet Sing (writer A)

*died. Was succeeded by his son Cardagoo Sing who died after reigning about 14 months.
His son Nownnee all Sing was killed on the day of his Father's death, in returning from
the Funeral by the fall of a Beam in one of the Gateways of Lahore, suspected to have
been affected by his Enemies. There followed a Regency of about 6 months when Runjeet
Sing's widow Shana Cour exercises the Supreme Power, Dyang Sing being Prime
Minister. Shere Sing a reputed Son of Runjeet Sing then succeed to the throne, putting
to death Shanacour shortly after his succession. He with his Prime Minister Dyang Sing
was killed by Adjeet Sing in August 1843, together with the whole of the Wives and
family of Runjeet Sing. Adjeet Sing was in his turn killed by Heera Sing the son of the
old Minister Dyang Sing by whom Dulheeb Sing, a child of 7 years of age and son of
one of Rajah Sing's Wives was placed on the Throne, Heera Sing being Prime Minister.
Dulheeb Sing's Mother's name is Jhinda a great beauty and his father is said to be a
Musulman. Dulheeb is on the Throne* (Writer B).

Formerly owned by Joshi Shankar Nath ('writer A'; astrologer to Ranjit
Singh) from whom it passed to J. D. Sims ('writer B'; Indian Civil Service,
Madras 1842–1875) and thence to Mr and Mrs T. W. F. Scott, Kensington.

Note: See p. 74.

Ranjit Singh's posture in this picture recalls Osborne's description:

'Cross-legged in a golden chair, dressed in simple white, wearing no ornaments but a single string of enormous pearls round the waist, and the celebrated Koh-y-nur, or mountain of light, on his arm—the jewel rivalled, if not
surpassed, in brilliancy by the glance of fire which every now and then shot
from his single eye as it wandered restlessly round the circle—sat the lion of
Lahore.'[1]

(2) *Fig. 26.* Maharaja Ranjit Singh. Lithograph after an original drawing by
Emily Eden, Lahore, December 1838. Published: Emily Eden, *Portraits of the
Princes and People of India* (London, 1844), pl. 13.

Emily Eden was greatly charmed by Ranjit Singh and appended the following comment to this plate: 'He retained a perfect simplicity or rather plainness
of appearance, while his chiefs and courtiers around him wore the most brilliant
draperies and a rich profusion of jewels. His manners were always quiet. . . . He
had a curious and constant trick, while sitting and engaged in conversation, of
raising one of his legs under him on the chair, which he used in compliance
with the customs of his European visitors, and then pulling off the stocking

[1] Osborne, *Court and Camp*, 93.

130

from that foot. He had the use only of one eye, which age and a hard life of exposure and excesses had dimmed at the period now spoken of, but it still retained the traces of the vigour and penetration for which he was remarkable.'

(*3*) *Fig. 25*. Maharaja Ranjit Singh seated in a chair, Raja Dhian Singh standing before him. Sikh, Punjab Plains, *c*. 1845.
Archaeological Museum, Bikaner, Rajasthan, 738–56.
Note: The posture of Ranjit Singh is modelled in reverse on the drawing (figure 26) by Emily Eden.

8. *Fig. 20*. Raja Hira Singh (*c*. 1816–1844). Sikh, Punjab Plains, *c*. 1838–1840.
Size: 209 × 143 mm; with border 268 × 202 mm.
Margin dark blue with white and red rules, Guler-Kangra type floral scroll in white and gold; border pink, flecked with red.
Inscribed on flap in English (same hand as in no. 5): *Rajah Heera Singh*: and in *nāgarī* characters: *srī rāja hīrā singhājī kī.*
Formerly in the collection of Lord Auckland (Governor-General of India 1836–1842) and brought by him to England in 1842. Given to the Victoria and Albert Museum by Auckland's great-nephew, O. E. Dickinson. From the same collection as nos. 5, 6, 7, 9, 10 and 11.
Victoria and Albert Museum, I.S. 115–1953.

Description: Hira Singh, in slate blue turban, green wrap, white coat and orange trousers, is seated in a chair on a terrace with a dark green carpet edged with pink and patterned with floral motifs in white, red and pale green. He faces right. An attendant in white dress and green turban stands before him. White balustrades, orange canopy. Background greyish white with a patch of blue sky and clouds at the top.

Comment on character:

As boy-favourite of Ranjit Singh from about 1826 to 1839 Hira Singh attracted much attention. See Osborne, *Court and Camp*, 77–78, quoted pages 35–36.
Of his later career (1843–1844) as chief minister to the child Maharaja Dalip Singh, McGregor records:
'Heera Singh had succeeded his father as prime minister. He had been the especial favorite of the Maharajah Runjeet Singh. He was always near him, and allowed to be seated in his presence, an honour denied to even Dhyan Singh. In appearance, he was rather effeminate, and did not resemble his father, who

131

was a fine, tall, powerful man. Little of energy was expected from him, but his first act showed that his intercourse with Runjeet Singh had conferred advantages on Heera Singh which made up for any deficiency in natural talents. His measures were prudent and such as the crisis demanded. He had utterly destroyed the powerful family of the Scindinwalas who had murdered his father, and cherished a deep-rooted hatred to Shere Singh, which however had been smothered for a time by the favours lavished on the members of it by the Maharajah. But Heera Singh had injudicious and interested advisers, and it was soon discovered that a Pundit named Julla possessed an entire influence over the Rajah, who followed the advice of this cunning Hindoo in all matters of state. In order to reconcile the army and render it subservient to his wishes, Heera Singh was obliged to make promises which he could not possibly fulfil. The Treasury was exhausted, and the more he bestowed on an idle and discontented soldiery the greater were its demands. Discontent followed, and the Rajah, no longer able to stem the march of anarchy, endeavoured to escape, but it was too late, he was pursued and both he and his favourite Pundit were killed.'[1]

Note: In figure 62, Pandit Jalla is the person seated next to Hira Singh.

Portrait for comparison:

(*1*) *Fig. 35.* Raja Dhian Singh (1796–1843) seated on a terrace facing, right to left, Maharaja Kharak Singh (1802–1840), Nau Nihal Singh (1821–1840) and Hira Singh (*c.* 1816–1844). Sikh, Punjab Plains, *c.* 1840.

Inscribed on reverse in Telegu characters; and in English by two different hands, the first (writer A) being the same as the writer of the notes in Telegu, the other (writer B) continuing the notes with further comments

(1) *Raja Dana Sing* (writer A)
or *Deyan Sing—the prime minister of Runjeet Sing and afterwards of Shere Sing and killed with him by Adjeet Sing* (writer B).

(2) *Maharaja Kadga Sing* (writer A)
or *Cadooga Sing. Son of Runjeet Sing, succeeded him and died after a reign of 14 months* (writer B).

(3) *Son Noumee Hall Sing* (writer A)
Son of Cadooga Sing, succeeded him, but was killed in returning from the funeral of his father, on the day of his accession, by the fall of a beam of a gateway (writer B).

(4) *Raja Dana Sing Son Hera Sing* (writer A)
Raja Dana Sing or Deyan Sing, the Prime Minister of Runjeet Sing and afterwards of Sher Sing, along with whom he was assassinated by Adjeet Sing. His son Hera Sing is

[1]McGregor, *History*, II, 25–26.

now Prime Minister of Dulheb Sing, a child of 7 years of age, now on the Throne (writer B).

Formerly owned by Joshi Shankar Nath ('writer A'; astrologer to Ranjit Singh); from whom it passed to J. D. Sims (writer 'B'; Indian Civil Service, Madras, 1842–1875) and thence to Mr and Mrs T. W. F. Scott, Kensington.

Note: For a discussion of Joshi Shankar Nath, Sims and 'writers A and B', see pages 33–34, 37 and Note X, page 74.

The present picture clearly distinguishes Hira Singh (figures 19, 20 and 29) from Nau Nihal Singh (figures 24, 32).

While each possesses a slightly beaked nose, the head of Hira Singh in profile is flat and broad, that of Nau Nihal is high and narrow.

9. *Fig. 21.* Maharaja Kharak Singh (1802–1840) on horseback. Sikh, *c.* 1838–1840.
Size: 205 × 127 mm; with borders 260 × 183 mm.

Dark blue margin with thin white rules, pattern as in no. 5; border pink, flecked with red.

Inscribed on flap in English (same hand as in no. 5): *Rajah Khurruck Singh.*

Formerly in the collection of Lord Auckland (Governor-General of India 1836–1842) and brought by him to England in 1842. Given to the Victoria and Albert Museum by Auckland's great-nephew, O. E. Dickinson. From the same collection as nos. 5, 6, 7, 8, 10 and 11.

Victoria and Albert Museum, I.S. 113–1953.

Description: Kharak Singh, in yellow turban, dark green coat, white dress and green trousers rides a white stallion with dark red saddlecloth edged with gold. He faces left. An attendant in white with reddish-brown turban and red trousers, carries above him a dark red umbrella patterned with white spots. Foreground green, stippled. Background pale blue. From the same series and workshop as no. 5.

Comments on character:

Contemporary accounts are unanimous in stressing Kharak Singh's weak mentality and character.

Osborne, after meeting Ranjit Singh, wrote on 2 July 1838: 'Kurruck Sing, his son and heir, was with him this morning. He is the worst looking of the Sikhs I have yet seen, and if report speaks true, is little better than an imbecile; but of this I had no opportunity of personally judging. His manners, however, appear to be awkward and unconciliatory, and he is but little liked or respected in the Punjab.'[1]

Four months later (28 November 1838) his aunt, Emily Eden, recorded much the same opinion: 'Kurruck Singh is apparently an idiot; some people say he only affects it, to keep Runjeet from being jealous of him, but it looks like very unaffected and complete folly.'[2]

On the events following Ranjit Singh's death on 27 June 1839, the succession of Kharak Singh and his brief reign, McGregor and Latif give sharply differing accounts.

McGregor concedes Kharak's limitations but tends to view him with pitying charity: 'The immediate successor of Runjeet Singh was his eldest son, Khurruk Singh, who possessed none of his father's qualifications for rule, though resembling him strongly in feature; and it was soon apparent that Nonehal Singh, the son to the heir of the throne of Lahore, would be, in reality, the Ruler of the Punjab. . . . The first act of the new ruler (Khurruk) was an unpopular one and gave great dissatisfaction. Instead of allowing the Rajah Dhyan Singh to remain as Wuzeer or prime minister, he raised a creature of his own to that high appointment. This man, named Chet Singh, had nothing to recommend him but arrogance and sycophancy. His good fortune was of short duration. Dhyan Singh, at the instigation, it was supposed, of Shere Singh, entered the Durbar and slew the prime minister before his master's eyes. After this act of violence, Khurruk Singh shut himself up; and, though he occasionally attended the Durbar, he never forgave the insult. His intellect, never very powerful, became impaired, and the management of public affairs thus fell into the hands of Nonehal Singh, who had always shown a dislike to the British, and now made preparations in the vicinity of Lahore for hostilities against that power. After a short reign of a little more than twelve months, Khurruk Singh died of a broken heart.'[3]

In comparison, Latif is almost brutally harsh: 'The funeral solemnities of Ranjit Singh being over, Kharak Singh, his eldest legitimate son, ascended the throne and was acknowledged Maharaja of the Panjab. He was a man of weak intellect, and was more addicted to opium than his father. He was in the habit of taking the drug twice a day, and passed the whole of the time in a state of semi-inebriety. Physiognomically he was the counterpart of his royal sire, but he possessed none of his diplomatic qualifications. One Chet Singh, who had hardly anything to recommend him but arrogance and sycophancy, attained such an ascendancy over the weak mind of the new Maharaja that

[1] Osborne, *Court and Camp*, 192–193.
[2] Eden, *Up the Country*, 197.   [3] McGregor, *History*, II, 4–5.

he became a mere puppet in his hands. One of Kharak Singh's first acts was to deprive Raja Dhian Singh and his son, Hira Singh, of the privilege of free admission into the king's zenana, so that the minister was unable to make important representations on State affairs privately to the king. Chet Singh was raised to the dignity of wazir, and a plot was made to assassinate Dhian Singh. Chet Singh lived in the fortress with his master, Kharak Singh, and had recently raised two battalions of bodyguards, with whom he conspired to despatch Dhian Singh one morning as he entered the fort. The plot was known to Dhian Singh, who succeeded not only in preventing the accomplishment of the treacherous act, but, having won over Kanwar Nau Nehal Singh to his side, revenged himself on Chet Singh so completely that all his plans were frustrated, and he himself met a melancholy and fatal end.

A rumour was set afloat that Kharak Singh had formed a league with the British Government and had consented to acknowledge their supremacy, to pay a tax of six annas per rupee, to disband the Sikh army, and to do away with the sardars, who were to be replaced by English officers. This rumour was soon circulated through the town, and became the chief topic of conversation in the markets and streets. The civil and military freely vented their indignation at this supposed treacherous compact. Kharak Singh was openly calumniated, and the soldiery began to look upon him as a traitor, unworthy of his position. Nau Nehal Singh, who for some time before his father's accession to the throne resided at Peshawar, was hastily recalled, together with Raja Gulab Singh. He entered the city the avowed enemy of his father. So strong was the feeling against Kharak Singh that even his wife, Chand Kour, the mother of Nau Nehal Singh, became his bitterest enemy, and gave her full consent and connivance to her husband's dethronement.'[1]

There follows a vivid account of Chet Singh's murder on 8 October 1839, Kharak Singh's abdication and the confinement and ill-treatment of him by Nau Nihal. As a result of these measures, Latif adds:

'Kharak Singh's intellect became impaired, and, broken-hearted and afflicted by the revolting and insulting conduct of his only son, he lingered on a bed of sickness for some nine months, suffering from colic, during which time his son showed the greatest possible indifference in regard to his treatment, and, with the design of hastening his end, committed him to the care of specially appointed quacks and mountebanks, who had their own parts to play in the tragedy.'[2]

Note: Unlike his father, Ranjit Singh, who was rarely portrayed facing left owing to the blindness in his left eye, Kharak Singh was shown in Sikh

[1] Latif, *History*, 497.   [2] *Ibid.*, 499.

portraits facing either left or right. In further contrast to his father, his beard was also always shown black.

10. *Fig. 24.* Raja Nau Nihal Singh (1821–1840) in a chair with Raja Dhian Singh (1796–1843), seated on the ground before him. Sikh, Punjab Plains, *c.* 1840.

Size: 203 × 146 mm; with border 257 × 198 mm.

Margin dark blue with white and red rules and Guler-Kangra type floral scrolls in white and gold; border pink, flecked with red.

Inscribed on flap in English (same hand as no. 5): *Now Nahal Singh & Raja Dhen Singh.*

Formerly in the collection of Lord Auckland (Governor-General of India 1836–1842) and brought by him to England in 1842. Given to the Victoria and Albert Museum by Auckland's great-nephew, O. E. Dickinson. From the same collection as nos. 5, 6, 7, 8, 9 and 11.

Victoria and Albert Museum, I.S. 116–1953.

Description: Nau Nihal Singh, son of Kharak Singh, in white turban, coat and wrap and with green trousers is seated in a gold chair. He faces left and holds a pink flower. Dhian Singh sits on the ground before him on an oval rug, dark green with golden edge. He wears white, except for yellow trousers. A bow is in his right hand. Terrace carpet dark red with green, blue and white floral motifs. White arch and balustrade. Pale green background with an orange blind edged with yellow. In the centre a shrub with white flowers. Style and composition, similar to no. 7.

Comments on character:

For Nau Nihal Singh's relations with his father, Kharak, see comment to no. 9.

McGregor describes his character and sudden death, the day after his father's, as follows: 'All eyes were now turned towards the favourite of the Sikhs, the grandson of their great ruler, whom he resembled in features and disposition. He was popular with the army, for he had been a soldier from his boyhood, and was of a brave and indomitable spirit, united, at the same time, to great caution, discretion, and forethought. Runjeet Singh was very proud of Nonehal, and fondly anticipated that in him the Sikhs would find a successor worthy of filling the throne of Lahore, and preserving his kingdom entire. But this fond hope was not destined to be realized. Nonehal Singh, on return-ing from the obsequies of his father, was killed by a stone falling on his head from one of the gateways of Lahore, while passing under it in his howdah. Oodum Singh, the eldest son of Rajah Goolab Singh, of Jummoo, who was on the same elephant, shared the same fate.'[1]

Latif queries this account and gives the following version of the accident: 'The news of Kharak Singh's death was conveyed to the prince at his favourite hunting-ground in Shah Bilawal, in the environs of Lahore, where he was at the time engaged in a shooting-party. He received the intelligence with open demonstrations of joy, and did not even condescend to leave his amusement for the full space of two hours after the tidings first reached him, when orders were quietly passed for the performance of Kharak Singh's funeral obsequies.

Two of Kharak Singh's ranis and eleven of his slave-girls burnt themselves alive on his funeral pile. The ceremony took place in the open space opposite the *samadh* of Maharaja Ranjit Singh, in the presence of Nau Nehal Singh and the Court. The young Maharaja appeared to look on with the utmost *sang froid*, and before the body of his father was half consumed, he retired from the scene, accompanied by his sardars, with whom he bathed in a nallah, a short distance from the pyre, the elephants and other paraphernalia of royalty following close behind. The party were not mounted, ostensibly out of reverence for the dead monarch. Having bathed, the prince with his suite made his way back to the fort. As he approached the archway of the northern gate of the Hazuri Bagh, close to the *samadh*, he took the hand of Mian Udham Singh, the eldest son of Gulab Singh and nephew of Dhian Singh. They continued walking on slowly, the prince making some humorous remarks to his companion, quite unconscious of the fateful moment which awaited him. As both entered the archway, a loud crash was heard, and it was found that a fragment of the upper wall had fallen and crushed the two young men, who were walking close under it.'[2]

Note: An inscription on figure 28 (Maharaja Ranjit Singh cross-legged on a throne) alleges that the fall from the archway was 'suspected to have been affected by his enemies'.

11. *Fig. 30.* Raja Dhian Singh (1796–1843). Sikh, Punjab Plains, *c.* 1838–1840.
Size: 185 × 102 mm; with border 236 × 155 mm.
Margin dark blue with white oval-and-stroke pattern as in no. 3; border pink with red rules.
Inscribed on flap in English (same hand as in no. 5): *Rajah Dhen Singh.*
Formerly in the collection of Lord Auckland (Governor-General of India 1836–1842) and brought by him to England in 1842. Given to the Victoria and

[1] McGregor, *History*, II, 5–6. [2] Latif, *History*, 499–500.

Albert Museum by Auckland's great-nephew, O. E. Dickinson. From the same collection as nos. 5–10.

Victoria and Albert Museum, I.S. 117–1953–1840.

Description: Raja Dhian Singh in red turban and trousers, white coat and yellow wrap is seated on a golden chair facing left. A black shield is on his back. He holds a pink flower in his right hand. Terrace carpet pale yellow with blue pattern. A bunch of grapes and a melon are on a dish. White balustrade. Background pale blue.

Portraits for comparison: Figures 23, 24, 30, 33 and 35.

12. *Fig. 22.* Kharak Singh (1802–1840). Sikh, Punjab Plains, *c.* 1835–1840.

Size: 143 × 84 mm; with border 202 × 142 mm.

Margin dark blue with small round blobs in white and gold; border pink with red rules.

Inscribed on reverse in pencil in English: *Cadooga Sing Maharajah.*

Victoria and Albert Museum, Sir William Rothenstein collection, I.S. 338–1951.

Note: 'R' and 'k' are pronounced in the Punjab like the English letters 'd' and 'g'. 'Kharak' thus becomes 'Khadag', or, as in the present case, 'Cadooga'. For a similar spelling of Kharak Singh, see inscriptions on a Sikh series in the T. W. F. Scott collection, London, figures 28 and 35.

Description: Kharak Singh in a dark green coat speckled with gold, green turban and black beard, sits in a gold chair beneath an arch on a white terrace. He holds a rose in his right hand and faces left. Flat red background with pale band of white and blue at the top.

Comment: The fact that the inscription refers to Kharak Singh as 'Maharaja' suggests that the picture was obtained after his accession in June 1839, but possibly before his death on 5 November 1840. Its date of execution would therefore be not later than 1840. The red Guler-style background, an unusual feature in Sikh portraits, suggests that the painter was at the time a comparatively new arrival from Guler. If the sitter is taken to be in his thirties and the portrait contemporary, its likely date is between 1835 and 1840.

Portraits for comparison: Figures 21 and 35.

13. *Fig. 23.* Raja Suchet Singh (1801–1844) seated with Raja Dhian Singh (1796–1843). Sikh, Punjab Plains, *c.* 1840.

    Size: 206×151 mm; border trimmed away.

    Inscribed on reverse with three couplets in Persian.

    Victoria and Albert Museum, I.S. 264–1953. Given by Robert Skelton.

Description: Raja Dhian Singh in orange trousers and white dress edged with crimson, sits on a terrace facing left. He leans against a green cushion. His younger brother, Raja Suchet Singh, is seated opposite him in dark yellow turban, yellow dress and trousers and orange wrap. White balustrade. Carpet dark green, patterned with floral motifs in white, red and pale green and edged with pink. Pale blue background streaked with white. On either side is a frail tree with pink flowers.

    Portraits of Dhian Singh for comparison: Figures 24, 25, 30, 35.

14. *Fig. 27.* Maharaja Ranjit Singh (1780–1839). Sikh, Punjab Plains, *c.* 1840.

    Size: 203×134 mm; with border 261×197 mm.

    Margin dark blue; border pink, flecked with red; red rules.

    Inscribed on the flap in English: *Maharaja Ranjeet Singh but not a very good likeness.*

    Formerly in the collection of Queen Mary. With nos. 15, 16, 17 and 18 given by Queen Mary to the Victoria and Albert Museum, 1936. I.M. 56–1936.

Description: Ranjit Singh, dressed entirely in green, bestrides a white stallion with red fetlocks. He faces right. Crimson saddle-cloth edged with yellow. An attendant in white vest with orange turban and drawers and yellow scarf bears a crimson umbrella over him. Green foreground. Background pale greyish blue. At the top blue sky.

Comment: Similar in style and composition to no. 6 with which Ranjit Singh himself tallies. Inscriptions on nos. 15 and 16 from the same group (*Maharaja Kharak Singh son of Ranjeet Singh and nominal ruler of the Panjab*; and *Kunwar Nao Nahal Singh grandson and the virtual ruler of the Panjab*) suggest that the first British owner acquired the series between October 1839 when Nau Nihal deposed his father and November 1840 when he died. Its likely date would, therefore, be 1840.

15. *Fig. 31.* Maharajah Kharak Singh (1802–1840). Sikh, Punjab Plains, *c.* 1840.

Size: 157 × 100 mm; with border 208 × 152 mm.

Margin dark blue with continuous creeper pattern in white; pink border with red rules.

Inscribed on the flap in English (in same hand as no. 14): *Maharaja Kharak Singh son of Ranjeet Singh and nominal ruler of the Panjab.*

Formerly in the collection of Queen Mary. With nos. 14, 16, 17 and 18 given by Queen Mary to the Victoria and Albert Museum, 1936. I.M. 57–1936.

Description: Kharak Singh in orange turban, yellow vest and trousers and green coat is seated left leg crossed on an oval rug against an orange cushion edged with green. The rug is mauve with pale yellow border. He holds a short sword, point downwards, in his left hand. Terrace floor pink, white balustrades. Whitish blue background; the whole set in an orange oval rim.

Comment: From the same standard portrait set as no. 16.

16. *Fig. 32.* Nau Nihal Singh (1821–1840). Sikh, Punjab Plains, *c.* 1840.

Size: 155 × 102 mm; with border 208 × 154 mm.

Margin dark blue with continuous creeper pattern in white; pink border with red rules.

Inscribed on the flap in English (in same hand as no. 14): *Kunwar Nao Nahal Singh grandson and the virtual ruler of the Panjab.*

Formerly in the collection of Queen Mary. With nos. 14, 15, 17 and 18 given by Queen Mary to the Victoria and Albert Museum, 1936. I.M. 58–1936.

Description: A companion picture to no. 15; comparable in pose and composition. The oval rug, however, is deep blue rimmed with bright yellow; Nau Nihal wears a green turban, yellow trousers, yellow scarf and mauve coat; his right arm is outside the sleeve and his left hand rests on his left knee. Terrace, background and oval orange rim as in no. 15. Each faces right. Small-pox marks on Nau Nihal's face clearly discernible.

Comment on character:

MCGREGOR

'Nonehal Singh is not a handsome man; for his countenance, like that of his grandfather, is strongly marked by the small-pox, yet there is a steady, determined look about him, which points him out as a person likely at some future period to emulate the present ruler of the Panjab and though Khurruk Singh will, no doubt, ascend the throne on the death of his father, it seems very doubtful how long he will be able to retain it.'[1]

17. *Fig. 33.* Raja Dhian Singh (1796–1843) on horseback. Sikh, Punjab Plains, *c.* 1840.

Size: 175 × 133 mm; with border 225 × 184 mm.

Margin dark blue with continuous creeper pattern in white as in nos. 15 and 16; pink border flecked with red.

Inscribed on the flap in English (same hand as no. 14). *Raja Dhian Singh the nominal minister and favourite of Ranjeet Singh.*

Formerly in the collection of Queen Mary. With nos. 14, 15, 16 and 18 given by Queen Mary to the Victoria and Albert Museum, 1936. I.M. 59–1936.

Description: Raja Dhian Singh in white dress, green turban, green trousers and orange wrap—a black shield on his back—bestrides a chestnut stallion with black fetlocks. He faces left. Red saddle-cloth with gold and grey surrounds. An attendant in orange turban, white vest and yellow trousers holds a red umbrella above him. Green foreground and hummocks. Pale bluish white background.

Comment: Closely similar in style to figure 34.

Portraits for comparison: Figures 9, 23, 24, 25, 30, 35.

Note: For a companion portrait of his elder brother Gulab Singh on horseback, see figure 34. The two brothers can be distinguished by the following marked differences: nose pronouncedly beaked, beard short, square, and with tip up-tilted (Gulab Singh), beard long, and flowing (Dhian Singh).

18. *Fig. 29.* Hira Singh (*c.* 1816–1844). Sikh, Punjab Plains, *c.* 1840.

Size: 175 × 133 mm; with border 225 × 184 mm.

Margin dark blue as in no. 15; border pink, flecked with red; red rules.

Inscribed on flap in English (in same hand as no. 14): *Raja Heera Singh son of Dhian Singh.*

Formerly in the collection of Queen Mary. With nos. 15, 16 and 17 given by Queen Mary to the Victoria and Albert Museum, 1936. I.M. 60–1936.

[1] McGregor, *History*, I, 252.

Description: Hira Singh in white vest, crimson trousers and slate blue turban and wrap—a black shield on his back—sits cross-legged on a dark green carpet leaning against an orange cushion edged with yellow. He faces right. Two pillows in orange, edged with yellow lie beside him. He holds a flower in his left hand. Pale whitish blue background. A single white balustrade.

Portraits for comparison: Figures 19, 20 and 62.

19. *Fig. 36.* Sikh sardar, perhaps Lehna Singh Majithia, receiving petitions. Sikh, Punjab Plains, *c.* 1840.

Size: 247 × 211 mm; with border 308 × 272 mm.

Margin dark blue with Guler-Kangra type floral scroll in white and gold, black rules; border pink flecked with red; red rules.

Inscribed in pencil on left border in *gurmukhi* characters: *ram chanda bhuti*
Victoria and Albert Museum, I.S. 43–1960.

Note: The pencil inscription seems to be corrupt.

Description: A Sikh sardar in white turban, white dress and yellow trousers—a black shield strapped to his back—sits on a carpeted terrace facing left. He holds a rosary in his hands. To the left is a secretary with white beard, reading out a petition, and marking the place with a reed-pen. Beside him on the carpet are a yellow pen-case and cloth bag used for keeping documents. In the bottom left-hand corner are ten soldiers in red, blue, green and yellow, handing up petitions. Red carpet with blue, green, white and yellow floral pattern. White balustrades and archway. Orange blind with green border. Pale green background with white and pale blue sky at the top. On either side two trees—one with thick branches and dark foliage, the other with frail branches and pink flowers.

Comment: In style, clearly related to figure 19 with which it shares similar balustrades, carpet, archway, blind, background and a tree with pink flowers. A noteworthy detail is the dark tree on the left where leaves are shown like blunt fingers outlined with white prickles. This idiom also occurs in a *Bhāgavata Purāna* series, author's collection and in figure 35.

For an inscribed portrait of Lehna Singh Majithia closely resembling the present figure in nose, lips, eyes and features, see Punjab Museum, Chandigarh, collection received on transfer from Lahore (Gupta, *Catalogue of Paintings in the Central Museum, Lahore,* 49).

The case for regarding this picture as a portrait of Lehna Singh Majithia is argued at pages 20–21.

20. *Fig. 37.* Maharaja Gulab Singh (1792–1857) of Jammu taking his bath prior to doing worship. Sikh, Punjab Plains, *c.* 1835.

Size: 210×242 mm; with border 268×302 mm.

Dark blue margin with Guler-Kangra floral scrolls in grey and gold, black rules. Border pink flecked with red.

Victoria and Albert Museum, P. C. Manuk and Miss G. M. Coles collection, I.S. 37–1949.

Description: Gulab Singh, bare save for a white *dhoti*, stands on a footstool in an open room backed by a terrace with views of flowering trees, a river and low hills. A boy servant in yellow vest and drawers pours water on his shoulders. Behind them, to the left, are four other servants—one, in the foreground, fills a pitcher with water, a second holds a white cloth, a third carries a sword and black shield, a fourth fetches a basket of clothes. On the right are laid out the ingredients of *pūjā* (worship). They include brass vessels, a small stool, supporting a basket containing a flower garland, and a second stool on which is laid a jewelled casket enclosing a *shālagrām* (a black oval stone sacred to Vishnu) adorned with a tiny crimson umbrella. A *gomukha* (an L-shaped cloth bag containing a rosary) is set out on a yellow pillow. In the foreground a *pūjārī* (priest) prepares sandal-wood paste, while, in the background, a second priest sits waiting in an alcove, some sticks of incense burning beside him. Clothes, predominantly white and yellow, a few of them pink and bluish green. Terrace floor pale grey. Two baskets, one top left, the other, centre foreground, dark red.

Comment: For Gulab Singh's practice of eating alone after taking his bath, see Honigberger's account quoted in the text, page 54.

For notes on Gulab Singh's character, see pages 52–56. Like his brothers, Dhian and Suchet, Gulab Singh wore Sikh dress but adhered to the Rajput religion.

Portraits for comparison:

(1) *Fig. 34.* Gulab Singh on horseback. Sikh, Punjab Plains, *c.* 1840–1845. Inscribed on fly-leaf in Persian characters: *srī rāja mahārāja bahādur gulāb singh* and in English: *Maharaja Golab Sing.*

India Office Library, London, Add. Or. 707.

From the private papers of Herbert Edwardes, Assistant to Henry Lawrence, Lahore, 1847 to 1848.

Note: For further portraits, see figures 15, 34, 50, 52, 53, 55, 57.

21. *Fig. 46.* A Hill prince smoking, attended by a group in Sikh dress. Sikh, Punjab Plains, *c.* 1840.

Size: 229×275 mm; with margin 237×292 mm.

Margin dark blue with cursive scroll in gold, white rules; border trimmed away. Upper portion rubbed and damaged.

Inscribed at top in *nāgarī* characters: *durathāīān phate chanda katocha.* (The audience (?) of Fateh Chand Katoch.)

Victoria and Albert Museum, Sir William Rothenstein collection, I.S. 193–1951.

Description: A Hill prince in white turban, white dress and orange-red trousers sits smoking a hookah before six visitors. Two are standing, the remaining four sit on a dark green rug. The foremost visitor leans against a large brownish yellow cushion edged with green. Below him is a large oval rug in blue with yellow surround. Behind him is an attendant in white waving a white cloth. Background orange brown with pale blue band at the top. Above the gathering is a red canopy edged with green. Since the prince is smoking, it is likely that his visitors are Rajputs but in Sikh dress.

Comment: With nos. 22–25, part of a distinctive group of pictures collected by Sir William Rothenstein, characterised by inscriptions with hints of Kangra and Jammu affiliations, a large-scale treatment of heads and cushions and the use of large oval rugs. They are perhaps the work of Kangra-Sikh painters at Lahore—a surmise which would account for the presence of Sikh costume, the tendency to enlargement (a Kangra fashion in the period 1820 to 1830) and the mysterious blending of seemingly unrelated subjects.

The inscription in the present case—identifying the subject as Fateh Chand (brother of Raja Sansar Chand of Kangra) is unacceptable since Fateh Chand had different features and also wore different styles of turban. (See M. S. Randhawa, 'Maharaja Sansar Chand: the patron of Kangra painting', *Roopa Lekha* (1961), XXXII, no. 2, page 10, figure 18.) The subject may, none the less, be a member of the Kangra royal house. Ludar Chand, son of Fateh Chand, gave his daughter to Hira Singh (boy favourite of Ranjit Singh) on the occasion of the Kangra marriage fiasco of 1828 and, like his father, was *persona grata* with the Sikhs (see page 24 above). In this view, the writer of the inscription may have correctly connected the sitter with Kangra but perhaps confused father and son.

22. *Fig. 47.* A Hill prince smoking, Sikh, Punjab Plains. *c.* 1840.

Size: 220×155 mm; border trimmed away.

Uninscribed. Faded and discoloured.

Victoria and Albert Museum, Sir William Rothenstein collection, I.S. 190–1951.

Description: A Hill prince in blue turban and wrap, white vest and yellow drawers, sits smoking a hookah on a terrace floor. He leans against a white cushion edged with green and sits on a large oval rug, orange red with yellow surround. He faces left. In front of him squats a hookah-bearer and behind him stands an attendant waving a white cloth. Grey background. White balustrade and archway.

Comment: In appearance similar to the subject of no. 21. The turban in Sikh style implies close association with the Sikh court though the hookah is once again an obstinate relic of Rajput customs.

The vast oval rug and general posture connect the picture in style with nos. 21, 23, 24 and 25.

23. *Fig. 48.* A Hill prince seated. Sikh, Punjab Plains, *c.* 1840.

Size: 168×124 mm; with margin 175×131 mm.

Margin dark blue with white rule; border trimmed away.

Inscribed on reverse in English: *(13) Raja Sansar Chand of Kangra Valley. Three. £1/2/–*; and in Persian characters: *rāja sansar chand.*

Victoria and Albert Museum, Sir William Rothenstein collection, I.S. 189–1951.

Description: A Hill prince in mauve dress and turban with green trousers and orange-red waistband sits on a terrace floor facing left. He leans against a large green cushion and holds in his right hand a bow. At his waist, a sword in blue scabbard. In the foreground an orange-red pillow. White balustrades. Terrace carpet ivory with minute floral pattern, in green and red. Mauve edge. Pale blue background with archway at the top.

Comment: Despite the inscription, which may have been written by a dealer, the subject bears little resemblance to Raja Sansar Chand (1775–1823) of Kangra (see Randhawa, *op. cit.* especially figures 24 and 28). Some connection with the Kangra family, however, may be possible, and in that case Mian Ranbir Chand, son of Raja Anirudh Chand and grandson of Sansar Chand, may be considered. Following his father's death in 1833, he made overtures to Ranjit Singh, and was granted an estate, which he held until his death in 1847. The bow, held firmly in the right hand, is perhaps a flattering tribute to the family's

145

previous royal status. For the gift of a bow as a mark of respect, see Burnes, *Travels*.

24. *Fig. 51.* Prince in Sikh costume seated on a chair. Sikh, Punjab Plains, *c.* 1840.

    Size: 245 × 170 mm; with margin 263 × 189 mm.

    Dark blue margin with white rule; border trimmed away.

    Inscribed on reverse in English (in same hand as in no. 23): *Old Maharaja of Ponch. Rs 35/– £2/–/–*

    Victoria and Albert Museum, Sir William Rothenstein collection, I.S. 192–1951.

Description: A young man in white coat and turban with yellow scarf and orange-red trousers sits in a black chair. He holds a long sword in a green scabbard. He faces left—a black shield on his back. On the floor is a white carpet with large floral patterns in green, blue and red, blue surround, white archway. To the rear a grey wall with door—a grey blind tied up above it and beyond it a pale blue background.

Comment: In appearance the sitter bears a strong resemblance to Raja Gulab Singh of Jammu, especially in the unusually long and hooked nose (see figures 52 and 55). His age, however, can hardly be more than twenty-five and since Gulab Singh was born in 1792 the picture if contemporary would need to have been painted in about 1820. This seems far too early a date and it is perhaps more reasonable to treat it as a later portrait, commemorating Gulab Singh's youthful entry into Ranjit Singh's service.

    Punch was acquired by the Sikhs in 1819, held by Dhian Singh (Gulab's brother) until 1843 and absorbed by Gulab Singh in 1846. This may account for the inscription, which as in no. 23, seems to be by a dealer.

25. *Fig. 50.* Maharaja Gulab Singh (1792–1857) of Jammu and Kashmir. Sikh, Lahore, *c.* 1846.

    Size: 270 × 209 mm; with black border trimmed away in places, 297 × 234 mm.

    Victoria and Albert Museum, Sir William Rothenstein collection, I.S. 194–1951.

Reproduced: L. Heath, *Examples of Indian Art* (London, 1925), pl. 10; W. G. Archer, 'Sir William Rothenstein and Indian Art', *Art and Letters* (1951), XXV, no. 1, pl. 7; K. Khandalavala, *Pahari Miniature Painting* (Bombay, 1958), no. 306; W. G. Archer, *Indian Miniatures* (New York, London, 1960), pl. 98; P. S. Rawson, *Indian Painting* (Paris, London, 1961), page 147 (col.); G. Lawrence, *Indian Art: Paintings of the Himalayan States* (Paris, London, 1963), pl. 15 (col.).

Description: Gulab Singh, a massive figure clothed in a white dress edged with green and gold, sits kneeling on a terrace carpet of pale yellow flecked with leaf patterns and triple-petalled flowers—the petals blue, the flower centres red. He wears a multi-coloured turban composed of white, green, gold and orange-red bands. His large knees, covered in orange-red trousers, protrude beneath the long sword in dark green scabbard which he holds hilt upwards in his left hand. He leans against a massive pink cushion with green spots and green ends. His right hand, holding a sprig of flowers appears from behind, revealing that the cushion is tucked between his right arm and side. A large black shield, reinforcing the effect of brutal might, is loosely strapped to his back. Face, three-quarter view, the eyes glancing searchingly to the left. Blue background.

Comment: Part of a group which has, in common, idioms such as a pale terrace carpet flecked with leaf and flower patterns (figures 48, 51, 58), a long sword (figures 48, 51, 58), a shield on the back (figure 51), a great cushion (figures 46, 48, 51) and jagged angular edges to the dress (figure 58). In style a Sikh continuation of Kangra painting of the 1820 to 1830 period (compare Archer, *Kangra Painting*, pl. 8), but obtaining greater strength and vigour through massive simplification. As in figure 57, the face is keenly rendered with acute insight into character and sensitivity to detail.

The great head (the largest in Sikh miniature painting), the bold arresting pose and strong compulsive rhythm can be paralleled in Emily Eden's *Portraits of the Princes and People of India*, especially pl. 7, portrait of Hira Singh (present figure 49). This book, a collection of lithographs based on original drawings, some of them made in December 1838, was published in London in 1844. Copies must doubtless have reached Lahore through British missions in 1845 (as is shown by figure 25, a Sikh portrait in gouache repeating in reverse a portrait by Emily Eden of Ranjit Singh, figure 26).

Although formerly identified by Basil Gray as Kharak Singh ('Painting', *The Art of India and Pakistan*, no. 572, page 134; repeated Archer, *Art and Letters*, *op. cit.*) the subject is clearly Gulab Singh, eldest of the three Dogra brothers, and an important contributor to Ranjit Singh's legend. The cult of Gulab Singh in 1846, following his rescue of the Sikh state from the British, is discussed in detail at pages 52–56. This sudden focusing of Sikh interest on

Gulab Singh's role in the Punjab may account for the glamorous magnification evident in the present portrait.

For comments on character, see text, pages 52–56.

Portraits for comparison:

(*1*) *Fig. 52.* Maharaja Gulab Singh seated.
Lithograph after an original drawing by C. S. Hardinge, Lahore. February 1846.
Published: C. S. Hardinge. *Recollections of India* (London, 1847), part II, plate 14.
Entitled: *Gulab Sing.*

(*2*) *Fig. 53.* Maharaja Gulab Singh with attendant and child.
Water-colour by William Carpenter, Kashmir, *c.* 1855.
Lettered on mount: *Gholab Singh late Maharaja of Kashmir.*
Victoria and Albert Museum, I.S. 153–1882.
Note: Significant as a contrast to figure 52 and for rendering sharply clear the differences of feature between Gulab Singh and his youngest son, Ranbir (portrayed by Carpenter, figure 54).

William Carpenter (*c.* 1818–1899), son of the woman artist, Margaret Sarah Carpenter, worked in India from 1852 to 1856, painting mainly portraits, historical and genre subjects but also a few landscapes. He went to Calcutta via Ceylon and travelled up-country to the Punjab, often dressing and living in Indian style. He visited Afghanistan while accompanying the Punjab Irregular Force. On his travels he made numerous sketches which he elaborated into finished oils on his return to England. Many of these were exhibited at the Royal Academy between 1857 and 1866. From 1857 to 1858 he contributed to the *Illustrated London News.* For a further collection of his paintings see Victoria and Albert Museum, nos. 54 to 193 of 1880 I.S.; nos. 33 to 166 of 1882 I.S.; no. 80 of 1885 I.S.

26. *Fig. 57.* Maharaja Gulab Singh (1792–1857) of Jammu and Kashmir seated with his third, surviving son, Ranbir Singh (?–1885). Sikh, Lahore, *c.* 1846–1847.
Size: 222 × 156 mm; with border 298 × 240 mm. Dark blue margin with white rules. Border pink, red rules.
Victoria and Albert Museum, I.S. 13–1956.

Description: Gulab Singh, left, sits kneeling, facing his third son, Ranbir Singh, who kneels before him to the right. Each is dressed in white—Gulab Singh having touches of crimson on his coat and Ranbir Singh traces of dark green. Behind Gulab Singh is a crimson cushion edged with green. Beneath him is a green oval rug rimmed with orange-red. He wears orange-red trousers and a turban composed of white, green, gold and red strands. Ranbir Singh has dark yellow trousers lined with red and a white turban streaked with pink and gold. His hands are folded together in respect, his left arm supporting a sword in a crimson scabbard. He wears a black shield on his back and leans against an orange-red cushion. Terrace carpet pale yellow flecked with green leaf patterns and red and blue flowers. White balustrade. Orange-red canopy. Background pale blue with streaks of blob-like cloud.

Comment: In style the picture shares certain idioms—oval rug, pale carpet with leaf pattern, dresses with jagged edges, long sword pointing downwards, multi-coloured turbans—with the group of portraits (nos. 21–24) which culminate in the massive study (no. 25) of Gulab Singh. In certain other respects, however—hardness of execution, a canopy on vertical poles, flat background, blob-like clouds, smaller heads and general palette—it resembles the more standard style of Guler artists at Amritsar or Lahore. A portrait study of Gulab Singh's two other sons, Udham and Sohan Singh (figure 56), is not unlike the present picture and is even more clearly in this latter style.

Related Examples:

(*1*) *Fig. 55*. Maharaja Gulab Singh with his two eldest sons, Udham Singh (?–1840) centre and Sohan Singh (?–1844), left. Sikh, Lahore, *c.* 1840–1846. British Museum, 1915–9–15–01.

Reproduced: Mulk Raj Anand, 'Painting under the Sikhs', *Marg* (1954), VII, no. 2, figure 1 (but captioned 'Dhyan Singh with two nobles, perhaps his sons').

Comment: Similar dotted cushion and oval rug as in no. 21. Dress, sword and turbans as in no. 26.

(*2*) *Fig. 56*. The first and second sons of Maharaja Gulab Singh; left, Udham Singh (the senior-most), right, Sohan (Randhir) Singh (middle son). Sikh, Lahore, *c.* 1840–1846.
Originally inscribed on fly-leaf in Persian characters: *udham singh randhir*; and in English: *Meah Oodum Sing and Sohun Sing, late sons of Maharaja Gulab Sing*.
India Office Library, Add. Or. 708. With figure 34, from the private papers of Herbert Edwardes, Assistant to Henry Lawrence, Lahore, 1846 to 1848.
Canopy, carpet, dress and turbans as in figure 57. Margin with Guler-style floral pattern. Striped trousers as in figure 55.

(*3*) *Fig. 58*. Ranbir Singh seated on a terrace conversing with a secretary, the latter's pen-case and papers beside him. Sikh, Lahore, *c*. 1846. British Museum, 1915–19–15–02.

Reproduced: I. Stchoukine, *La Peinture Indienne* (Paris, 1928), pl. 91 ('Two Sikh nobles').

Dress, turban, sword, cushion and oval rug as in figures 55, 56, 57. The carpet with leaf and floral patterns, and large cartouches as in figures 59 and 60 (the second Lahore Darbar of 26 December 1846). Ranbir Singh as in figures 57, 59 and 60.

(*4*) *Figs. 59 and 60*. The second Lahore Darbar of 26 December 1846 showing from left to right, front row, Henry Lawrence, Lord Gough (Commander-in-Chief), Lord Hardinge (Governor-General), Sheikh Imam-ud-din (ex-Governor of Kashmir), Ranbir Singh (proxy for Gulab Singh), one person unidentified, Dalip Singh (child Maharaja), Frederick Currie (Foreign Secretary). Sikh, Lahore, *c*. 1846–1947.

British Museum, P. C. Manuk and Miss G. M. Coles collection, 1948–10–9–0109.

Reproduced: Anand, *Marg* (1954), VII, no. 2, figure 8 ('The signature of the Treaty of Lahore, 1846').

Discussed in detail at pages 14–16 above.

Comment: In style a blend of Kangra-Guler painting at Lahore (compare pose and treatment of Sikh figures, carpets as in figure 58, canopies as in figures 56 and 57) with later Mughal idioms such as the schematic disposition of tent screens and awnings (an idiom practised at, amongst other centres, Farrukhabad, Oudh, *c*. 1760–1770, see Victoria and Albert Museum picture I.S. 200–1949).

For reasons given in the text, the central figure facing Lord Hardinge can only be Ranbir Singh and the occasion the second (rather than the first) Lahore darbar of 1846. At the first darbar held on 9 March to ratify the first treaty of Lahore, signed the previous day, both Sir Charles Napier, Gulab Singh, and Count Waldemar were present, while Sheikh Imam-ud-din was absent. At the second darbar held on 26 December to ratify the second treaty signed on 16 December 1846, Napier, Gulab Singh and Waldemar were absent and Imam-ud-din was present. Ranbir Singh also attended since he had returned from Kashmir with Lawrence to represent his father, attend the trial of Lal Singh, and obtain public confirmation that Kashmir was Gulab Singh's.

For proof that the fourth figure in the front row, shown full-face, is Sheikh Imam-ud-din, see Hardinge's inscribed portrait (*Recollections of India* (London,

1847), pl. 26) where the straight nose and eye-brows, style of beard and head-dress with side-cloths, draping the shoulders, tally exactly with the figure in our present picture.

A side-light on Sikh culture is afforded by the presence in the picture of two distinct styles of chair. Those occupied by the main British party, though of Indian make, are in British taste of the Regency period.[1] Each arm joins the rear support some six inches below the chair back and the Governor-General's chair is dignified with formal tigers, their tails serving as chair-arms. In contrast, the chair occupied by Currie is in Sikh style, the arm connecting not with the support but curving round in a loop to join the chair back at its top. The inclusion of this 'looping' arm (markedly present in almost all Sikh chairs, see figures 10, 13, 19, 20, 22, 24, 25, 30, 41, 61, 65, 66, 93, 94, 95) may illustrate Ranjit Singh's ability to adopt alien fashions, yet give them a strongly Sikh air.

For variants of standard Sikh chairs, see figures 11, 12, 15, 51. It is noteworthy that in the sketch of Ranjit Singh in December 1838, Emily Eden gives the chair British-style arms (figure 26), but these are converted into Sikh style in the Indian version based upon it (figure 25). Helen MacKenzie, on the other hand, in her drawing, figure 66, is careful to give Dalip Singh a chair in full Sikh style.

Portraits of Ranbir Singh for comparison:

(1) *Fig. 54.* Maharaja Ranbir Singh of Jammu and Kashmir, with attendants. Water-colour by William Carpenter, Kashmir, *c.* 1855.
Lettered on mount in English: *Rumbir Singh, Maharajah of Kashmir, and Shere Surun, son of the Wazeer.*
Victoria and Albert Museum, I.S. 154–1882.

(2) *Fig. 95.* Maharaja Ranbir Singh of Jammu and Kashmir, seated on a chair. Sikh, Lahore, *c.* 1860. Water-colour.
Inscribed in English: *Maharaja Rambir Sing King Kashmir.*
India Office Library, London, Add. Or. 1402b.
From an album entitled *Punjab Portraits*, illustrating Sikh rulers, characters, trades and occupations of the Punjab.
Note: For Ranbir and Gulab Singh's sharp differences of face, nose, beard and moustaches, compare figures 54 and 92 (Ranbir) with figures 34 and 52 (Gulab). In marked contrast to Gulab Singh's curved nose, tipped beard and very slightly upturning moustache, Ranbir can be distinguished by a straight nose, untipped beard and, above all, by a pair of bristling moustaches, rising sharply on each cheek to at least eye-level in stiffly waxed points. A careful look

[1] Compare Clifford Musgrave, *Regency Furniture* (London, 1961).

at the two faces, as shown in cat. no. 26, figure 57, disposes of any possibility that the central figure, eyeing Lord Hardinge in 'The second Lahore darbar of 26 December 1846' (figures 59, 60), can be Gulab Singh.

27. *Fig. 70.* Two Sikhs on horseback. Sikh, Punjab Plains, *c.* 1835.

Size: 247×179 mm; with border 310×238 mm.

Dark blue margin with floral scroll in gold and slate blue, white rules; pink border flecked with red.

Inscribed on reverse in Persian characters: *tasvīr ardaliyān-ī-khās sarkār daulatmadār māharājā sāhib lāhaur* (picture of the personal orderlies of the exalted ruler the maharaja sahib of Lahore).

Victoria and Albert Museum, D. J. Elliott collection, I.S. 479–1950.

Description: Two Sikh horsemen, armed with lances, riding together. The first, on the left, has a black mount with white head and fetlocks and orange-red saddle-cloth. He wears a green coat, pale blue dress and yellow trousers. His companion (behind him on the right) bestrides a white horse with red fetlocks and blue saddle-cloth. He wears a pink turban, white dress and orange-red scarf. A black shield is strapped to his back. Pale green sword. Misty blue background.

Comment: In style close to Guler painting of the 1820 to 1830 period and like no. 2, perhaps painted soon after Guler artists had settled in the Punjab Plains.

The Sikh passion for horses resulted in standard horsemen sets (compare nos. 29, i–iv) of which this present picture may be an early precursor.

For a lancer in somewhat similar pose, see W. G. Osborne, *The Court and Camp of Runjeet Sing* (London, 1840), 64.

28. *Fig. 71.* A seated groom with saddled horse. Sikh, Punjab Plains, *c.* 1840.

Size: 245×185 mm; with border 272×208 mm.

Narrow mauve margin with black rules; red border with white rule.

Inscribed in pencil on reverse in handwriting of J. C. French: *Sikh. Amritsar.*

Victoria and Albert Museum, J. C. French collection, I.S. 201–1955.

Obtained by French in Amritsar.

Description: A Sikh groom in white dress with orange-red turban and scarf squats beside a grey stallion with black mane, tail and fetlocks. He holds a fly-whisk in his right hand and a red bridle in his left. The horse has an orange-red saddle and saddlecloth with gold surround. In the foreground, a band of grey water. Background dull green with tiny trees and slopes in the distance. On the skyline crinkly white clouds and deep blue sky.

Comment: For a similar study of horse and groom, see Emily Eden, *Portraits of the Princes and Peoples of India* (London, 1844), pl. 14. 'Horse of Runjeet Singh'.

29 (i–iv). *Figs. 72 to 75.* Four Sikh riders on horseback from a Sikh horse-man set. Sikh, Punjab Plains, *c.* 1840–1845.

Victoria and Albert Museum, 03534 (i–iv). Transferred from the India Office to the South Kensington Museum, 1880.

29 (i). *Fig. 72.* Sikh lancer in chain-mail on horseback.
Size: 253 × 204 mm; with border 285 × 235 mm.
Brick red border with black and white rules.
Victoria and Albert Museum, 03534 (i) I.S.

Description: A lancer in chain-mail bestrides a white stallion. He faces right. A blue quiver with arrows is at his waist and behind it on the further side is a bow. He carries a lance in his right hand, a dagger at his left side and on his back, a black shield. Orange saddle-cloth with gold edging. The background is a curving green hillside with a stream. At the top, dark blue sky with white clouds.

29 (ii). *Fig. 73.* Sikh horseman.
Size: 258 × 202 mm; with border 290 × 233 mm.
Brick red border with black and white rules.
Victoria and Albert Museum, 03534 (ii) I.S.

Description: A Sikh horseman with rounded beard in white dress and green trousers bestrides a brown stallion, with white fetlocks. Orange saddle-cloth. In the foreground a dark green field with tufted plants; below it a stream. Pale blue background with a curving rim of white cloud and dark blue sky.

29 (iii). *Fig. 74.* Sikh warrior with breast-plate on horseback.
Size: 253 × 203 mm; with border 284 × 233 mm.

Brick red border with black and white rules.
Victoria and Albert Museum, 03534 (iii) I.S.

Description: A Sikh warrior in white and mauve dress and red trousers bestrides a bluish grey stallion. He wears a helmet on his head, a breast-plate on his chest and a shield on his back. He faces left and carries a lance in his right hand. Yellow saddle-cloth. Green hill side with a stream and clumps of plants. At the top, a curving rim of white clouds and dark blue sky.

Comment: A note attached to *Indian Scenes and Characters* (London, 1859), pl. 8, 'Cavalcade of Sikh Chieftains' shows how much Sikh cavalry impressed European visitors. 'Prince Soltykoff', it relates, 'was reminded by this vast assemblage of Sikh cavaliers, superbly dressed in chain armour of Raffaele's fresco in the Vatican which represents an invasion of Huns. The whole plain, which consisted of green corn-fields, was covered with masses of horsemen. Most conspicuous amongst these were the cuirassiers of the Body Guard, in plate armour and plumed helmets. Their flags were of green silk of a triangular shape and covered with figures of Indian deities; and kettle drums sounded in front of them. At a little distance from them in detached groups or single rode the most renowned Sikh warriors, some of them in chain armour and helmets and armed with bows of prodigious strength, others in cloth of gold, silk and velvet. The personages of highest rank rode on elephants, superbly caparisoned with cloth of gold and bearing seats of massive gold and silver. In strange contrast with the noblemen so seated whose dresses blazed with precious stones, were the grooms and other servants who sat behind them, some of whom were entirely naked or wore only a slender covering of dirty linen. And among the glittering cavaliers rode or ran groups of half-naked men, whose rags contrasted oddly with the rose-coloured silken vest of the chiefs. Not the least curious part of the throng were the bands of elfish lads who ran beside the horsemen and turned over on their hands and feet in the dust, a practice well known in countries further West.'

29 (iv). *Fig. 75.* Sikh warrior in chain-mail on horseback.
Size: 252 × 204 mm; with border 282 × 233 mm.
Brick red border with black and white rules.
Victoria and Albert Museum, 03534 (iv) I.S.
Description: A Sikh warrior in chain-mail bestrides a dark brown stallion with black fetlocks. He faces left and is armed with a black sword at his side, a dagger at his waist, a black shield on his back and a gun on his shoulder.

Yellow saddle-cloth, sage-green hillside with clumps of tufted plants and at the top, a curving rim of white clouds and blue sky.

Comment: For a comparable series executed in water-colour on English paper, perhaps for the British, see India Office Library, Add. Or. 1347–1396. Interest in uniforms and types of horseman was not confined to the Sikhs but seems to have engaged British as well as other travellers in the Punjab.

30 (i-iii). *Figs. 78, 77.* Three paintings from a set of Punjabi characters. Sikh, Punjab Plains, *c.* 1840–1850.
    Approximate size: 154×110 mm; with border, 181×138 mm.
    Narrow gold margins. Red borders with white rules.
    Victoria and Albert Museum, D. J. Elliott collection, I.S. 489–1950, 488–1950 and 487–1950.

30 (i). *Fig. 78.* Two Akalis.
    Inscribed on reverse in Persian characters: *akāliyān amritsar*; and in pencil in English: *Akali Sikh*.
    Victoria and Albert Museum, I.S. 489–1950.

Description: Two Akalis, bare save for slate blue turbans, drawers and scarves, confront each other. They wield blue clubs, and have swords at their waists and steel bangles on their right wrists. Conical turbans with steel quoits. In the foreground a green field with patch of water. Background pink with curving rim of crinkly white clouds and blue sky.

Comment: Akalis haunted the precincts of the Golden Temple, Amritsar, and were a ferocious and dreaded nuisance to all pilgrims and visitors to the city. Schoefft's unlucky brush with them has already been described (pages 45–47); but even Metcalfe, British envoy to the Sikhs in 1809, was molested by them and his life saved with difficulty.

Cunningham gives the following sober account of their rise to power and influence in the eighteenth century: 'Besides the regular confederacies, with their moderate degree of subordination, there was a body of men who threw off all subjection to earthly governors, and who peculiarly represented the religious element of Sikhism. These were the "Akalees," the immortals, or rather the soldiers of God, who, with their blue dress and bracelets of steel, claimed for themselves a direct institution by Govind Singh. The Gooroo had called upon men to sacrifice everything for their faith, to leave their homes and to follow the profession of arms; but he and all his predecessors had likewise denounced the inert asceticism of the Hindoo sects, and thus the fanatical feeling of a Sikh took a destructive turn. The Akalees formed themselves in their struggle to reconcile warlike activity with the relinquishment of the world. The meek and humble were satisfied with the assiduous performance of menial offices in temples, but the fierce enthusiasm of others prompted them to act from time to time as the armed guardians of Amritsir, or suddenly to go where blind impulse might lead them, and to win their daily bread, even single-handed, at the point of the sword. They also took upon themselves something of the authority of censors, and, although no leader appears to have fallen by their hands for defection to the Khalsa, they inspired awe as well as respect, and would sometimes plunder those who had offended them or had injured the commonwealth. The passions of the Akalees had full play until Runjeet Singh became supreme, and it cost that able and resolute chief much time and trouble, at once to suppress them, and to preserve his own reputation with the people.'[1]

Almost every foreign visitor to the Punjab was scared of their unpredictable rages and their almost inexhaustible capacity for taking umbrage. Jacquemont visited the Golden Temple in October 1832 but took good care to go by elephant and to be protected by Sikh cavalry. 'The fanaticism and madness of the Akalis or warrior monks with whom this holy place is always crowded', he said, 'would threaten almost certain danger to any European who was to visit it, unless he had a powerful guard.'[2]

He summarised their principal traits as follows: 'The Akalis, or Immortals, are properly speaking Sikh faqirs. Their rule compels them to be dressed in blue and always to carry arms. The sacred pool at Amritsar is their head-quarters, but they often spread themselves over the Punjab in large and formidable parties. Ranjit wisely turns their ferocity to his own advantage. He enlists them in his armies, and employs them, preferably against his Mussalman enemies. He has at the moment about 4,000–5,000 of them in the army which he maintains at Attock, ready to march against another fanatic the Syed. I have only seen two of them in the streets of Amritsar; it was evening, their arms glittered in the light of the torches and the matches of their muskets hung ready lighted. I had never seen more sinister-looking figures.'[3]

A little later, he felt that even this picture was too rosy and hastened to retract: 'I was wrong when I mentioned earlier that Ranjit had formed several regiments of Akalis which he was using against the Syed. They are quite uncontrollable and the only way to deal with them is to exterminate them. After

[1]Cunningham, *History*, 117–118.   [2]Jacquemont, *Letters*, 262.
[3]Garrett, *The Punjab*, 28.

Amritsar their favourite headquarters is Lahore. One sees them chiefly on the outskirts of the city among the ruins of the Mughal palaces and mosques. This is their lair. Nearly all of them are mounted on ponies and armed with a spear or matchlock, others have only a bow or a sword. They are dressed in tattered blue clothes and most of them wear a long pointed head-dress of the same colour, surrounded at its base with a polished steel ring like the brim of a hat. They are hideous to behold. They live on what they can take if it is not given to them, and hurl insults at those whom they dare not plunder. M. Allard, who has wisely made them friendly by his liberality, has nevertheless on one occasion been attacked by them; but for my escort I should have been obliged to beat a hasty retreat. Sometimes they collect in parties of hundred and mingle among the Rajah's attendants, and when they think themselves strong enough, they threaten him and demand money. They have more than once held him up to ransom in this way, but Ranjit has never ventured to take vigorous measures against them. When a campaign takes place, he urges them to go on active service and gives a general order to put them in positions from which they have little chance of returning, and they usually come back in smaller numbers for they fight with desperate courage.'[1]

For Phula Singh Akali and his feats of derring-do, see Biographical Notes and no. 66.

30 (ii). *Fig. 77.* Two Sikh cultivators.

Inscribed on reverse in Persian characters: *ābā ajadā(d) sikhān.* (Sikh ancestors(?)); and in English in pencil: *For . . . book.*
Victoria and Albert Museum, I.S. 488–1950.

Description: Two figures, nude save for white loincloths, black-striped wraps and white turban-bands, proceed left across a field. Each carries a forked stick. Foreground green with a patch of water. Background blue with curving rim of crinkled white cloud and blue sky.

Comment: Sikh cultivators are mainly Jats, termed by Cunningham, 'the finest rural population in India'. Renowned as 'industrious and successful tillers of the soil', they were 'hardy yeomen equally ready to take up arms and to follow the plough'. It was oppression by Muslim landlords which led many of them to adopt Sikhism.

For a comparable study which also includes the same type of forked stick, see *Punjabi Characters*, 'Jats' (India Office Library, Add. Or. 1376).

[1] *Ibid.*, 53.

157

30. (iii) Two gentry.

Inscribed on reverse in Persian characters: *chaudhrī muhammad vāris va chaudhrī nūr muhammad. zamīndāran dalkha saka khohāla. dalkhān kih zamindār sardār mulk bahar dalkhān būdand.* (Chaudhri Muhammad and his son, Chaudhri Nur Muhammad, landlords of Dalkha, residents of Khohala. The Dalkha landlords are lords of the Dalkha country.)

Victoria and Albert Museum, I.S. 487–1950.

Description: An old man with white turban, beard and *jāma* sits on a pale crimson rug beneath a tree, facing left and addressing an oldish man, also in white, who stands before him. In the foreground, a green field with patch of water. In the tree, five white paddybirds. Pale brown background with curving rim of crinkled white clouds and blue sky.

II SKETCHES

31. *Fig. 80.* Sikh sardar. Sikh, Punjab Plains, *c.* 1835–1845.
Size: 130 × 120 mm.
Unfinished drawing partly primed and coloured.
Inscribed in top in damaged *nāgarī* characters: *sardār . . . . . singh . . . vālā.*
Victoria and Albert Museum, I.S. 11–1957.

Description: The subject seated and facing right, a black shield at his back. White dress edged with green. Green trousers. Crimson scabbard.

32. *Fig. 79.* Sikh sardar. Sikh, Punjab Plains, *c.* 1835–1845.
Size: 125 × 140 mm.
White priming; partly coloured.
Uninscribed.
Victoria and Albert Museum, I.S. 9–1957.

Description: The subject, facing left, is seated on a brick red rug with green border, his left arm resting on a dark red cushion. He wears a yellow turban, crimson trousers and white coat. Black beard, snub nose.

33. *Fig. 83.* Ajit Singh Sandhawalia (?–1843) seated with a companion. Sikh, Punjab Plains, *c.* 1835–1840.
Size: 155 × 175 mm.
Line drawing with white priming.
Inscribed on front in *tākrī* characters: (*a*) *jīt sīngh sandhaubalīajī.*
Victoria and Albert Museum, I.S. 171–1953. Given by Miss M. W. Patterson.

Description: The subject, facing right, is seated on the ground leaning against a cushion. A companion faces him.

Portrait for comparison: W. G. Osborne, *The Court and Camp of Runjeet Sin* (London, 1840), 70.

159

34. *Fig. 81.* Dina Nath seated holding a petition and facing right. Sikh, Punjab Plains, *c.* 1840–1845.

Size: 140 × 131 mm.

Tinted line drawing, in white, black and brown. To the right of the face, a second profile, also Dina Nath's.

Inscribed on reverse in Persian characters: *dīnanāth daftarī*; and in *tākrī* characters: . . *thārī dīnanatha.*

Victoria and Albert Museum, I.S. 174–1953. Given by Miss M. W. Patterson.

Description: Dina Nath, Finance Minister of Ranjit Singh, member of Dalip Singh's Regency Council and adviser to Henry Lawrence, sits on the ground, facing right, a pen case and cloth—bundle of documents, in front of him. As in most other portraits, he holds a long sheet of paper.

Comments on character:

GRIFFIN

'Among the men who rose to power during the latter days of the Maharaja's life, no one was more remarkable than Raja Dina Nath. He has been well and happily styled the Talleyrand of the Punjab, and his life and character bear a strong resemblance to those of the European statesman. Revolutions in which his friends and patrons perished passed him by; dynasties rose and fell but never involved him in their ruin; in the midst of bloodshed and assassination his life was never endangered; while confiscation and judicial robbery were the rule of the State, his wealth and power continually increased. His sagacity and far-sightedness were such, that when, to other eyes, the political sky was clear, he could perceive the signs of a coming storm which warned him to desert a losing party or a falling friend. Honest men do not survive many revolutions, and the Raja's falseness was the measure of his success. He was patriotic, but his love of country was subordinate to his love of self. He hated the English with a bitter hatred for they were stronger than he or his country; but his interests compelled him to serve, like Samson, the Philistines he hated. He was not without his own notions of fidelity, and would stand by a friend as long as he could do so with safety to himself. Even when he deserted him it was from thoughts of danger to his wealth and influence than from personal fear, for Raja Dina Nath was physically brave, and also possessed, in an eminent degree, moral courage; though it did not lead him to do right regardless of conse-quences. He possessed immense local knowledge and as vast a capacity for work; but his desire of keeping power in his own hands had an evil effect on the progress of business. He was an accomplished man of the world, courteous and considerate; well educated, though nothing of a scholar, and in conversation with Europeans he would express himself with a boldness and apparent candour that were as pleasant as they are unusual in Asiatics.

It was only in 1834 that Raja Dina Nath was made Finance Minister, for which his qualifications were exceedingly high, but the Maharaja had for many years reposed great confidence in him, and he was on all occasions of importance one of his most trusted advisers. After the death of his master he retained great influence with the chiefs and the army, and on the British occupation of Lahore was appointed to the Council of Regency, of which he was a most able and useful member. Although his position at the head of the Financial Department gave him many opportunities of enriching himself at the public expense, of which there is every reason to believe he availed himself, he still worked more disinterestedly than others, and was of great service to the Resident at Lahore. Without his clear head and business-like habits it would have been almost impossible to disentangle the Darbar accounts, and after the annexation of the Punjab Dina Nath's aid in revenue and jagir matters was almost as valuable as before. At the time of the revolt of the Sikh army in 1848, it was asserted by some that Raja Dina Nath was a traitor at heart; that he had himself encouraged the rising; and that had he not been a wealthy man, with houses and gardens and many lakhs of rupees in Lahore, convenient for confiscation, he would have joined the rebels without hesitation; but these stories were perhaps invented by his enemies. Certain it is that on his being recalled to Lahore he zealously carried out the wishes of the British authorities in confiscating the property of the rebels and in counter-acting their schemes.'[1]

Portrait for comparison:

(*1*) *Fig. 64.* Henry Lawrence, British Resident at Lahore, 1846–1848, dictating instructions to Dina Nath.

Style of Hasan-al-din, Sikh, Lahore, *c.* 1847.

Inscribed in Persian characters: *rāja dīnanāth. Karnil Larens sāhib bahādur.*

India Office Library, London (Photo).

Note: For other portraits, see figures 61, 62, 81 and 108–111.

35. *Fig. 82.* Sikh sardar. Sikh, Punjab Plains, *c.* 1835–1845.

Size: 97 × 86 mm.

White priming, partly coloured. Uninscribed.

[1] Griffin, *Ranjit Singh,* 127–129.

Victoria and Albert Museum, I.S. 10–1957.
Description: The subject faces right. White turban, red cloak, green trousers.

36. *Fig. 87.* Sikh sardar. Sikh, Punjab Plains, *c.* 1835–1845.
  Size: 124×110 mm.
    Primed and partly coloured. Uninscribed.
    Victoria and Albert Museum, I.S. 12–1957.

Description: The subject, white bearded, seated and facing left. White dress, edged with green. Crimson trousers and scabbard. Black shield on back. Front of turban yellow.

37. *Fig. 84.* Brahmin(?) Sikh, Punjab Plains, *c.* 1835–1845.
    Size: 103×112 mm.
    Primed and partly coloured. Uninscribed.
    Victoria and Albert Museum, I.S. 14–1957.

Description: The subject, with partly shaven beard, seated and facing left. Black hair. White dress, grey wrap.

38. *Fig. 88.* Sikh sardar. *c.* 1835–1845.
    Size: 113×112 mm.
    Primed and partly coloured. Uninscribed.
    Victoria and Albert Museum, I.S. 13–1957.

Description: The subject, with long black beard, seated and facing right. Crimson trousers, white coat, green and gold wrap.

Portrait for comparison: A. K. Coomaraswamy, *Boston Catalogue, V.,* pl. 125, page 241 (but hardly Ranjit Singh as tentatively proposed).

39. *Fig. 86.* Sikh sardar. Sikh, Punjab Plains, *c.* 1835–1845.
    Size: 114×114 mm.
    Primed and partly coloured. Uninscribed.
    Victoria and Albert Museum, I.S. 15–1957.

Description: The subject with rounded black beard seated and facing left: green turban, white dress edged with crimson, yellow-green trousers, crimson scabbard, black shield at back.

40. *Fig. 85.* Sikh sardar. Sikh, Punjab Plains, *c.* 1835–1845.
    Size: 118 × 113 mm.
    Primed and partly coloured. Uninscribed.
    Victoria and Albert Museum, I.S. 16–1957.

    Description: The subject with greying beard, seated and facing left. White turban and dress, green trousers, crimson scabbard, black shield and strap.

41. *Fig. 91.* Sikh sardar. Sikh, Punjab Plains, *c.* 1835–1845.
    Size: 135 × 135 mm.
    Partly primed and coloured. Uninscribed.
    Victoria and Albert Museum, I.S. 172–1953. Given by Miss M. W. Patterson.

    Description: The subject faces left; head and torso only. White turban and dress. White beard.

42. *Fig. 89.* Sikh sardar. Sikh, Punjab Plains, *c.* 1835–1845.
    Size: 128 × 110 mm.
    Primed and partly coloured. Uninscribed.
    Victoria and Albert Museum, I.S. 17–1957.

    Description: The subject, with black beard seated and facing left. Brick red trousers, white dress, crimson scabbard, black shield on back.

43. *Fig. 90.* Raja Dhian Singh (1796–1843). Sikh, Punjab Plains, *c.* 1835–1840.
    Size: 99 × 83 mm.
    Water-colour. Uninscribed.
    Victoria and Albert Museum, F. B. P. Lory collection, I.S. 92–1960.

    Description: The subject faces left and is seated on an oval crimson rug, edged with blue. On the back a black shield. The oval rug as in nos. 10, 15, 16, 22 and 26.

    Comment: Identical with W. L. McGregor, *The History of the Sikhs* (London, 1846), II, pl. at page 2, entitled *Rajah Dhiyan Singh.*

III GLASS

44. *Fig. 69.* Maharaja Ranjit Singh (1780–1839), nimbate. Sikh, Lahore, 1849.
    Size: 508 × 406 mm.
    Inscribed at foot in Persian characters: *amali kehar singh musavir lahori samvat 1906.* (The work of Kehar Singh, painter, Lahore, A.D. 1849.)
    Victoria and Albert Museum, 03530 I.S. Transferred from the India Office to the South Kensington Museum, 1880.

Description: Ranjit Singh, nimbate, sits in a chair facing half right. Both eyes are visible, the left and blind eye being shown further to the right. Brown face heavily pitted with small-pox scars. Yellow turban much bejewelled. Dress white with green coat elaborately embroidered with gold edgings and lavish white floral designs. In the left hand is a gold-edged cloth and in right the gold hilt of a sword. Long grey beard, partly white. The chair is in Sikh style, the nearer arm rising to a loop at the back. Deep blue background. Blue halo.

Comment: As in nos. 89–91, a marked departure from standard portrayals of Ranjit Singh—the painter ruthlessly depicting the blind left eye and treating the face with almost gross realism. The presence of the British may have led to this strange insistence on accuracy while the use of a new material, glass —itself a western medium—also points to British influence. Glass painting was a feature of British art from about 1780 onwards and appears to have reached India in the eighteen-thirties.

Portrait for comparison:

   (*1*) *Fig. 68.* Maharaja Ranjit Singh (1780–1839), full face. Lithograph (London, 1837) after a drawing by G. T. Vigne, Lahore, March 1837.
    Lettered: *The Maharajah Runjeet Singh. Aged 58. King of the Sikhs and Ruler of the Punjab, Ladak, Kashmere and Peshawar. From an original Portrait now in England and taken during the visit of His Excellency General Sir Henry Fane G.C.B. Commander*

164

in chief of the King's and Honble Compy's Army in India to Lahore, for the purpose of attending the marriage of No Nepal (sic) Singh, the Maharajah's Grandson at the Ataree in the Punjab on the 8th March 1837. G.T.V. del. Inscribed on back: *Received from Secretary, Feby 2nd, 1838, Library.* Commonwealth Relations Office, London.

Note: Of Ranjit Singh's character and appearance, Vigne recorded the following impression:

'The diminutive size of his person, and the comparative simplicity of his attire—consisting of a turban, usually large only over the forehead, with the end hanging down the back, folded à la Sikh; a kind of frock or tunic, padded so as to give an extraordinary breadth to his naturally wide shoulders; the kumerbund tied round his waist; and pair of close-fitting trowsers, of the same colour, yellow or pea-green; and all of Kashmirian manufacture—did not prevent anyone, who entered the Durbar for the first time, from instantly recognising the Maharajah. The contour of his face was square; his complexion was a light olive, his forehead was wide and Napoleon-like: his right and only eye, large and prominent, for he had lost the other by the small-pox, with which he was slightly marked, was incessantly roving; his nose was slightly retroussé; his nostrils expanded and contracted, as his conversation became animated; and decision and energy were pre-eminently imprinted on his thick but well-formed lips. A grey moustache, blending with his white beard, added character to the very expressive countenance of this extraordinary man.'[1]

[1] Vigne, *Personal Narrative*, 255–256.

IV IVORIES

Note: For a general discussion of Indian water-colour paintings on ivory, see Archer, *Indian Painting for the British* (London, 1955). Sikh paintings on ivory are discussed at pages 65–68 above.

45. *Fig. 104.* Maharaja Sher Singh (1807–1843). Sikh, Lahore, *c.* 1850–1870.
Size: 40 × 40 mm; shape round.
Inscribed on reverse in English: *Maharajah Shere Singh.*
Victoria and Albert Museum, I.S. 162–1954.

Description: Three-quarters view, head and shoulders, facing right. Figure heavily clothed, the chest covered with jewels. Thick moustaches curling inwards at the tips. Background green and pale yellow.

Comments on character:

JACQUEMONT

'Ranjit has two sons; the elder, Kharak Singh, is 26 or 28, is very like his father to look at, but is very feeble-minded. The other, Sher Singh, is less than 20 and is not at all like his father but is very intelligent.'[1]

OSBORNE

'Sher Sing is a fine manly looking fellow and was richly dressed. He is a supposed son of the Maharajah, though the latter strongly denies the paternity.'[2]

VON ORLICH

'Shere Singh is rather above the middle height; he is very corpulent and strongly built, but is light in his movements; his features are expressive of good-nature and a love of pleasure, and his fine dark eye beamed with kindness and affection: his black beard was very carefully dressed.'[3]

[1]Garrett, *The Punjab*, 55. [2]Osborne, *Court and Camp*, 64. [3]Von Orlich, *Travels*, I, 124.

EMILY EDEN

'A very jolly dog.'[1]

LATIF

'Sher Singh was addicted to pleasure and had been in the habit of indulging in the use of spirituous liquors to an immoderate extent before he assumed the reins of Government. Firmly established in his kingdom, he gave himself up to his favourite pursuits, hunting and wrestling, paying but little attention to affairs of State, which were left entirely in the hands of his prudent Minister, Raja Dhian Singh. He was brave and of a mild and affable disposition. He, however, sometime after, became a complete libertine and an open drunkard, indulging especially in champagne. The marble palace garden, opposite the royal mosque of Aurangzeb, was his favourite resort of pleasure; and here he used to sit on his bed of roses, with wreaths of flowers hanging over the beautiful marble arches, and rose and musk water sprinkled on the ground, while bands of musicians discoursed sweet music. "Eat, drink and be merry" was the maxim of the royal sage, Sardanapalus, of ancient celebrity and the same maxim might with truth have been attributed to the voluptuous Sher Singh.'[2]

Portraits for comparison:

(*1*) *Fig. 38.* Maharaja Sher Singh seated on a bed after bathing; to the left a Kangra lady, to the right, a Sikh man-servant. Kangra, *c.* 1830, gouache.
Inscribed at the top in *nāgarī* characters: *mahārājā sher singh.*
Punjab Museum, Chandigarh (on transfer from Central Museum, Lahore).
Reproduced: S. N. Gupta, 'The Sikh School of Painting', *Rupam* (1922), pl. 2, page 126.
Note: Sher Singh was Sikh Governor and Administrator of Kangra, 1830 and 1831.

(*2*) *Fig. 39.* Maharaja Sher Singh. Lithograph (London, 1842) after an original drawing by G. T. Vigne, Punjab, 1838.
Published: G. T. Vigne, *Travels in Kashmir, Ladak, Iskardo* (London, 1842), I, frontispiece. Inscribed: *Sher Singh, the present Maharajah of the Punjub.*

(*3*) *Fig. 40.* Maharaja Sher Singh. Sikh, Punjab Plains, *c.* 1840, gouache.
Inscribed on reverse in English by writer A (see Note X, page 74): *Maha Raja Share Sing*; and by writer B (James Duncan Sims): *Received from M. R. R.*

---

[1]Eden, *Up the Country,* 210. [2]Latif, *History,* 507–508.

167

Sunkanada Johestree, a Native of Travancore, for several years Chief Astrologer at the Court of Lahore, during Runjeet Sing, Cadagoo Sing and Shere Sing's reigns.

Mr and Mrs T. W. F. Scott collection, London.

In view of inscriptions on figures 28 and 35 in the same hand as writer B's, we can infer that Sims obtained this and four other Sikh portraits from Joshi Shankarnath (pages 37, 74) in 1844. By then the latter had ended his career as court astrologer, Lahore, and returned to South India.

From a standard portrait set by Guler painters in the Punjab Plains at Amritsar or Lahore.

(4) *Fig. 41.* Maharaja Sher Singh seated in a chair. Sikh, Punjab Plains, *c.* 1840–1845.

British Museum, 1956–10–13–03.

From a standard portrait set by Guler artists in the Punjab Plains. Notable for including huge jewels on Sher Singh's left arm and turban and for the sharply in-curling moustache-ends—as characteristic of Sher Singh as the bristling upward-pointing moustache-ends are of Ranbir Singh (figures 54 and 57).

(5) *Fig. 42.* Maharaja Sher Singh. Lithograph after an original drawing by Emily Eden, Lahore, December 1838. Published: Emily Eden, *Portraits of the Princes and People of India* (London, 1844), pl. 2.

Inscribed: *Maharaja Shere Singh.*

'Shere Singh came to my tent to sit for his picture—such a gorgeous figure! all over diamonds and emeralds . . . He made a very good picture.' Emily Eden, letter dated 20 December 1838 (*Up the Country*, 223).

(6) *Figs. 44 and 45.* The Dasahra festival at the court of Lahore; Sher Singh greeting Ranjit Singh as he returns on horseback from a hunting expedition.

Oil painting by August Theodor Schoefft, Vienna, *c.* 1845–1850, after original drawings made by the artist at Lahore, 1841.

Sikh Museum, Lahore, Pakistan. Formerly owned by Louis Philippe of France, Maharaja Dalip Singh, Princess Bamba Sutherland.

Discussed pages 48 and 49 above.

Bibliography: F. A. Khan, *The Princess Bamba collection (antiquities of the Sikh period)*, (National Museum of Pakistan, Karachi, 1961), pl. 12; Sir William Foster, 'Some Foreign European Artists in India', *Bengal Past and Present* (July–December 1930), XL, 79–98.

(7) *Fig. 43.* Maharaja Sher Singh, seated, a drawn scimitar in his right hand.
Oil painting by August Theodor Schoefft, Vienna, *c.* 1845–1850, after a version made by the artist at Lahore, 1841.
Sikh Museum, Princess Bamba collection, Lahore, Pakistan.
For posture, compare figures 108, 109, and 110 (popular woodcuts).

(8) *Fig. 92.* Maharaja Sher Singh seated on an oval rug.
Water-colour. Sikh, Lahore, *c.* 1860.
Inscribed in English: *Maharaja Sher Singh.*
From an album entitled *Punjab Portraits*, India Office Library, London, Add. Or. 1454.
Similar scimitar as in (7).

46. Maharaja Sher Singh, Sikh, Lahore, *c.* 1850–1870.
Size: 50 × 50 mm.
Mis-inscribed on reverse in English: *Faquir chiragh-ud-din religious chief of the Sikh.*
Victoria and Albert Museum. I.S. 159–1954.
Description: Three-quarter view, head and shoulders facing right. Turban mauve, coat green, scarf brown. Heavily be-jewelled. Thick moustaches curling at the tips. Background pale blue.
Comment: Inscription perhaps by a curio dealer. Subject as in no. 45.

47. *Fig. 100.* Pratap Singh, son of Sher Singh. Sikh, Lahore, *c.* 1850–1870.
Size: 38 × 38 mm; shape round.
Inscribed on reverse in English: *Pertab Singh.*
Victoria and Albert Museum, I.S. 144–1954.
Description: Profile, head and shoulders, facing left. Turban and dress reddish brown. Background white and pale blue.

Portrait for comparison:

(1) Lithograph after an original drawing by Emily Eden, Lahore. December 1838. Published: Emily Eden, *Portraits of the Princes and People of India* (London, 1844), pl. 19.
Inscribed: *Purtaub Singh.*
'We had little Pertab to sketch this morning, and he was very pleasant. I asked him to fix his eyes on Captain M., who was acting interpreter. After a

time he began to fidget, and his stern old Sikh tutor (you don't want a Sikh tutor for your boys by chance?—if so, I can safely recommend this man for a remarkably good manner of teaching, besides having a beard half a yard long) reproved him for it. Pertab declared he could not help it,—he was told to fix his eyes on M., and "this is the way he moves his head,"—and then he mimicked M. turning from one to the other and interpreting, in such a funny little way. We gave him a diamond ring, which seemed to delight him.'[1]

Comments on character:

Besides Osborne's impressions quoted above (p. 41), Emily Eden's account of a dinner party is too charming to be omitted:

'To our horror, Shere Singh offered himself again for dinner yesterday. We had four strange officers as it was, and this promised to be an awful dinner; but it turned out very well. He brought his little boy, Pertab Singh, seven years old, with eyes as big as saucers, and emeralds bigger than his eyes; and he is such a dear good child! G. gave the little boy a box containing an ornamented pistol, with all sorts of contrivances for making bullets, all of which Pertab knew how to use. We accused Shere Singh of having taken a watch that had been given to his little boy; and he pretended to put this pistol in his sash, and it was very pretty to see the little fellow's appeal to G.; but in the middle of it all, he turned round to his father and said—"But you know, Maharaj Gee (your Highness), what is yours is mine, and what is mine is yours; I will lend it to you whenever you like." Shere Singh thought the child was talking too much at one time, and made him a sign, upon which the boy sunk down in the eastern fashion, with his legs crossed and his hands clasped, and he fixed his eyes like a statue. None of us could make him look or hear, and we asked his father at last to let him play, as we were used to children at home. He said one word, and the way in which Pertab jumped up was just like a statue coming to life.'[2]

The grim sequel, five years later, is recounted by Latif:

'(After killing Sher Singh) the assassins then repaired to the garden close by, in search of the heir-apparent, Partab Singh, a lad twelve years of age. The prince was engaged in his prayers and in giving alms to the Brahmins in the garden, when the ferocious Lahna Singh advanced towards him, with a drawn sword in his hand. The boy was terrified, and trembling threw himself at the ruffian's feet and implored forgiveness, saying, "Spare my life, for God's sake; oh! uncle, I will serve as a menial for removing the dung of your horses." "An uncle at such a time?" was the reply of the bloodthirsty Lahna Singh, who,

[1] Eden, *Up the Country*, 217.   [2] *Ibid.*, 210–211.

170

as he uttered these words, severed the boy's head from his body. The villanous soldiers then cut the boy's body to pieces with their sabres.'[1]

48. *Fig. 106.* Suchet Singh. Sikh, Lahore, *c.* 1850–1870.
Size: 60×48 mm; shape oval.
Inscribed: *Rajah Suchet Singh.*
Victoria and Albert Museum, 03605 I.S. Transferred from the India Office to the South Kensington Museum, 1880.
Description: Three-quarter view, head and shoulders, facing right. Yellow turban and wrap. Dark green coat. Background white and pale blue.

Comments on character:

Younger brother of Dhian and Gulab Singh.
'He likes the English far better than his brothers do; and they do not, it is said, like him the better for that. He is effeminately handsome and is always splendidly dressed.'—Vigne, *Personal Narrative*, 251.
The division of roles between the three brothers is assessed by Cunningham: 'The smooth and crafty Golab Singh ordinarily remained in the hills, using Sikh means to extend his own authority over his brother Rajpoots, and eventually into Ludakh; the less able but more polished, Dhian Singh, remained continually in attendance upon the Muharaja, ever on the watch, in order that he might anticipate his wishes; while the elegant Soochet Singh fluttered as a gay courtier and gallant soldier, without grasping at power or creating enemies.'[2]
Emily Eden has her usual tart phrase: 'the great dandy of the Punjab'.[3]
It is left to McGregor to express indignation at his murder: 'Soochet Singh was the *beau idéal* of a Sikh soldier. In his youth, and before debauchery had spoiled his looks, he was a very handsome man: muscular, agile, and well skilled in the use of the sword and matchlock; an excellent horseman: in short, a complete soldier. In his dress, Soochet Singh was particularly gorgeous, and wore a profusion of jewels; while his arms and horse-trapping were magnificently ornamented with gold and tinsel. Though thus a gallant soldier, he was of a mild and pleasing disposition; affable to strangers, and a universal favourite with the army. Possessed of such qualifications, it is not to be wondered at, that his nephew should have become jealous of his power and influence; and desirous of ridding himself of a man so much superior to him in every respect,

[1]Latif, *History*, 514.　[2]Cunningham, *History*, 190.　[3]Eden, *Up the Country*, 147.

171

save cunning: for Soochet's was not a suspicious nature; he was frank, free, and ingenuous. In compassing the death of his uncle, it was universally believed, that Heera Singh had acted under the advice, and at the instigation of the Pundit Julla. The cruel act had the effect of estranging the Rajah of Jummoo, who became suspicious of his nephew's protestations of friendship, while his hands were yet red with the blood of his uncle.'[1]

Portraits for comparison:

(1) See Biographical Notes.

(2) Suchet Singh in a garden. Sikh, Punjab Plains, dated 1839. Inscribed in provincial *nāgarī* characters resembling *tākrī: jamyāla rājā sru cet siha iha cītra najar kītā catere prāge sam(vat) 1896 hāpra 8.* (This picture of Raja Suchet Singh of Jammu was offered as a nazar (present) by the painter in samvat 1896, i.e. A.D. 1839.)

Museum of Fine Arts, Boston, 15.55.

Reproduced: Coomaraswamy, *Boston Catalogue,* V, 236, pl. 123 ('Suchet Singh' mistransliterated 'Sri Chet Singh').

49. *Fig. 96.* Maharaja Dalip Singh (1837–1893). Sikh, Lahore, *c.* 1850–1870.

Size: 50 × 50 mm; shape round.

Inscribed on reverse in English: *Dhulleep Singh ex-King of the Punjaub.*

Victoria and Albert Museum, I.S. 143–1954.

Description: Three-quarter view, head and shoulders, facing right. Left hand holding a flower. Turban and vest pink, coat green. Background pale blue.

Portraits for comparison:

(1) *Fig. 62.* Maharaja Dalip Singh in darbar, November 1843. Seated clockwise from left to right: (1)? (2) Labh Singh (3)? (4)? (5) Pandit Jalla (6) Hira Singh (7) standing attendant (8) Maharaja Dalip Singh petting a lap-dog (9) Dina Nath (10) Jawahir Singh (11) Lal Singh (12) Tej Singh (13) Gulab Singh (14) Suchet Singh (15) Chattar Singh Atariwala (16) Sher Singh Atariwala.

Style of Hasan-al-din, Sikh, Lahore, *c.* 1843. Mrs A. E. Anson collection, Chiswick, London.

Note: Uninscribed. For identifications see biographical notes. Pandit Jalla (5) was close adviser to Raja Hira Singh and perished with him in December 1844. Hira Singh (6) follows the portrait of him in the British Museum

[1] McGregor, *History,* II, 26–27.

172

(1945–11–10–07) obtained from Lady Invernairn, from the collection of E. A. Prinsep (Indian Civil Service, 1847–1874).

(2) *Fig. 61.* Maharaja Dalip Singh in darbar, December 1845.

Seated from left to right: (1) Labh Singh (2) standing attendant with cloth and yak's tail fly-whisk (3) Tej Singh (4) Maharaja Dalip Singh, a shot-gun in the left hand, his pet lap-dog at his feet (5) Dina Nath (6) Nur-ud-din.

By Hasan-al-din, Sikh, Lahore, *c.* 1845–1846.

Inscribed on reverse in Persian characters: *hasan-al-din musavir* (artist Hasan-al-din).

India Office Library, London, Add. Or. 710.

From the private papers of Herbert Edwardes, Assistant to Henry Lawrence, Lahore, 1847 to 1848.

(3) *Fig. 66.* Maharaja Dalip Singh seated on a chair with four attendants. Lithograph from an original drawing by Helen C. (Mrs Colin) Mackenzie, Lahore, 1849.

Published: Helen C. Mackenzie, *Illustrations of the Mission, the Camp and the Zenana* (London, 1854), pl. 6. Inscribed on lithograph in English: *Maharaja Dhalip Sing Lahore 1849 H.C.M.* Entitled: *His Highness the Maharaiah Dhalip Sing.*

Comment to plate: 'The young Prince was the last occupant of the throne of Ranjit Sing, which in the short interval since the death of its founder, had been stained by the blood of six of his successors, and the ascent to which was slippery with the gore of all who had aspired to it. The outbreak which followed the murder of Mr Agnew, and Lieutenant Anderson, showed that annexation was the only remedy left for the misery and bloodshed caused by the want of a ruling power, capable of controlling the mutual jealousies and hatred of the Chiefs, and the lawlessness of the Sikh Soldiery. The young Maharajah was therefore sent to Fattihghar with a Pension of £20,000 a year, and being placed under the charge of Dr Login, he soon learned to know Christianity by its fruits, and openly joined the Christian Church. This sketch was taken before he left Lahore, when he was about twelve years old. His regal manner, and perfect self-possession were very remarkable. It being the cold season, and his apartments open on one side to the outer air, he wore a yellow velvet mantle embroidered with silver, and cashmere socks and gloves; yellow being the sacred colour of the Sikhs predominated in his costume. A closer garment of red and gold is seen underneath. His ornaments were magnificent pearls and emeralds, his turban fringed with silver, his chair of gold, with crimson and yellow velvet cushions; the seats provided for his visitors being only of silver. Behind him stands his aged confidential attendant, Mian Kima, and he is surrounded by other members of his scanty suite.'

(*4*) *Fig. 67.* Maharaja Dalip Singh enthroned. Lithograph from an original drawing by C. S. Hardinge, Lahore, 1846.
Published: C. S. Hardinge, *Recollections of India* (London, 1847), part I, pl. 1 entitled: *The Maharajah Dhulip Singh.*

Hardinge describes his first sight of Dalip Singh as follows:
'We went with Currie and Lawrence, our Foreign Secretary and political agent, on elephants to receive him as he came in with his minister Gulab Singh. He shortly appeared in his howdah with Gulab, when a succession of salaams took place on both sides. The poor child (he is only eight years old, and a most intelligent looking boy) appeared rather frightened at our array of troops, and almost clung to Gulab Singh for protection. On dismounting from his elephant, the Rajah took him up in arms and brought him up into the tent where the Governor-General, the Commander-in-Chief, and their respective staffs were assembled.

Sir Henry met the child at the door, and, kissing his cheek, led him to his chair, where, after declaring publicly his satisfaction at receiving the heir to the Sovreignty of the Punjab under his protection, he had different presents, such as shawls, musical boxes, etc., laid before him, while he impressed upon his minister the necessity of entering into such terms with the British as would ensure the speedy termination of hostilities.'

Further comments on character:

In Sikh mythology and folk-lore, Dalip seems to have remained for ever 'the child maharaja', even popular wood-cuts (figure 110) featuring him with the same pet lap-dog as in figures 61 and 62.

At the risk of breaking the spell, Latif's impassioned indictment of his subsequent career as an adult may be cited: 'Under the wise ministration and guidance of (his tutor) Dr Login, Dulip Singh embraced Christianity and became an English country gentleman, owning extensive estates in Suffolk. He conducted himself with dignity and prudence and the Queen regarded him with sympathy and honoured him with invitations to select dinner parties. On public occasions he appeared in rich oriental costume and decorated with the richest gems. He was a frequent visitor at court. He married an Egyptian Christian lady, by whom he had issue. Thus for many years he continued to pass his life in peace and luxury when a sudden change became perceptible in his temper. Having expressed a desire to visit his home, the Panjab, he obtained the permission of the Government to make a journey to India. Immediately afterwards he not only took the Pahal of the Guru and re-embraced his old religion but opened a suspicious correspondence with certain old Panjab sardars. The Government disapproved of this action on the part of one who had been brought up on English bread and ordered him to return to England but he contrived to make his way to Russia and France, the Governments of which countries showed themselves quite indifferent to his fate. His Christian wife died in England of sorrow. His turbulent mother, the notorious Chand Kour (or Jindan) whose ambition and intrigues had mainly conduced to the rapid fall of the Empire of Ranjit, having become nearly blind, broken in heart and subdued in spirit, had previously died in England, in 1863, and found her last resting-place in a London suburb.'

In Russia, Latif continues, Dalip strove to gain the Czar's ear by alleging influence in the Punjab. No notice was taken by the Russian Government but the British Government discontinued Dalip's pension of £40,000 a year. Dalip, at length, 'thought it his best policy to profess repentance to the Queen. Gifted as Her Royal Majesty is by nature, with a noble and magnanimous heart and a philanthropic disposition, she was most graciously pleased to extend her pardon to him and permitted him to return to England. His pension was generously restored and the arrears discharged. It being the Queen's personal command that Dulip Singh's return to his former position in England should be made as easy and as gentle as possible, his subsequent prayer to be restored to the order of the Star of India, as a G.C.S.I., was also graciously granted. . . . As a Continental journal pointed out, 'he would have led a happier life, upon the whole, if he had continued to entertain shooting parties at Thetford Hall, instead of running about all over Europe with a bee in his bonnet.'[1]

50. Dalip Singh. Sikh, Lahore, *c.* 1850–1870.
    Size: 58 × 44 mm; shape oval.
    Inscribed on reverse in English: *Maharajah Dhulleep Singh.*
    Victoria and Albert Museum, 03598 I.S. Transferred from the India Office to the South Kensington Museum, 1880.
    Description: Front view, looking slightly left; head and shoulders. Reddish brown turban. Blue coat with gold trimmings. Background white and pale blue.

51. *Fig. 97.* Rani Jindan (?–1863). Sikh, Lahore, *c.* 1850–1870.
    Size: 60 × 50 mm; shape oval.

[1] Latif, *History*, 573–574, 628.

Inscribed on reverse in English: *Maharanee Jhundan*.

Victoria and Albert Museum, 03597 I.S. Transferred from the India Office to the South Kensington Museum, 1880.

Description: Three-quarter view, head and shoulders, facing left. Yellow veil and wrap. Brownish red blouse. Behind, part of a cushion. Background white and pale blue.

Comment on character:

GRIFFIN

'Another woman who rose to fame, or rather to notoriety, after the death of the great Maharaja, was Jindan, the reputed mother of Maharaja Dhulip Singh. She was the daughter of Manna Singh, a trooper in the service of the palace, and as a clever mimic and dancer, she attracted the notice of the old Maharaja and was taken into the zenana, where her open intrigues caused astonishment even in the easy Lahore court. A menial servant, a water-carrier, of the name of Gulu, was generally accepted as the father of Dhulip Singh. At any rate, the father was not Maharaja Ranjit Singh, who was paralysed several years before the birth of the child. Nor did he ever marry Jindan by formal or informal marriage. Many believed that Dhulip Singh was not born of Jindan at all; but was brought into the palace to favour an intrigue of the Jammu Rajas, Gulab Singh and Dhyan Singh, who required a child to put forward when all the other possible heirs, real or reputed, of the Maharaja should have perished; and it is certain that Jindan and the child were for some time sheltered at Jammu and only produced at a convenient time. However this may be, in the wild anarchy which succeeded the death of Sher Singh, when all the scum of the pot rose to the surface, Jindan, with her professed lover, Raja Lal Singh, played a conspicuous and infamous part, and her debaucheries and her unworthy paramour were in large part the cause of the Sutlej war and the ruin of the Sikh kingdom. Dhulip Singh, a child of nine years, was the titular Maharaja when the British army reached Lahore after the campaign; and as it was convenient to accept the status quo and as a nominal ruler was required for a country which the English Government had then no desire to annex or permanently occupy, the reputed child of the servant-maid and the water-carrier was confirmed on the throne of the Lion of the Punjab. Fortune, with her ever-turning wheel, must have laughed at the transformation.'[1]

52. Rani Jindan. Sikh, Lahore, *c.* 1850–1870.

    Size: 50×50 mm; shape round.

[1]Griffin, *Ranjit Singh*, 109–110.

Inscribed on reverse in English: *Runjeet Singh's ranee or queen.*
Victoria and Albert Museum, I.S. 158–1954.
Description: Three-quarter view, head and shoulders, turning left and leaning on a green cushion. Veil dark brown. Background white and pale blue.
Portraits for comparison: Cat. nos. 51, 53, 89, 90.

53. Rani Jindan. Sikh, Lahore, *c.* 1860–1870.
Size: 50×50 mm; shape round.
Inscribed on reverse in English: *Boomi Runjeet Singh's Ranee or Queen.*
Victoria and Albert Museum, I.S. 160–1954.
Description: Three-quarter view, head and shoulders, facing to the left and leaning back against a grey cushion. Green dress, brown shawl. Background pale blue.
Comment: Another version of no. 51.

54. Rani of Ranjit Singh. Sikh, Lahore, *c.* 1850–1870.
Size: 47×47 mm; shape round.
Inscribed on reverse in English: *Har Day Runjeet Singh's queen.*
Victoria and Albert Museum, I.S. 152–1954.
Description: Three-quarter view, head and shoulders, facing left. Purple veil, green dress, red cushion. Background pale blue.
Comment: Khushwant Singh (*Ranjit Singh*, 185) includes a certain 'Har Devi' among the names of the many women who, he says, 'appear in the records as having some sort of relationship with the Maharajah'. He explains: 'There were many women in the royal harem some of whom had been admitted after some sort of ceremony; others (usually widows) simply took residence in the palace because the Maharajah had cast his mantle over them; and there were yet others who came as maidservants but having caught Ranjit's fancy became his mistresses.' Dalip Singh, he says, described himself as 'the son of one of my father's forty-six wives'.

55. Rani of Ranjit Singh. Sikh, Lahore, *c.* 1850–1870.
Size: 36×36 mm; shape round.
Inscribed on reverse in English: *Runjeet Singh's wife.*
Victoria and Albert Museum, I.S. 164–1954.
Description: Three-quarter view, head and shoulders, facing left. Spotted crimson veil and blouse. Behind, a cushion. Background white and pale blue.

56. Rani of Ranjit Singh. Sikh, Lahore, *c.* 1850–1870.

Size: 48 × 48 mm; shape round.

Inscribed on reverse in English: *Runjeet Singh's Ranee or Queen.*

Victoria and Albert Museum, I.S. 163–1954.

Description: Profile, head and shoulders, facing right. Green veil, crimson blouse. Background white and pale blue.

57. *Fig. 101.* Nur-ud-din. Sikh, Lahore, *c.* 1850–1870.

Size: 58 × 48 mm; shape oval.

Inscribed on reverse in English: *Fakeer Noor Deen.*

Victoria and Albert Museum, 03596 I.S. Transferred from the India Office to the South Kensington Museum, 1880.

Description: Three-quarter view, head and shoulders, facing left. Green turban and coat. Yellow wrap. Brownish-red cushion. Background pale blue.

Portrait for comparison: Figure 61.

Note: Nur-ud-din, younger brother of Aziz-ud-din, was Ranjit Singh's physician and later a trusted adviser.

58. Sher Singh Atariwala. Sikh, Lahore, *c.* 1850–1870.

Size: 50 × 50 mm; shape round.

Inscribed on reverse in English: *Shere Singh the General.*

Victoria and Albert Museum, I.S. 145–1954.

Description: Profile, head and shoulders, facing left. Mauve turban and coat. White straps and necklaces. Background white and pale blue.

Portrait for comparison:

(*1*) *Fig. 93.* Sher Singh Atariwala seated on a chair. Sikh, Lahore, *c.* 1860. Water-colour. Inscribed in English: *Shaeer Sing belongs Atari.* India Office Library, London, Add. Or. 1404b. From an album entitled *Punjab Portraits,* illustrating Sikh rulers, characters, trades, occupations and monuments in the Punjab.

For other portraits see figures 62, 108, 109.

Note: General, second Anglo-Sikh war, 1848–1849. Son of Chattar Singh Atariwala.

59. Sher Singh Atariwala. Sikh, Lahore, *c.* 1850–1870.

Size: 60 × 48 mm; shape oval.

Inscribed on reverse in English: *Sirdar Shere Singh Attareewala.*

Victoria and Albert Museum, 03593 I.S. Transferred from the India Office to the South Kensington Museum, 1880.

Description: Profile, head and shoulders, facing left. The right hand holds the hilt of a sword. Green turban and coat. Yellow wrap. Background white and pale blue.

Portraits for comparison: Figures 62, 93, 108, 109.

60. Sham Singh Atariwala. Sikh, Lahore, *c.* 1850–1870.

   Size: 50×50 mm; shape round.

   Inscribed on reverse in English: *Shan Singh.*

   Victoria and Albert Museum, I.S. 151–1954.

   Description: Three-quarter view, head and shoulders, facing slightly right. White beard, black moustaches. Yellow dress and turban. Blue background.

Comment on character:

   Sikh general killed at battle of Sobraon, February 1846.

   Latif (*History*, 546, 547) describes how Sham Singh deplored the Sikh decision to fight the British and adds, 'But the admonitions of the hoary headed chief were not heeded. The brave old soldier thereupon announced to the desponding Khalsa his resolution to die in the first combat with the enemy.'

   [Thereupon, on the battle-field of Sobraon] 'remembering his vow to his countrymen, he dressed himself in a garment as white as his long snowy beard, galloped forward and cheering on his ardent followers, led them to the attack, reviving their spirits with the promise of everlasting bliss made to the brave by their great Guru. Thus fighting . . . thus scorning death to the last did this veteran soldier fall a martyr and his memory is held in the greatest esteem by his countrymen to this day.'

Portrait for comparison:

   (*1*) *Fig. 94.* Sham Singh Atariwala seated on a chair. Sikh, Lahore, *c.* 1860. Water-colour. Inscribed in English: *Sham Sing belongs Atari.* India Office Library, London, Add. Or. 1403a. From an album entitled *Punjab Portraits,* illustrating Sikh rulers, characters, trades occupations and monuments in the Punjab.

61. Sham Singh Atariwala. Sikh, Lahore, *c.* 1850–1870.

   Size: 62×52 mm; shape oval.

   Inscribed on reverse in English: *Sirdar Sham Singh Attareebalah.*

179

Victoria and Albert Museum, 03591 I.S. Transferred from the India Office to the South Kensington Museum, 1880.

Description: Three-quarter view, head and shoulders, gazing right. Dark blue turban and wrap. White coat with gold strap. Background white and pale blue.

Portraits for comparison: Cat. no. 60 and figure 94.

62. *Fig. 99.* Chattar Singh Atariwala. Sikh, Lahore, *c.* 1850–1870.

Size: 62 × 52 mm; shape oval.

Inscribed on reverse in English: *Sirdar Chutter Singh Attareewalah.*

Victoria and Albert Museum, 03592 I.S. Transferred from the India Office to the South Kensington Museum, 1880.

Description: Profile, head and shoulders, facing left. Yellow turban, Reddish brown wrap. Dark green coat. Purple cushion. Black shield at back. Background, brownish pink, white and pale blue.

Portraits for comparison: Figures 62, 108, 109, 110.

Note: Father of Sher Singh Atariwala. General, second Anglo-Sikh War, 1848–1849.

63. Chattar Singh Atariwala. Sikh, Lahore, *c.* 1850–1870.

Size: 50 × 50 mm; shape round.

Inscribed on reverse in English: *Chutter Singh, Shere Singh's father.*

Victoria and Albert Museum I.S. 156–1954.

Description: Profile, head and shoulders, facing left; white beard, black moustaches. Yellow turban, white dress. Background pale blue.

Portraits for comparison: Figures 62, 99, 108, 109, 110.

64. *Fig. 98.* Tej Singh. Sikh, Lahore, c. 1850–1870.

Size: 60 × 48 mm; shape oval.

Inscribed on reverse in English: *Teq Singh.*

Victoria and Albert Museum 03595 I.S. Transferred from the India Office to the South Kensington Museum, 1880.

Description: Profile, head and shoulders, facing left. Dark blue turban and wrap, white coat with green edge. Black shield at back. Background white and pale blue.

Portraits for comparison: Figures 61, 62.

Note: Commander-in-chief Sikh army, 1845.

65. *Fig. 102.* Lal Singh. Sikh, Lahore, *c.* 1850–1870.

Size: 60 × 48 mm; shape oval.

Formerly inscribed on reverse in English: *Lall Singh.*

Victoria and Albert Museum, 03608 I.S. Transferred from the India Office to the South Kensington Museum, 1880.

Description: Profile, head and shoulders, facing right. Pink turban and coat, with traces of yellow. Black shield on back. Background white and pale blue.

Comment on character:

Hardinge (*op. cit.*, pl. 13) cites the following sketch of Lal Singh's life and character from a writer in *The Calcutta Review*: 'A Brahmin of Rhotas, between the Indus and the Jylum, Lal Singh early came, as an adventurer, to the capital to try his fortune. He brought with him, as stock in trade, an athletic person, of unusual height, even among the Sikhs, an open merry countenance, with rather a sensual expression, a bold manly bearing, great ambition, and no scruples. His first footing within the precincts of the court was in the humble capacity of assistant in the Toshak-khana or Treasury of Regalia, and a mule's load of the Royal chattels was the first charge of the future Minister. Raja Dhian Singh afterwards selected him as a fit instrument to be set up in opposition to Misr Beni Ram, the head of the Toshak-khana, and he gave him a separate treasury of his own. But it was not until after Dhian Singh's death, and when Hira Singh was in the zenith of his power, that, tired of her old lovers, Rani Junda cast her eyes on the gallant figure of Misr Lal Singh, and commenced an amour, which, though it had drawn down the envy of the young adventurers at the Court, the shame and reprobation of the old Sirdars, and the ribald jests of the people, has raised the object of it to the Wizarut, and all but regal power in the Punjab. Misr Lal Singh now began to have some weight in the scale of parties. He intrigued alternately with and against the Jamu Rajahs (Gulab Singh being the uncle of Hira Singh), and no sooner did his bias become consistently hostile, than his intimacy with the Rani was made an excuse for removing him from the Toshuk-khana, to the control of which he had succeeded on the death of Beni Ram. The disgrace of her lover gained for Hira Singh the implacable enmity of the Rani, and the issue was that bloody revolution which led to the foul murder of young Hira Singh and his Minister.'

Hardinge adds: 'The later history of Lal Singh is well known. It is unnecessary to relate how, as Prime Minister and favourite of the Rani, he was for a while almost absolute in the Punjab. His power survived the defeats of the Sikh army on the banks of the Sutlej, and it was not until his intrigue with the Governor of Kashmir, in direct contravention of the Treaty of Umretsir, was discovered, that he was deposed from his authority. The late treaties made in consequence of that event are before the public. Lal Singh is now an exile in the territory of British India.'

Portraits for comparison:

(*1*) *Fig. 62.* Darbar of Dalip Singh. Eleventh figure from left.

(*2*) *Fig. 63.* Jawahir Singh (?–1845), brother of Rani Jindan, in darbar. Seated from left to right: (i) Labh Singh (ii) Lal Singh (iii) Jawahir Singh. Lithograph after a Sikh painting in style of Hasan-al-din (figures 61, 62), Lahore, *c.* 1845. *Published:* W. L. McGregor, *The History of the Sikhs* (London, 1846), II, frontispiece; entitled in English: *Lall Singh, Juwaheer Singh, Lab Singh*.

Note: Since the picture commemorates the rise to power of Jawahir Singh in 1845, Labh Singh's presence in it would seem to negative Latif's assertion (*History*, 527–531) that he was killed along with other members of Hira Singh's party in December 1844. For other portraits of Labh Singh, see figure 62 (second from left) and figure 61 (first on left).

For Jawahir Singh, see figure 62 (tenth from left).

(*3*) *Raja Lal Singh*. Lithograph from an original drawing by C. S. Hardinge, Lahore, 1846. *Published:* C. S. Hardinge, *Recollections of India* (London, 1847), part I, pl. 13. Entitled: *Rajah Lal Singh*.

66. *Fig. 103.* Phula Singh Akali. Sikh, Lahore, *c.* 1850–1870.
Size: 58×46 mm; shape oval.
Inscribed on reverse in English: *Phoola Singh Akaleea*.
Victoria and Albert Museum, 03589 I.S. Transferred from the India Office to the South Kensington Museum, 1880.
Description: Profile, head and shoulders, facing right. Blue conical turban with three iron quoits. Blue coat. White beard and black moustache. A bow on the right shoulder and two arrows in the left hand. White background.

Portraits for comparison: Figures 108, 109.
Note: A leading member of the fanatical sect which guarded the Golden Temple, Amritsar. Famous for his feats of wild daring.

67. *Fig. 105.* Mul Raj. Sikh, Lahore, *c.* 1850–1870.
Size: 40×40 mm; shape round.
Inscribed on reverse in English: *Moolraj Governor of Moolton*.

Victoria and Albert Museum, I.S. 142–1954.

Description: Profile, head and shoulders, facing right. Black beard. Brown and yellow dress and turban. Pale blue and white background.

Portraits for comparison: Figures 108, 109.

Note: Governor of Multan whose actions triggered off the second Anglo-Sikh war, 1848–1849.

68. Mul Raj. Sikh, Lahore, *c.* 1850–1870.

Size: 60×48 mm; shape oval.

Inscribed on reverse in English: *Diwan Moolraj.*

Victoria and Albert Museum, 03590 I.S. Transferred from the India Office to the South Kensington Museum, 1880.

Description: Profile, head and shoulders, facing right. Pink turban, yellow coat. Green cushion. Background white and pale blue.

Portraits for comparison: Figures 105, 108, 109.

69. Dina Nath. Sikh, Lahore, *c.* 1850–1870.

Size: 38×38 mm; shape round.

Inscribed on reverse in English: *Raja Deenanath.*

Victoria and Albert Museum, I.S. 161–1954.

Description: Profile, head and shoulders, facing right. White turban, beard and coat. Yellow wrap. Background pale blue.

Portraits for comparison: Figures 61, 62, 64, 108, 109.

Note on character: See cat. no. 34.

70. Dina Nath. Sikh, Lahore, *c.* 1850–1870.

Size: 60×52 mm; shape oval.

Inscribed on reverse in English: *Rajah Deena Nath.*

Victoria and Albert Museum, 03594 I.S. Transferred from the India Office to the South Kensington Museum, 1880.

Description: Profile, head and shoulders, facing right. Pale red coat. Background white and pale blue.

Note: See cat. no. 69.

71. Maharajah Ranjit Singh. Sikh, Lahore, *c.* 1850–1870.

Size: 50×50 mm; shape round.

Inscribed on reverse in English: *Runjeet Singh King of the Punjaub.*

Victoria and Albert Museum, I.S. 148–1954.
Description: Three-quarter view, facing right, both eyes (including the blind left eye) visible. Brownish white background.
Portraits for comparison: Figures 68, 69, 108, 109.

72. Maharaja Ranjit Singh. Sikh, Lahore, *c.* 1850–1870.
Size: 50×50 mm; shape round.
Inscribed on reverse in English: *Runjeet Singh.*
Victoria and Albert Museum, I.S. 167–1954.
Description: Profile, head and shoulders, facing left. Green turban and coat with gold and crimson straps. White beard. Black shield on left arm. In the right hand, a flower. Background pale blue.
Note: A reversal of the normal pose, showing the left eye as sound.

73. Maharaja Ranjit Singh. Sikh, Lahore, *c.* 1850–1870.
Size: 60×48 mm; shape oval.
Inscribed on reverse in English: *Maharajah Runjeet Singh.*
Victoria and Albert Museum, 03599 I.S. Transferred from the India Office to the South Kensington Museum, 1880.
Description: Three-quarter view, head and shoulders, facing right, both eyes visible. A gun in the right hand. Blue coat with gold trimmings. Green turban with pearls. White beard and moustache. Background white and pale blue.

74. Kharak Singh. Sikh, Lahore, *c.* 1850–1870.
Size: 50×50 mm; shape round.
Inscribed on reverse in English: *Khurk Singh Sikh Sirdar.*
Victoria and Albert Museum, I.S. 157–1954.
Description: Profile, head and shoulders, facing left. Crimson turban and coat with green strap. Black beard. In the right hand the hilt of a sword. Background white and pale blue.
Portraits for comparison: Figures 21, 22, 31, 35.

75. Kharak Singh. Sikh, Lahore, *c.* 1850–1870.
Size: 60×48 mm; shape oval.
Inscribed on reverse in English: *Maharajah Kurruck Singh.*

Victoria and Albert Museum, 03601 I.S. Transferred from the India Office to the South Kensington Museum, 1880.

Description: Profile, head and shoulders, facing right. Brownish yellow coat and turban. Red wrap edged with white and blue. Black shield on back. Background white and pale blue.

Note: See cat. no. 74.

76. Nau Nihal Singh. Sikh, Lahore, *c.* 1850–1870.
    Size: 50 × 50 mm; shape round.
    Inscribed on reverse in English: *Nao Rahall Singh one of the Sidars.*
    Victoria and Albert Museum, I.S. 146–1954.
    Description: Profile, facing left, holding a sword by the hilt. Yellow turban, white dress, pink scarf. Background misty white.
    Portraits for comparison: Figures 24, 32, 35.

77. Nau Nihal Singh. Sikh, Lahore, *c.* 1850–1870.
    Size: 48 × 48 mm; shape round.
    Misinscribed on reverse in English: *Hura Singh brother to Shere Singh.*
    Victoria and Albert Museum, I.S. 166–1954.
    Description: Profile, head and shoulders, facing left. Purple turban and coat with white and green straps. In the right hand the hilt of a sword. Background white and pale blue.
    Note: For identification, compare cat. nos. 76 and 78.

78. Nau Nihal Singh. Sikh, Lahore, *c.* 1850–1870.
    Size: 55 × 47 mm; shape oval.
    Inscribed on reverse in English: *Maharajah Nonihal Singh.*
    Victoria and Albert Museum, 03600 I.S. Transferred from India Office to South Kensington Museum, 1880.
    Description: Profile, head and shoulders, facing left. A flower in the right hand. Purple turban and wrap. Reddish brown coat. Background pale blue.
    Note: See cat. nos. 76 and 77.

79. Dhian Singh. Sikh, Lahore, *c.* 1850–1870.
    Size: 62 × 52 mm; shape oval.
    Inscribed on reverse in English: *Rajah Dhyan Singh.*

Victoria and Albert Museum, 03604 I.S. Transferred from India Office to South Kensington Museum, 1880.

Description: Profile, head and shoulders, facing left. Reddish brown turban. Dark green coat, the right hand holding the hilt of a sword. Background white and pale blue.

Portraits for comparison: Figures 15, 23, 24, 30, 33, 35, 90, 108, 109.

80. Dhian Singh. Sikh, Lahore, *c.* 1850–1870.

  Size: 50×50 mm; shape round.

  Inscribed on reverse in English: *Dhyan Singh a Sikh nobleman.*

  Victoria and Albert Museum, I.S. 165–1954.

  Description: Profile, head and shoulders, facing right. Green turban and coat. Black beard. The hilt of a sword held in the left hand. Background pale blue and white.

  Note: See cat. no. 79.

81. Hira Singh. Sikh, Lahore, *c.* 1850–1870.

  Size: 54×42 mm; shape oval.

  Inscribed on reverse in English: *Rajah Heera Singh.*

  Victoria and Albert Museum, 03607 I.S. Transferred from the India Office to the South Kensington Museum, 1880.

  Description: Three-quarter view, head and shoulders, facing left. Pink turban. Reddish brown wrap. Dark green coat. Traces of a yellow cushion. A shield at the back. Background pale blue.

  Portraits for comparison: Figures 19, 20.

82. *Fig. 107.* Gulab Singh. Sikh, Lahore, *c.* 1850–1870.

  Size: 50×50 mm; shape round.

  Inscribed on reverse in English: *Maharaja Goolab Singh King of Cashmere.*

  Victoria and Albert Museum, I.S. 149–1954.

  Description: Three-quarter view, head and shoulders looking right. White turban, coat and beard. Black shield. Blue background tinged with white.

  Portraits for comparison: Figures 15, 34, 50, 52, 53, 55, 108, 109.

83. Gulab Singh. Sikh, Lahore, *c.* 1850–1870.

  Size: 60×48 mm; shape oval.

  Inscribed on reverse in English: *Maharajah Golab Singh.*

Victoria and Albert Museum, 03603 I.S. Transferred from the India Office to the South Kensington Museum, 1880.

Description: Three-quarter view, head and shoulders, facing left. Black beard. Yellow turban. Green coat. White wrap. Traces of a supporting cushion. Background pale blue, yellow and white.

Note: See cat. no. 82.

84. Guru Nanak (first Sikh Guru). Sikh, Lahore, *c.* 1850–1870.

Size: 50×50 mm; shape round.

Inscribed on reverse in English: *Gooroo Nana founder of the Sikh's religion.*

Victoria and Albert Museum, I.S. 150–1954.

Description: Full face, head and shoulders. White beard. Coat reddish-brown. On the shoulders a multi-coloured patch work shawl. Blue and white background.

Portrait for comparison: Figure 1.

85. Dost Muhammad. Sikh, Lahore, *c.* 1850–1870.

Size: 50×50 mm; shape round.

Inscribed on reverse in English: *Dost Mahomed Khan King of Cabool.*

Victoria and Albert Museum, I.S. 147–1954.

Description: Three-quarter view, head and shoulders, facing left. White beard. Yellow and blue robe, white and gold turban. Background white and pale blue.

Note: Ruler of Afghanistan and enemy of the British.

86. Akbar Ali Khan. Sikh, Lahore, *c.* 1850–1870.

Size: 50×50 mm; shape round.

Inscribed on reverse in English: *Akbar Khan of the Kyber Pass massacre.*

Victoria and Albert Museum, I.S. 153–1954.

Description: Three-quarter view, head and shoulders, facing left. Black beard, crimson coat, yellow turban. Background pale blue.

Note: Afghan. Son of Dost Muhammad (no. 85). Died 1848.

87. Sikh sardar. Sikh, Lahore, *c.* 1850–1870.

Size: 50×50 mm; shape round.

Misinscribed on reverse in English: *Huree Singh Runjeet Singh's father.*

Victoria and Albert Museum, I.S. 155–1954.

Description: Profile, head and shoulders, facing left. Black shield on back, flower in right hand. Grey coat, crimson dress and turban. Background pale blue.

Note: The father of Ranjit Singh was Maha, not Hari, Singh.

88. Sikh sardar. Sikh, Lahore, *c.* 1860–1870.

Size: 50 × 50 mm; shape round.

Inscribed on reverse in English: *Gooro Nizam Singh a Sikh sardar.*

Victoria and Albert Museum, I.S. 154–1954.

Description: Three-quarter view, head and shoulders, facing left. Black beard and moustache. Red shawl and turban. Pale blue background.

V WOODCUTS

89. *Fig. 108.* Coloured woodcut depicting twelve heroes of the Sikhs. Popular Sikh, Lahore or Amritsar, *c.* 1870.

Size: 320 × 230 mm.

Inscribed in English: first row, *Maharaja Sher Sing, Maharaja Runjeet Sing (late King of Punjab), Maharaja Dulleep Sing son of Ma Ra Runjeet Singh*; second row, *Moolraj Governor of Mooltan, Golab Sing King of Jumoo and Cashmere, Jindan (late Queen)*; third row, *Raja Deena Nath, Sher Sing Atareewala (fought at Goojrat), Chuttur Sing Atareewala*; fourth row, *Raja Dhyan Sing, Dost Mohamed Ruler of Kabul, Phoola Sing of Umritsar.*

Victoria and Albert Museum, I.M. 2/56–1917.

Given by Rudyard Kipling from the J. Lockwood Kipling collection, 1917.

Description: Twelve portraits in four rows. Modelled on Sikh portraits on ivory, with oval shape and dark rims. Backgrounds silver grey. Colours brick-red, crimson, yellow, green. Size of each oval 70 × 60 mm. Nos. 1–3, 5 and 6 three-quarter view, 1 and 2 facing right, the other three facing left; remainder in profile.

Comment: Ranjit Singh's blind left eye clearly shown. Gulab Singh depicted with small in-curling moustache ends.

90. *Fig. 109.* Coloured woodcut depicting twelve heroes of the Sikhs. Popular Sikh, Lahore or Amritsar, *c.* 1870.

Size: 325 × 235 mm.

Inscribed in English: first row, *Maharaja Sher Singh, Maharaja Ranjit Singh late King of Punjab Maharaja Dulip Singh, son of Ma Ra Ranjit Singh*; second row *Raja Dhian Singh, Prime Minister, Gulab Singh of Jummoo and Kashmir, Jindan (late Queen)*; third row, *Chutter Singh Attariwala, Sher Singh Attariwala, Raja Dina*

189

Nath; fourth row, *Mulraj Governor of Multan, Dost Muhamad ruler of Kabul, Pula Singh of Amritsar.*

Victoria and Albert Museum, I.M. 2/119–1917.

Given by Rudyard Kipling from the J. Lockwood Kipling collection, 1917.

Description: Twelve portraits in four rows. Modelled on Sikh portraits on ivory, with oval shape and black rim. Backgrounds pale blue. Colours brick-red, crimson, slate blue, yellow. Size of each oval 70 × 60 mm. Nos. 1, 2 three-quarter view, facing right, nos. 3, 5, 6, 11 and 12 three-quarter view, facing left. Remainder profiles.

Comment: Similar in general style to no. 89. Gulab Singh, however, is given the upward-pointing moustache ends more typical of his son, Ranbir.

91. *Fig. 110.* Woodcut depicting twelve heroes of the Sikhs. Popular Sikh, Lahore or Amritsar, *c.* 1870.

Size: 380 × 300 mm.

Inscribed in English: first row, *Raja Shair Singh, Raja Ranjeet Singh, Raja Daleep Singh, Rani Jinda*; second row, *Raja Dhian Singh, Raja Golab Singh of Kashmir, Raja Shair Singh of Atari, Raja Chater Singh of Atari*; third row, *Raja Dina Nath, Mool Raj of Multan, Nawab Dost Mohamed Khan of Cabul, Phola Singh Nihaung.* Also inscribed in Persian and Punjabi characters.

Victoria and Albert Museum, I.M. 2/47–1917.

Given by Rudyard Kipling from the J. Lockwood Kipling collection, 1917.

Description: Twelve portraits in three rows. Modelled on poses current in standard portrait sets in gouache. Approximate size of each 125 × 80 mm. Nos. 1 and 2 three-quarter view, facing right; nos. 3, 4, 6, 11 and 12 three-quarter view, facing left. Remainder profiles.

Comment: Ranjit Singh's blind eye visible. Dalip Singh with lap dog.

Gulab Singh as in no. 82, figure 107—Portrait on ivory.

92. *Fig. 111.* Woodcut. Maharaja Ranjit Singh in darbar attended by his sons, ministers and rivals. Popular Sikh, Lahore or Amritsar, *c.* 1870.

From left to right (clockwise): (1) ?, (2) Sher Singh, (3) Kharak Singh, (4) standing attendant, (5) Ranjit Singh, (6) Dalip Singh, (7) Dhian Singh, (8) Gulab Singh, (9) Suchet Singh, (10) Tej Singh (thence right to left): (11) Dost Mumahammad, (12)?, (13)?, (14) Dina Nath, (15)?, (16)?

Size: 200 × 215 mm.

Victoria and Albert Museum, I.M. 2/16–1917.

Given by Rudyard Kipling from the J. Lockwood Kipling collection, 1917.

93. *Fig. 112.* Woodcut. Sikh Railway train. Popular Sikh, Lahore or Amritsar,
   c. 1870.
   Size: 305 × 460 mm.
   Victoria and Albert Museum, I.M. 2/51–1917.
   Given by Rudyard Kipling from the J. Lockwood Kipling collection, 1917.
   Description: Railway train in two sections. The upper has four coaches with
men and women passengers, Sikh and British. The lower has two coaches and
an engine. Sikh station-master, guard, booking clerk and signalman.
   Discussed pages 69–70.

94. A series of 13 woodcuts on miscellaneous Sikh subjects. Popular Sikh, Lahore
   or Amritsar, *c.* 1870. Sizes various.
   Victoria and Albert Museum, Indian Section.
   Given by Rudyard Kipling from the J. Lockwood Kipling collection, 1917.
   1. View of the Golden Temple, Amritsar. I.M. 2/50–1917.
   2. The ten Gurus. I.M. 2/11–1917.
   3. Guru Nanak with followers and attendants. I.M. 2/33–1917.
   4. Ranjit Singh on horseback, facing right, a follower holding a state umbrella.
      I.M. 2/63–1917 (right half).
   5. Guru Nanak, nimbate, seated with Mardana and Bala. I.M. 2/36–1917
      (upper half).
   6. The ten Gurus. I.M. 2/88–1917.
   7. Guru Govind Singh on horseback with hound and followers. I.M. 2/133–
      1917.
   8. Ranjit Singh on horseback facing left with hound and follower holding a
      state umbrella. I.M. 2/136–1917.
   9. Akali with wife and child. I.M. 2/137–1917.
   10. View of the Golden Temple, Amritsar. I.M. 2/153–1917.
   11. Guru Nanak with disciples. Inscribed in Persian characters: made at
      Amritsar. I.M. 2/154–1917.
   12. Battle between Sikhs and British. I.M. 2/151–1917.
   13. Guru Govind Singh baptising five converts. I.M. 2/179–1917

Plates

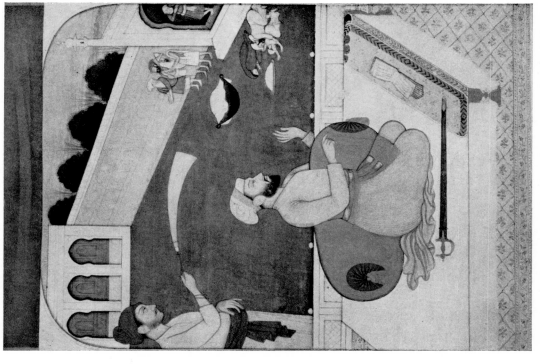

2. Guru Arjun (fifth Guru, 1581–1606) expounding the Granth. Guler, c. 1820. (Page 19)

1. Guru Nanak (b. 1469 d. 1529) conversing with Guru Govind Singh (tenth Guru, 1675–1708). Guler, c. 1820. (Page 19)

3. Guru Har Govind (sixth Guru, 1606–1645). Guler,   4. Guru Har Rai (seventh Guru, 1645–1661). Guler, *c.* 1820.

6. Guru Tegh Bahadur (ninth Guru, 1661–1675). Guler
c. 1820. (Page 19)

5. Guru Har Kishan (eighth Guru, 1661–1664). Guler,
c. 1820. (Page 19)

7. Guru Govind Singh (tenth Guru, 1675–1708). Guler, *c.* 1830. (Page 125)

8. Mian Amar Singh 'Darhiwala' of Kotla. Guler, *c.* 1825. (Pages 19, 125)

9. Raja Dhian Singh (1796–1843) on horseback with retainers. Sikh, *c.* 1830–1835.

10. Sikh sardar presiding at a wedding reception. Guler, *c.* 1815–1820. (Pages 19–20)

11. Sikh sardar carousing with a Guler lady. Guler, *c.* 1815–1825. (Pages 19–20)

12. Maharaja Ranjit Singh (1786–1839) carousing with a Kangra lady.
Kangra, *c.* 1830–1835. (Page 27)

13. Youth in Sikh dress dallying with a Kangra lady. Kangra, *c.* 1835.
(Page 27)

14. Maharaja Ranjit Singh (1780–1839) on horseback. Sikh, *c.* 1835–1840.
(Pages 126–127)

15. Maharaja Ranjit Singh (1780–1839) in darbar with his head astrologer and pandits. Sikh, *c.* 1830–1835.

16. The funeral of Ranjit Singh (1780–1839). Kangra, c. 1840. (Pages 27–30)

17. Maharaja Ranjit Singh (1780–1839) on horseback. Sikh, *c.* 1838–1840.
(Pages 127–128)

18. Maharaja Ranjit Singh (1780–1839) on horseback. Sikh, *c.* 1838–1840.
(Pages 128–129)

19. Maharaja Ranjit Singh (1780–1839) and Hira Singh (c. 1816–1844). Sikh, c. 1838–1840.
(Page 129)

20. Hira Singh (*c*. 1816–1844). Sikh, *c*. 1838–1840. (Pages 131–132)

21. Maharaja Kharak Singh (1802–1840) on horseback. Sikh, *c.* 1838–1840.
(Page 133)

22. Maharaja Kharak Singh (1802–1840) seated. Sikh, *c.* 1835–1840.
(Page 138)

23. Raja Suchet Singh (1801–1844) and Raja Dhian Singh (1796–1843). Sikh, *c.* 1840.
(Page 139)

24. Raja Dhian Singh (1796–1843), seated on the ground, with Raja Nau Nihal Singh
(1821–1840). Sikh, *c.* 1840. (Pages 136–137)

25. Maharaja Ranjit Singh (1780–1839) receiving Raja Dhian Singh (1796–1843). Sikh, *c.* 1845. (Pages 51, 131)

26. Maharaja Ranjit Singh (1780–1839) seated. Lithograph. Emily Eden, *Portraits of the Princes and Peoples of India* (London, 1844), plate 13. (Pages 51, 130, 131)

27. Maharaja Ranjit Singh (1780–1839) on horseback. Sikh, *c.* 1840. (Page 139)

28. Maharaja Ranjit Singh (1780–1839) seated. Sikh, *c*. 1840. (Pages 37, 129, 130)

30. Raja Dhian Singh (1796–1843) seated. Sikh,

29. Hira Singh (c. 1816–1844) seated. Sikh, c. 1840.

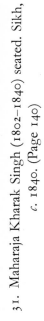

31. Maharaja Kharak Singh (1802–1840) seated. Sikh,
c. 1840. (Page 140)

32. Raja Nau Nihal Singh (1821–1840) seated. Sikh,
c. 1840. (Pages 140–141)

33. Raja Dhian Singh (1796–1843) on horseback. Sikh, *c.* 1840. (Page 141)

34. Raja Gulab Singh (1792–1857) of Jammu on horseback. Sikh, *c.* 1840–1845.
(Page 143)

35. Raja Dhian Singh (1796–1843) facing, right to left, Maharaja Kharak Singh (1802–1840),
Raja Nau Nihal Singh (1821–1840) and Hira Singh (c. 1816–1844). Sikh, c. 1840.
(Pages 37, 132, 133)

36. Sikh sardar receiving petitions. Sikh, *c.* 1840. (Pages 20, 21, 142)

37. Maharaja Gulab Singh (1792–1857) of Jammu bathing. Sikh, c. 1835–1840.
(Pages 53, 54, 143)

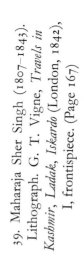

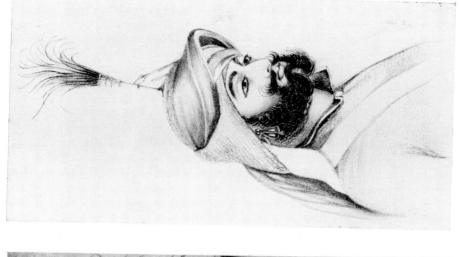

39. Maharaja Sher Singh (1807–1843). Lithograph. G. T. Vigne, *Travels in Kashmir, Ladak, Iskardo* (London, 1842), I, frontispiece. (Page 167)

38. Maharaja Sher Singh (1807–1843) seated on a bed after bathing. Kangra, *c.* 1830. (Pages 25, 26, 167)

40. Maharaja Sher Singh (1807–1843) seated. Sikh, *c.* 1840.
(Pages 37, 167, 168)

41. Maharaja Sher Singh (1807–1843) seated. Sikh, *c.* 1840–1845.
(Page 168)

42. Maharaja Sher Singh (1807–1843) seated. Lithograph. Emily Eden, *Portraits of the Princes and People of India* (London, 1844), plate 2. (Pages 42, 168)

43. Maharaja Sher Singh (1807–1843) seated. Oil. By August Theodor Schoefft. Vienna, *c.* 1845–1850. (Pages 48, 169)

44. Maharaja Sher Singh (1807–1843) returning from a hunt. Detail of Figure 45.

45. The Dasahra Festival at the Court of Lahore. Oil. By August Theodor Schoefft. Vienna, *c.* 1845–1850.

(Pages 48, 49, 168)

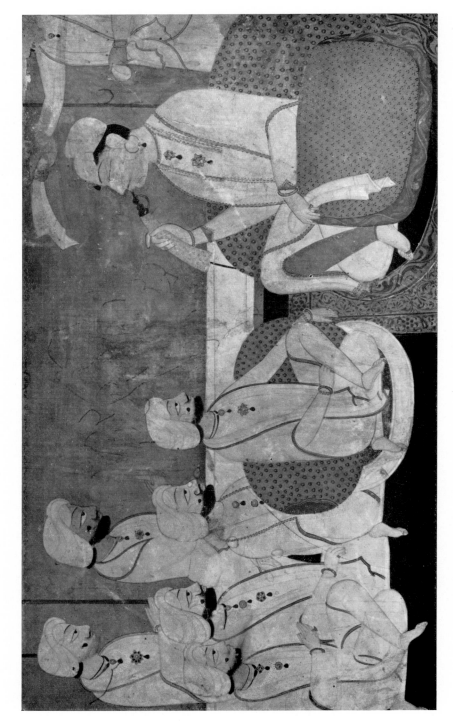

46. Hill prince smoking, attended by courtiers in Sikh dress. Detail. Sikh, c. 1835–1840. (Page 144)

48. Hill prince seated. Sikh, *c*. 1840. (Pages 145–146)

47. Hill prince smoking. Sikh, *c*. 1840. (Pages 144–145)

49. Hira Singh (*c.* 1816–1844) seated. Lithograph. Emily Eden, *Portraits of the Princes and People of India* (London, 1844), plate 7. (Page 51)

50. Maharaja Gulab Singh (1792–1847) of Jammu and Kashmir. Sikh, *c.* 1846.
(Pages 54, 146)

51. Prince in Sikh dress. Sikh, *c.* 1835–1845. (Page 146)

52. Maharaja Gulab Singh (1792–1857) of Jammu and Kashmir. Lithograph. C. S. Hardinge, *Recollections of India* (London, 1847), part II, plate 14. (Pages 56, 148)

53. Maharaja Gulab Singh (1792–1857) of Jammu and Kashmir. Water-colour. By William Carpenter (c. 1818–1899), Kashmir, c. 1855. (Pages 56, 148)

54. Raja Ranbir Singh (?–1885) of Jammu and Kashmir. Water-colour. By William Carpenter (c. 1818–1899), Kashmir, c. 1855. (Page 151)

55. Maharaja Gulab Singh (1792–1857) of Jammu and Kashmir with his sons, Udham Singh, centre, and Sohan (Randhir) Singh, left. Sikh, *c.* 1840–1846. (Pages 55, 149)

56. The first and second sons of Maharaja Gulab Singh (1792–1857) of Jammu and Kashmir: Udham Singh (?–1840) left, Sohan (Randhir) Singh (?–1844), right. (Pages 55, 149)

57. Maharaja Gulab Singh (1792–1857) of Jammu and Kashmir, left, facing his third son, Ranbir Singh (?–1885), right. Sikh, *c.* 1846. (Pages 55, 148)

58. Raja Ranbir Singh (?–1885) of Jammu, left, conversing with a secretary.
Sikh, *c.* 1846. (Pages 55, 150)

59. The second Lahore darbar of 26 December, 1846. Detail. (Pages 55, 150, 151)

60. The second Lahore darbar of 26 December, 1846. Front row, left to right, Henry Lawrence, Lord Gough, Lord Hardinge, Sheikh Imam-ud-din, Raja Ranbir Singh of Jammu, one person unidentified, the child Maharaja Dalip Singh, Frederick Currie. Sikh, *c.* 1846–1847. (Pages 55, 150, 151)

61. Maharaja Dalip Singh (1837–1893) in darbar, December, 1845. Seated, from left to right (1) Labh Singh (2) standing attendant (3) Tej Singh (4) Maharaja Dalip Singh (5) Dina Nath (6) Nur-ud-din. By Hasan-al din, Sikh, 1845–1846. (Pages 66, 173)

62. Maharaja Dalip Singh (1837–1893) in darbar, November, 1843. Seated clockwise from left to right: (1)? (2) Labh Singh (3)? (4)? (5) Pandit Jalla (6) Hira Singh (7) standing attendant (8) Maharaja Dalip Singh (9) Dina Nath (10) Jawahir Singh (11) Lal Singh (12) Tej Singh (13) Gulab Singh (14) Suchet Singh (15) Chattar Singh Atariwala (16) Sher Singh Atariwala. Style of Hasan-al din, Sikh, c. 1843. (Pages 65–66, 172–173)

63. Jawahir Singh (?–1845) in darbar. Seated, from left to right, (1) Labh Singh (2) Lal Singh (3) Jawahir Singh. Lithograph. W. L. McGregor, *The History of the Sikhs* (London, 1846), II, frontispiece. (Pages 66, 182)

65. Youth with attendant. Sikh, *c.* 1832–1835. (Page 125)

64. Henry Lawrence, British Resident at Lahore, 1846–1848, dictating to Dina Nath, ex-Finance Minister. Style of Hasan-al din. Sikh, *c.* 1847. (Pages 66, 161)

Within the image: *Maharaja Dhalip Sing. Lahore 1849.*

66. Maharaja Dalip Singh (1837–1893) seated with attendants. Lithograph. Helen C. Mackenzie, *Illustrations of the Mission, the Camp and the Zenana* (London, 1854), plate 6. (Pages 62, 173–174)

67. Maharaja Dalip Singh (1837–1893) enthroned. Lithograph, C. S. Hardinge,
Recollections of India (London, 1847), part I, plate 1. (Pages 62, 174)

THE MAHARAJAH RUNJEET SINGH.

AGED 58.

King of the Sikhs & Ruler of the Punjab, Ladak, Kashmere & Peshawar.

From an original Portrait now in England and taken during the visit of His Excellency General Sir Henry Fane G.C.B. Commander in Chief of the King's & Hon.ble Compa.nys Army in India to Lahore, for the purpose of attending the marriage of N. Nehal Sing the Maharajah's Grandson at the Staree in the Punjab on the 8th March 1837.

68. Maharaja Ranjit Singh (1780–1839). Lithograph (London, 1837) after a drawing by G. T. Vigne, Lahore, March 1837. (Pages 164–165)

کلل لر سنکھ مصور لا و ری سمہ ۱۹۰۹

69. Maharaja Ranjit Singh (1780–1839). Glass. By Kehar Singh, Sikh, Lahore, 1849.
(Page 164)

70. Mounted orderlies of Ranjit Singh. Sikh, *c.* 1835. (Page 152)

71. Horse and groom. Sikh, *c.* 1840. (Page 152)

73. Sikh horseman. Sikh, *c.* 1840–1845.
(Pages 40, 153)

72. Sikh lancer in chain-mail. Sikh, *c.* 1840–1845.
(Pages 40, 153)

75. Sikh rider in chain-mail with gun. Sikh, *c.* 1840–1845. (Pages 40, 154)

74. Sikh rider with shield and breast-plate. Sikh, *c.* 1840–1845. (Pages 40, 153)

76. Lady with Sikh lover. Kangra, *c.* 1830. (Page 26)

78. Two Akalis. Sikh, *c.* 1840–1845.
(Pages 155–157)

77. Two Sikh cultivators. Sikh, *c.* 1840–1845.
(Page 157)

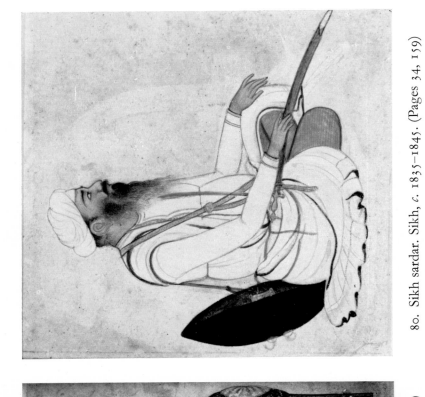

80. Sikh sardar. Sikh, *c.* 1835–1845. (Pages 34, 159)

79. Sikh sardar, Sikh, *c.* 1835–1845. (Pages 34, 159)

81. Dina Nath (?–1857). Sikh, *c.* 1840–1845.
(Pages 160–161)

82. Sikh sardar. Sikh, *c.* 1835–1845.
(Pages 34, 161)

83. Ajit Singh Sandhawalia (?–1843). Sikh, *c.* 1835–1840. (Page 159)

84. Brahmin (?). Sikh, *c.* 1835–1845.
(Page 162)

85. Sikh sardar. Sikh, *c.* 1835–1845.
(Pages 34, 163)

86. Sikh sardar. Sikh, *c.* 1835–1845.
(Pages 34, 162)

87. Sikh sardar. Sikh, *c.* 1835–1845.
(Pages 34, 162)

88. Sikh sardar. Sikh, *c.* 1835–1845.
(Pages 34, 162)

89. Sikh sardar. Sikh, *c.* 1835–1845.
(Pages 34, 163)

90. Raja Dhian Singh (1796–1843). Sikh,
c. 1835–1840. (Page 163)

91. Sikh sardar. Sikh, *c.* 1835–1845.
(Pages 34, 163)

92. Maharaja Sher Singh (1807–1843).
Sikh, *c*. 1860. (Pages 59, 169)

93. Sher Singh Atariwala. Sikh,
c. 1860. (Pages 59, 178)

94. Sham Singh Atariwala. Sikh,
c. 1860. (Pages 59, 179)

95. Maharaja Ranbir Singh (?–1885) of
Jammu and Kashmir. Sikh, *c*. 1860.
(Pages 59, 151)

96. Maharaja Dalip Singh (1837–1893). Sikh, *c.* 1850–1870. (Page 172)

97. Rani Jindan (?–1861). Sikh, *c.* 1850–1870. (Pages 175–176)

98. Tej Singh, Sikh, *c.* 1850–1870. (Pages 67, 180)

99. Chattar Singh Atariwala. Sikh, *c.* 1850–1870. (Pages 66, 180)

100. Pratap Singh (1831–1843). Sikh,
c. 1850–1870. (Pages 67, 169)

101. Nur-ud-din. Sikh, c. 1850–1870.
(Page 178)

102. Lal Singh. Sikh, c. 1850–1870.
(Page 181)

103. Phula Singh Akali. Sikh, c. 1850–1870.
(Page 182)

104. Maharaja Sher Singh (1807–1843).
Sikh, *c.* 1850–1870. (Pages 51, 166)

105. Mul Raj. Sikh, *c.* 1850–1870.
(Page 182)

106. Raja Suchet Singh (1801–1844). Sikh,
c. 1850–1870. (Page 171)

107. Maharaja Gulab Singh (1792–1857).
Sikh, *c.* 1850–1870. (Page 186)

108. Twelve Heroes of the Sikhs. Woodcut. Sikh, *c.* 1870. (Pages 68, 189)

Maharaja Sher Singh.

Maharaja Ranjit Singh,
late King of Punjab.

Maharaja Dulip Singh,
son of Mr Raja Ranjit Singh

Raja Dhian Singh, Prime Minister.

Gulab Singh King of Jumos & Kashmir.

Jindan (late Queen)

Chutter Singh Attariwala.

Sher Singh Attariwala.

Raja Dina Nath.

Mulraj Governor of Mooltan

Doctor, Mahamad ruler of Mooltan

Phula Singh of Amritsar

109. Twelve Heroes of the Sikhs. Woodcut. Sikh, *c.* 1870. (Pages 68, 189)

110. Twelve Heroes of the Sikhs. Woodcut. Sikh, *c.* 1870. (Pages 68, 190)

111. Maharaja Ranjit Singh (1780–1839) in darbar. Woodcut. Sikh, *c.* 1870. (Pages 69, 190)

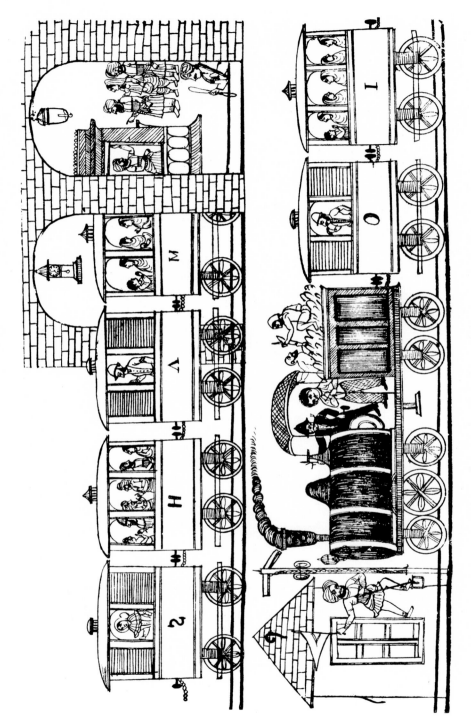

112. Sikh railway train. Woodcut. Sikh, c. 1870. (Pages 69, 191)

CONCORDANCE

Museum Number	Catalogue Number	Figure Number	Page Number	Museum Number	Catalogue Number	Figure Number	Page Number
03530 I.S.	44	69	164	I.M. 2/88–1917	94	—	191
03534 (i) I.S.	29 (i)	72	153	I.M. 2/119–1917	90	109	189
03534 (ii) I.S.	29 (ii)	73	153	I.M. 2/133–1917	94	—	191
03534 (iii) I.S.	29 (iii)	74	153	I.M. 2/136–1917	94	—	191
03534 (iv) I.S.	29 (iv)	75	154	I.M. 2/137–1917	94	—	191
03589 I.S.	66	103	182	I.M. 2/151–1917	94	—	191
03590 I.S.	68	—	183	I.M. 2/153–1917	94	—	191
03591 I.S.	61	—	179	I.M. 2/154–1917	94	—	191
03592 I.S.	62	99	180	I.M. 2/179–1917	94	—	191
03593 I.S.	59	—	178	I.M. 56–1936	14	27	139
03594 I.S.	70	—	183	I.M. 57–1936	15	31	140
03595 I.S.	64	98	180	I.M. 58–1936	16	32	140
03596 I.S.	57	101	178	I.M. 59–1936	17	33	141
03597 I.S.	51	97	175	I.M. 60–1936	18	29	141
03598 I.S.	50	—	175	I.S. 37–1949	20	37	143
03599 I.S.	73	—	184	I.S. 479–1950	27	70	152
03600 I.S.	78	—	185	I.S. 480–1950	4	14	126
03601 I.S.	75	—	184	I.S. 487–1950	30 (iii)	—	158
03603 I.S.	83	—	186	I.S. 488–1950	30 (ii)	77	157
03604 I.S.	79	—	185	I.S. 489–1950	30 (i)	78	155
03605 I.S.	48	106	171	I.S. 189–1951	23	48	145
03607 I.S.	81	—	186	I.S. 190–1951	22	47	144
03608 I.S.	65	102	181	I.S. 192–1951	24	51	146
I.M. 2/11–1917	94	—	191	I.S. 193–1951	21	46	144
I.M. 2/16–1917	92	111	190	I.S. 194–1951	25	50	146
L.M. 2/33–1917	94	—	191	I.S. 338–1951	12	22	138
I.M. 2/36–1917	94	—	191	I.S. 111–1953	5	17	127
I.M. 2/47–1917	91	110	190	I.S. 112–1953	6	18	128
I.M. 2/50–1917	94	—	191	I.S. 113–1953	9	21	133
I.M. 2/51–1917	93	112	191	I.S. 114–1953	7	19	129
I.M. 2/56–1917	89	108	189	I.S. 115–1953	8	20	131
I.M. 2/63–1917	94	—	191	I.S. 116–1953	10	24	136

GLOSSARY

Adi Granth	The first or prime Sikh bible.	*Kach*	Shorts.
Akālī	Immortal; beyond death. Name of a ferocious Sikh sect.	*Kalān*	Head.
		Kalm	Pen, brush.
		Kanghā	Comb.
Bhāī	Brother.	*Karā*	Iron bracelet.
Crore	100 lākhs, i.e. 10,000,000.	*Kesh*	Hair.
Daftarī	Book-keeper.	*Khalif*	Son.
Darbār	Court.	*Khālsā*	Pure; hence, the baptised Sikh community.
Dārhi	Beard.		
Dārhi wālā	'He of the beard.'	*Kirpān*	Sword.
Dasam Granth	The tenth book or bible.	*Lākh*	100,000.
Dhoti	A length of cloth used for draping a man's waist.	*Misl*	Equal; hence, confederacy, or band of the equal.
Gaddi	Shepherd caste.	*Mughal*	Muslim ruling community in India 16th–19th century.
Ghurcharā	Mounted bodyguard.		
Gomukha	Cloth-bag containing a rosary.		
		Nāyaka	Lover.
Granth	The Sikh bible.	*Nāyikā*	Woman in love.
Guru	Teacher.	*Nāzim*	Governor.
Hārem	Female quarters.	*Nihang*	Crocodile; a soubriquet for *Akālī*.
Havelī	Mansion.		
Jāt	Cultivating caste or class of the Punjab.	*Pahul*	Sikh baptismal rite.
		Pandit	Scholar.
Jāgīr	Freehold; rent-free grant of land.	*Pūjā*	Worship.
		Pūjārī	Priest.
Joshī	Astrologer.	*Rājā*	King or prince.

Rānī	Queen.	*Satī*	Woman who burns herself on her husband's funeral pyre.
Rājput	The supreme soldier caste.		
Rupiyā (rupee)	Silver coin, about one shilling and sixpence.	*Sawār*	Rider.
Sākan	Inhabitant.	*Sikh*	Disciple, learner.
Shālagrām	A black stone or fossil ammonite, worshiped as a symbol of Vishnu.	*Sīkhnā*	To learn.
		Singh	Lion.
		Srī	Respected.
Samādhī	Cenotaph.	*Vāris*	Heir, successor.
Sardār	Chief; hence, a Sikh term of respect.	*Vasant (Basant)*	Spring.
		Zenāna	Female establishment.

INDEX

Wt. 3530 K20

SO Code No. 29-1699*